Immersive, vivid, and chock full of idiosyncratic details, Jane Goette's A *River Road Memoir* is a rhapsodic, whimsical, witty, knowing, and spellbinding account of growing up in the American South. Goette, who reflects wisely and compassionately upon the astonishing conflicts surrounding race and privilege in mid-century Louisiana, is sure to delight, entertain, and educate any reader who picks up this book, while no doubt charming her way into their hearts.

-- **Matthew Vollmer,** author of *Permanent Exhibit* and *This World Is Not Your Home*

With unabashed honesty and poignant compassion, Jane Goette weaves together vivid images of her family's small-town life to paint a portrait of the deep south in the 1950s and 60s. Her narrative, *A River Road Memoir*, springs from the rich dirt of a deeply racist, yet vibrant Louisiana. Goette's colorful non-fiction stories ultimately craft an intimate, timely account of a place and its people at one of the great intersections of American history.

--**Charlotte Morgan,** author of *Protecting Elvis* and *Are You Gregg's Mother?*

A River Road Memoir

by

Jane Goette

DVille Press

A River Road Memoir

Copyright © 2022 by Jane Goette

All photos from the author's personal collection unless otherwise credited.

Layout and design by Write2Grow, LLC
Cover design by Gary Dauphin

ISBN: 978-1-7368172-2-3

DVille Press

Published by:
DVille Press, LLC
618 Mississippi Street
Donaldsonville, Louisiana 70346 USA
(225) 473-9319
www.dvillepress.com

For the unsung heroes of their families who died
before their stories were finished:

Eleanor "Candy" Goette and Josephine Sobral Goette

and

For the proudest legacy of my life:

Sarah, Sophie, and Carl David

Mother and son observe a cicada emerging from its shell:

It flew to the oak tree to breed and die, oblivious to the wake of wonder it had left behind. As I let that wonder wash over me I realized that this was the gift I really wanted to give my children, for what good are straight teeth and trumpet lessons to a person who cannot see the grandeur that the world is charged with?

Katherine Paterson
Gates of Excellence

Acknowledgments

Had it not been for Charlotte Morgan, my River Road stories might have sailed down the Mississippi into the Gulf of Oblivion. In later years, she and Mindy Quigley helped me finalize River Road for submission.

I'm indebted to the many women I've come to know from on-going writing groups in the New River Valley and summer retreats at Nimrod; you helped me become a better writer: Chelsea Adams, earth mother to scores of "Virginia Wolves" who gathered in living rooms and coffee shops scattered throughout the valley seeking a "room of her own" and finding it with each other; Maria, Anne, Simone, Lucy, Nancy, Kathie, Linda, Kristina, Charlie, Tracee, Megan and others; Debby Freed, who took me to Nimrod that first, long-ago summer; Frances Burch, who slapped sense into me, "Jane, your writing is beautiful, but your stories are boring"; Bonnie Soniat for recommending me to the Virginia Commission for the Creative Arts.

Special thanks to my education colleagues Doug Kingery, Linda Waggaman, and Heidi Dickens; Madison friends and Doty St. gang; Rosary Beck, my River Road research pal; Martha Lain and Debbie Buchanan who keep my mind, heart, and spirit alive and growing; Gene Sotile, steadfast friend from seventh grade; Linda Waggaman for touching up old family photographs and taking new ones.

From Oak Alley and Whitney Plantations on the River Road I learned missing, buried pieces of history that deepened my understanding of intersections between history and my own family. Special thanks to Jeanette Jefferson's daughters, Jospehine "Toot" Schonberg and Babbette Joseph, to Stanley Francis, and to Kathe Hambrick for illuminating the substantial and inspiring black history of my community, and to my sisters, our children, and grandchildren—we are Candy and Conrad's "living arrows."

Thank you, Tricia Scott for helping DVille Press and me with early explorations of cover design and enormous thanks to my editor Mary Gehman whose independent streak, curious, questioning mind, interest in history, literature, journalism, and writing made us a good match. Mary and I pushed each other to make this a better book.

Contents

Prologue:
Whispers in the Grass

My River Road memories begin in summertime. Shadows, whispers in the grass, ants crawling across my legs—a slight detour on their path from here to wherever it is ants go. The distant hum of a lawnmower, the scent of cow manure drifting across Mrs. Abadie's pasture. On the other side of the field, Mrs. Torres' figs spill to the ground, rotting in the late-afternoon sun on the Old River Road.

I lean against the wooden pole that holds the clothesline—it's a good place for daydreaming. Mosquito hawks perch on the line like a row of WWI fighter planes ready for take-off. Next door the Japanese plums on Miss Jambois' tree turn yellow. Blue hydrangeas flower on one side of her weathered cypress porch and bloom pink on the other. Her brother, Char*lie* (Chaw-*lee*) paces the length of the sidewalk that borders the Jambois yard, smoking his pipe in speechless serenity.

As I lie back under flapping towels, little-girl cotton panties, and starched petticoats, the clouds light up in infrequent flashes of heat lightning—like someone flicking the switch in a dimly lit room— like flickers of memory. Though I'm a scaredy-cat at night, I love being alone on these lazy afternoons to look out across Mrs. Abadie's pasture and the sugarcane fields beyond. I can see far across this flat land and feel the premonition of distant rain speeding toward me just as surely as I feel the future approaching.

I won't always be a little girl sitting under a clothesline with nothing much to do. But what child can imagine she will someday long for such moments? Time felt as heavy as an elephant back then, until the years became like the ants I barely noticed crawling across my legs before they disappeared in the grass.

I grew up on Louisiana's historic River Road in the heart of sugarcane country during the last days of segregation. My mother was a young newspaper woman from the North who married a middle-aged Catholic Brother from the Old South—an improbable and complicated union that produced four daughters. In 1951 Candy and Conrad Goette moved their young family to an old house on the River Road outside Donaldsonville, Louisiana, the same town where my father had spent his childhood, and my sisters and I would spend ours. Nothing much seemed to have changed, except the movies my father saw at the Grand were silent and ours were "talkies."

In many ways, mine was an idyllic childhood steeped in freedom and adventure, peopled by memorable characters, both white and black, living together and apart in the shadow of slavery's history. At the time my parents moved to Donaldsonville, its population was forty percent black and sixty percent white. Sugar production remained the main industry of the river parishes, as it had during early settlement days until the 1960's when chemical plants began sprouting along the Mississippi between Baton Rouge and New Orleans, transforming "The Golden Horn" into "The Cancer Corridor."

Reconstruction seemed but a bump in the River Road, a blip on history's screen. After the Feds pulled out in 1877, Confederate monuments went up, and so did some families' fortunes *if* they were white. My great grandfather bought Oak Alley Plantation in 1881, restored its sugarcane farming, and ran it profitably until after the Spanish American War when the U.S. gained control of Cuba, causing sugar prices in Louisiana to plummet.

My grandmother, Josephine Sobral, postponed her marriage to Sidonius Goette in order to help her family figure out its future. It proved impossible to rein in her father and brothers' lavish ways and stubborn refusal to adapt to a changing world. Josephine and Sidonius postponed their wedding until they'd help negotiate the sale of the plantation, which was finalized a few weeks after their Oak Alley wedding on January 3, 1905. My father was born eight months and twenty-seven days later.

Two World Wars had ended before I was even born, but childhood on the River Road changed very little from my grandmother's River Road youth at Oak Alley and mine in an old house 10 miles upriver. Like Josephine Sobral and my father Conrad Goette, my sisters and I grew up playing on the banks of the Mississippi—in a place of constant tension between water and land, history and justice—but the winds of the River Road were consistently sweet and comforting for a white child, one era to another. For me, that began to change as I approached adolescence.

By the early 1960's, the Goettes didn't need Bob Dylan to tell us the times were changing. The voices around us grew louder. Angry, resentful whites shouted, "segregation forever!" Hopeful, emboldened black people marched in the streets of northern cities, singing "We Shall Overcome," while in rural Louisiana, black people crowded together in small churches up and down the river, praising Jesus and praying for the Promised Land. Both, northern protests and southern spirituals, are testament to the united, indomitable spirit of black Americans.

My mother was an integrationist who wrote liberal editorials in *The Donaldsonville Chief*. My father was the principal of the white public schools, elementary, middle and high school from 1951 until 1965 when he became a supervisor, finally retiring in 1972. His principal years coincided with a time in the South when the line in the sand was school desegregation. My parents shared a belief in racial equality but argued about how and when integration could be realized. Mother was an outsider whose controversial politics could be tolerated in the pages of a newspaper. My father's career put him in the hot seat of the most divisive issue of our time. Politics was a constant conflict in our home; my three sisters and I were often caught in the middle.

From eighth grade until I left for the University of Wisconsin, I experienced an ever-growing restlessness socially and politically. One summer I was Christopher Columbus leading expeditions through the cane fields in search of a new world; the next summer I couldn't remember how to play pretend anymore. One summer I wanted to live on the River Road with my parents and sisters for the rest of my life; the next summer I thought I would die if I couldn't fly away soon. One summer I read *Gone with the Wind*; the next, *Cry the Beloved Country* and *The Ugly American*.

Mrs. Kahn's 5th grade class introduced me to history. When we read about the Children's Crusade and early world explorers, I wanted to be them. From eighth grade on I read newspaper stories about young people risking their lives in a cause I understood and longed to join. The Civil Rights movement had started, and I was stuck in Donaldsonville far from where the action seemed to be happening, far from the possibility of finding kindred spirits, becoming a participant in something important, making a difference to history.

Meanwhile, across the levee, the Mississippi River continued its journey to the sea, as it had for thousands of years. Our human struggles don't mean a thing to a river that has all the time in the world. It will endure. But our lives are short, a fact made painfully clear in June 1979 when, at age 55, my mother died. I didn't have a single memory of her ever being sick. Candy Goette had never missed a day of work in her life. Until lung cancer, my mother had not seen a doctor in 28 years, not since my youngest sister was born. How could she be walking down a sidewalk too fast for me to follow and then be dead six months later? No one who knew her could imagine it, least of all my father. He lost his will to live and died ten months later leaving my sisters and me needing each other in new ways and with greater intensity.

I lost my mother, my father, and my Louisiana home just as I was beginning my own family in Blacksburg, Virginia. My children would never know their grandparents, would never know the friends that hung out every Friday night at our River Road house; the storytelling and heated political debates, the cigarettes and beer consumed—except for my coffee-drinking mother. When the hour grew later and the pontificating began: Harry, about Aristotle `and Socrates; Daddy, with his Huey Long, and J.P., anxious to talk about Ho Chi Minh. When the pontificating started, Mother quietly drifted to the back of the house and returned in her bathrobe and curlers, unmistakable signal the evening was over. I couldn't imagine it would all be over so soon.

I'd spent my childhood tramping through sugarcane fields, swimming in irrigation ditches, and playing cowboys on the levee. It was exhilarating to fall from a horse, shot dead in the heart, voices of childhood companions swirling around me as I lay in the cool, bee-rich clover. When I grew tired of being dead, resurrection was easy. All it took was the desire to rise and rejoin the game. The only way to resurrect the dead now—the people, the times, the place—

is to tell the stories. I didn't want the flesh and blood of my parents to become shadows. I didn't want the distinct voices of my River Road to become whispers disappearing in the grass.

Goette sisters: Ann, Kay Kay, Gretchen, and Jane
dressed for Easter Mass, 1957

Jane Goette

Candy and Conrad

In Donaldsonville, Louisiana, if you were not immediately recognized by an adult, an interrogation would begin. "Who ya mama and daddy?" It was the first and most important question. We didn't much care for strangers in our town, and a child possessed no identity at all until he or she had been attached to a family.

When I identified my parents, "Candy and Conrad Goette," the inquisitors studied me as carefully as I studied them. Those might be the only words we exchanged, but sometimes another question would follow. "How ya mama like it here?"

In the polite but pointed code of Donaldsonville discourse, I learned early to read between the lines. Everybody loved my daddy. But not my mother.

Candy Goette was Not-From-Here, which seemed to be the most alarming label you could slap on a person. It was acceptable to be crazy or lazy, dishonest or disabled, fickle or feeble, but if you were Not-From-Here, people didn't know what to make of you. Worst of all, my mother was a Yankee.

Sometimes I didn't know what to make of my mother either, but it wasn't because she was a Yankee. At night when she read poetry or Winnie the Pooh to my sisters and me, her voice was soft and tender. During the day, our constant presence in the house got on her nerves, and if we spilled a glass of milk, she made her "witch face" and yelled "goddamit!"

Every day, my parents read the morning and evening papers together at the kitchen table, drinking coffee and smoking cigarettes. They exchanged opinions about the news as easily as they traded sections of *The Morning Advocate* and *The Times Picayune*. Daddy might relate a funny exchange with Twitchy Mistretta at the Post Office and Mother, her own encounters downtown with Gaston Hirsch or Bubba Lemann. They laughed at each other's stories. At such mundane moments, I knew my parents were friends, but it didn't always seem so.

Whenever Daddy caught a red light coming into town, Mother pounced on him, firing abuse as stinging as buckshot. "Goddamn it,

Conrad, you drive like an old man! You could have made that light!"

Though it never seemed to faze our father, my sisters and I grew anxious each time the family car approached the corner of Mississippi and Lessard. As we watched Mother's shoulders tighten and her face twist into a worried frown, we wished Daddy would step on the gas. But he never did.

Like the Mississippi River, which was also called "old man," Daddy seemed always to know where he was going and that he would reach his destination despite twists and turns along the way. There was no need to race through the journey.

Mother walked, talked and thought faster than most people in our town. She was a Progressive and believed that progress necessitated a certain speed if it was to overcome its greatest obstacle, inertia. Sometimes her self-imposed forward march seemed as puzzling to my father as that proverbial Yankee habit of listening for the "point" and missing the story.

World War II was still in progress when my parents' destinies converged in Alexandria, Louisiana. That such an improbable couple would decide to marry was as surprising as the circumstances of their first meeting.

Eleanor Jean Canright was nineteen years old when she arrived in Louisiana, having left Wisconsin and her first fulltime newspaper job at *The Waukesha Daily Freeman* to take a position as a reporter for *The Alexandria Town Talk*. At that time, Brother Jerome had spent twenty-three years of his life in the service of God. He was thirty-seven years old, had already had a long and successful career in Catholic education, and was the director of a prestigious Catholic prep school located in the burgeoning Louisiana military town of Alexandria. The country had entered the third year of its greatest foreign war.

"Eleanor Jean" was the only name my grandparents would ever acknowledge, and the one Mother used when she wrote for the newspaper, but in high school her friends started calling her "Canni." It seemed sassy, young, and stylish. She liked it as much as she'd disliked being associated with homely old Eleanor Roosevelt. Although Mother's attitudes changed toward both these names, in Louisiana they called her "Candy," and there was nothing she could do about it, not even when she turned 40 and felt ridiculous with a name that seemed more fitting to a teenager in bobby socks or a New Orleans stripper.

Mother was an avid newspaper reader her entire life and had her first piece of writing published in the local paper when she was still in elementary school. The summer after she graduated from Waukesha High, Mother began working at *The Waukesha Freeman*, a newspaper founded by Abolitionists. It's ironic that Mother started her career writing for a paper associated with the Underground Railroad but went on to spend the rest of her life in the heart of "Dixie" writing for newspapers that supported an established order she abhorred.

In 1943, while Mother tapped away at a typewriter nine to five and lived with her parents, her best friend, Marion Schmookie— who had not yet found a job—went down South to visit her brother. He was stationed in Alexandria, Louisiana for training before shipping out. Though it had been intended as a visit only, Marion found work and an exciting new social life. There were no lingering signs of the Depression in this booming town full of "help wanted" ads, dance clubs, and handsome young men. These last items were especially rare back in Waukesha where Mother and her friends complained that it was easier to find a one-legged hunchback than an eligible young man to date. Marion wrote to Mother urging her to drop everything and head South: "Things are hoppin' down here! Hurry up and come, Canni, before the war ends!"

In that historical moment, American G.I.s were fighting across the maps of Europe and Asia. A world war was ending the Great Depression and creating more jobs than there were men to fill them. The country was bustling again. For Mother's generation, it wasn't a pink slip or an eviction notice that propelled their moves as it had been for their parents. Winter was over. The old world had exploded and a new one would take its place. These children of the Great Depression were the cicadas of early summer, newly emerged from the chrysalis, making noise, ready to swing. Jazz, Big Band, Fireside Chats and train engines; this is what they heard. Young people crowded bus stations and train depots; they crossed state lines; flew over oceans; sailed across dance floors.

Meanwhile, "Canni" was still stuck in Waukesha missing everything, still hiding her Chesterfields from her disapproving mother, still leaning into the radio each time it played "Begin the Beguine," still waiting for her life to begin.

Mother was as restless as the keys of her typewriter when she tapped out her escape plan. She started saving her paychecks, stopped buying lunch downtown, avoided dress shops, stayed home and listened to the radio instead of going to the movies. A few months after giving her notice to the *Freeman*, in the spring of 1943 Mother bought a train ticket to Alexandria, Louisiana. It was the last line of Marion's letter she kept thinking about: "The town is swarming with good looking guys in uniform!" She didn't mean the kind my father wore.

On the eve of her departure, Mother walked down Hartwell Avenue to the corner drugstore, bought two Hershey bars, her favorite magazines, and a new tube of lipstick.

The next morning she boarded a train carrying a handbag and one suitcase which Grandpa placed on the overhead rack above her seat. Grandma watched, smiling nervously and twisting the embroidered handkerchief she'd meant to give her daughter. There were no kisses, just a swift, stiff embrace followed by an encouraging pat on the shoulder. This was the way they did it up North.

A whistle sounded. Eldon and Stella Canright headed down the narrow aisle and descended the steps to the platform. As the train lurched forward, my mother waved goodbye to her parents through the window and never looked back.

On that long journey from Waukesha, Wisconsin to Alexandria, Louisiana in 1943, train tracks crisscrossed like shiny ribbons, tying North and South, East and West. Between Milwaukee and Alexandria, Mother changed trains, crossed rivers, and watched the slow transformation of landscape. Like all travelers, she wanted to know where she was headed, but change was the needle guiding her compass, steering her toward a future with my sisters and me, steering her towards our daddy and a life in the Deep South.

Because I know what she could not, I have wondered about my mother's journey. I've imagined her train traversing fields where a Canright and a Sobral might once have battled—Mother's great grandfather, fighting for the Union; Daddy's grandfather, for the Confederacy. Until she moved to Louisiana, The Civil War had seemed a long-ago, far-away war remembered only by a dwindling number of white-bearded veterans, stick figures who appeared every 4th of July in Waukesha's parades. These ancient men seemed improbable heroes; their battles were names written in the dust-covered pages of history, in cemeteries and in old fashioned poems like "The Blue and The Gray," by Francis Miles Finch (1827-1907):

> By the flow of the inland river,
> Whence the fleets of iron have fled,
> Where the blades of the grave-grass quiver,
> Asleep are the ranks of the dead:
> Under the sod and the dew,
> Waiting the judgment day;
> Under the one, the Blue,
> Under the other, the Gray.

As far as Mother was concerned, romantic notions of the past belonged in poetry books. WWII was her generation's war. They were FDR's children, fearing only "fear itself," ready to live and die for something more than "making ends meet."

At nineteen, when she steered her life south, Mother was seeking romance, dance floors, and perhaps a handsome young soldier sporting shiny medals on his chest. Instead, she found a middle-aged monk dressed in a plain black robe with a shiny, silver cross dangling from his neck.

* * *

By the time my mother arrived in Alexandria to begin her adult life, my father was 37 years old and being groomed to assume leadership of his religious order when its superior, my father's mentor, retired from Sacred Heart. From age fourteen until my father was released from his vows, he had been known as "Brother Jerome." During those years, he'd had lots of teaching posts as he rose through the ranks to the more prestigious head job at Menard in Alexandria. The assignment he had loved most took place early in his career when, as a young Sacred Heart Brother, he had been posted to its mission school in Muscogee, Oklahoma to teach young Native American boys.

Until seven years ago, I had assumed that my father's love for Native Americans originated with that chance posting near an Oklahoma reservation. But when an elder Louisiana cousin shared his collection of historical records and newspaper clippings, I learned of a life-sized, wooden, tobacco shop Indian that had stood inside the entrance of the Bel House, my father's boyhood home. The statue had been purchased by my grandfather, Sidonius Goette, and donated to the New Orleans Cabildo sometime after his death. Tobacco shop Indians were men. Despite the brown and yellow aging of the newspaper clipping, this small image was arresting. The wooden statue depicted a beautiful Indian woman who—except for garb—might have been the Madonna. She was special, radiant. I had to see that statue.

A few months later when I saw her at the Cabildo, I experienced a "Blink" moment, a surprising flash of understanding as if I were looking at her through the eyes of that lonely little boy who longed for a mother he could not remember. A child will imagine what he most wants and cannot have. This Indian woman with a face like the Madonna was the mother figure my father saw every day in his home. She was always kind, calm, and beautiful; her arms, always opened wide to embrace her son—if only she could.

Disparate pieces of a family puzzle tumbled into place like they'd been waiting all these decades for me to open my eyes and see. The distance between my father and me, the past and the present, fell away. The Oklahoma chapter in my father's life had not been accidental; Brother Jerome had *requested* that posting to Muskogee.

Conrad Goette's childhood "Madonna"

When Daddy told us about his time with the Native Americans in Muscogee, his face assumed a far-away expression and his voice grew quiet. He made the Indians seem like heroes. After his stories, I could never cheer when the cowboys shot the Indians dead on the big screen of the Grand Theater in Donaldsonville.

Out in Oklahoma, the Sacred Heart mission school boarded the children from the reservation, allowing one day a month for their families to visit. The parents of Daddy's students didn't have cars, trains or even horses. In order to reach the school, they left the reservation before dawn and walked hours to sit quietly in a large, crowded room, side by side with their sons for a visit that lasted perhaps two hours, during which they rarely spoke.

At the end of visiting time, a Brother returned to lead the boys back to their residential quarters. The parents sat and watched their sons file through the doorway past pictures of white-faced saints and a statue of a white god, the one nailed to a cross. Those weathered, Native American faces never changed expression. After their sons reached the end of the long hall and disappeared behind another door, the parents stood up and walked back to the reservation.

More amazing to me than all that walking was Daddy's description of the visit. "They would sit together for those two hours and not exchange a single word. They didn't smile, they didn't hug, and they didn't cry."

I could not fathom such behavior. "Didn't they love their children?" I asked. Daddy's brow furrowed as he shot me a look that said I had asked a "stupid jackass" question. "Of course they loved their children. Why in the Sam Hill do you think they walked all that way to see them?!"

Though my father had been born into a privileged class, they were not the people with whom he identified. He seemed to have an intuitive understanding of kids who didn't fit, young people who were hurting, even when that pain was masked by bad behavior. He knew a thing or two about that, though it was his polished demeanor that propelled his rise through the ranks of Sacred Heart.

My father's upbringing had instilled him with lifelong, impeccable manners and a social ease and charm that were useful to the Brothers of the Sacred Heart, especially when courting generous donors to their coffers and causes. It had been my father's idea to transform Menard from a sleepy, hundred-year-old Catholic institution into a progressive, military-prep boarding school that would be competitive and would attract the best students from the region—Catholic, Protestant and Jewish.

When my parents met in Alexandria, "Brother Jerome," Conrad, had been with Sacred Heart for more years than my mother had lived. Everybody, including Daddy, assumed he would remain "Brother Jerome" for the rest of his life, so when my grandfather, Sidonius Goette, died in 1923 leaving a considerable fortune, Daddy hadn't thought twice before giving his entire inheritance to the Brothers of the Sacred Heart—another reason he was their "fair-haired boy." Though he was only 18 at the time, his commitment to life within his religious order never wavered until the day he met a young reporter from Wisconsin.

When Mother's train finally arrived in Alexandria in the spring of 1943, Marion was there waving from the platform. Two high school girlfriends from Waukesha had left home to pursue independent lives in a booming military town farther from home than either of them had ever considered possible. Marion had found an apartment they would share on the second floor of a duplex with outside stairs leading up to their front door. Now Mother had to find a job. She was young, but an innate "newshound" with experience writing for the Waukesha Freeman. In Alexandria, Louisiana in 1943, newspaper writers were in short supply.

Mother was hired. During the first week on her new job at the Alexandria *Town Talk*, Mother sat at a desk with her pen and paper diligently crafting a first-draft version of the story she'd been assigned. Her editor startled her in the middle of a perfect sentence composed in her best penmanship.

"Candy, you've got 10 minutes to have that story typed and on my desk!" ("Canni" had already been transformed to "Candy" by Louisiana ears.) From that moment on, Mother composed at the typewriter and became one of the fastest writers I've ever known.

Mother's most dramatic experience as a reporter for *The Town Talk* occurred in the early days of her reporting career when she witnessed a shooting. She'd just completed an interview with an old, distinguished Alexandria judge. I don't remember his name, only that he was white-haired and diminutive. My mother was a regular in the courthouse, always equipped with pen, paper and good questions. This judge liked her very much and often took her to lunch after an interview.

On this particular day, Mother and the judge had just left the restaurant and were heading down the street toward her office when she noticed an enormous brute of a man half a block away barreling toward them. As the man drew closer Mother realized that his crazy, fiery eyes were fixed on the judge. "I'm gonna kill ya, you old son of a bitch!" he shouted at the judge, marching toward him with clinched fists.

The judge was visibly shaken but remained calm. "You'd better stop right where you are," he warned, "you're under a restraining order!"

But the man didn't stop. With one hand the judge pushed Mother aside, and with the other, drew a pistol from the waist pocket of his jacket. "Stay back," he warned and aimed his gun. "I'm going to shoot if you come any closer."

The judge's threat fueled the man's fury rather than caution, and his pace accelerated. "Stop, goddamit!" the judge shouted one last time before firing the first bullet. Two bullets later, the ex-con fell to the sidewalk inches away from the judge's feet. He lay like a felled redwood, but the red pooling around this tree-sized man was all too human.

Mother's instincts as a reporter immediately kicked in. She ran to the nearest phone booth and with shaking hands, dialed her editor's number at *The Town Talk*. "There's been a shooting at..." she gave the address, "You'd better send a reporter right away!" Through the receiver, her boss bellowed, "Candy, you *are* a reporter!"

By chance, Mother had fallen into the kind of dramatic news story reporters dream about, the hard-edged or important events *never* assigned to a woman. The few female journalists who worked in that era were usually relegated to the society page; they reported on weddings, debutante balls, and garden parties. But Mother's editor liked and respected her. Though she was young, she was sharp, professional, and energetic. He admired her writing skills and recognized her newshound instincts. Candy was curious, wasn't afraid to look people in the eye, and asked smart questions. Though he would never have chosen her to cover the story of the shooting, afterwards, he gave her meatier assignments than women's social news.

So, when the leading families of Alexandria started sending their eldest sons to Menard instead of better-known private schools, it stirred curiosity and became a story of interest to the *Town Talk*. With Menard about to celebrate its centennial, it seemed the opportune time to make the school's history and dramatic transformation the cover story of the Sunday edition. Mother's editor assigned her the story. She called Menard and set up an interview with its head, Brother Jerome.

***

I can't help imagining more about my parents' meeting than either of them ever told:

I see Brother Jerome sitting at his desk that morning, re-reading Menard's latest applications for the next academic year, deciding which boys to squeeze in and which to place on the wait list. I see his dark, wavy hair and satisfied face as he rocked back and forth in his swivel chair—a simple pleasure he enjoyed the rest of his life. There had been twice as many applications as the previous year. The applicants were good, strong students, too—just the types Sacred Heart had hoped to recruit. Some of them came from the best families in Avoyelles Parrish.

It's easy to imagine that under his long robe, Brother Jerome might have planted one black shoe on the floor and used the other to swivel his chair from side to side. The hands of the clock had not yet reached noon, but already it had been a great day for him. Earlier that morning along with glowing letters from students' parents, the postman had also delivered a letter from Brother Superior praising him for his "vision." Once again, Jerome had exceeded his mentor's highest hopes. The man had a right to feel proud.

But vision has its limitations. As he bent to sign the last letter on his desk, he had no idea what was about to happen...but I do. My time-traveling imagination watches as his pen glides across that last paper with the ease of an ice-skater on a frozen pond— completely oblivious to his impending fate—still unaware that a moment later he would slide across the edge into another life. He puts down his pen, touches the cross on his chest, thumps his fingertips together and lets a wonderful feeling wash over him.

The season was changing. Summer's stifling heat was giving way, and Brother Jerome surely felt a change in the air. The window was opened and the breeze coming through ruffed the hair on his forehead. He turns his head toward the window to enjoy the delicious touch of fresh air on his face. He closes his eyes as if trying to remember something...as if he were waiting.

Then, a soft knock on the door. His secretary peeks in and announces, "Brother Jerome, Miss Canright is here from *The Town Talk*."

My mother steps through the door into a pool of sunshine. My father swivels around in his chair to greet her just as a breeze stirs the soft waves of her shoulder-length hair and lifts her skirt a few inches. The vision startles him; something catches inside his chest. He stops breathing or thinking or remembering who he is and what he is supposed to do. Like Paul on the road to Damascus, like Van Gogh beholding that field of sunflowers, he sees the light ... and it is my mother.

"Jesus, God, I'm a goner!" Brother Jerome exclaims to himself. And it is true.

Candy on the steps of her Alexandria apartment

Ootie's Kitchen

My parents' courtship began immediately, although it took a marriage proposal—they were both Catholic—for my mother to realize it. The day after her visit to Menard, Candy heard someone coming up to her apartment. When she looked out, she was surprised to see Ootie trudging up the steps, concentrating on whatever he was carrying in both hands.

Ootie was Menard's head cook, as well as the school's official driver. Mother had met him the day before, the day of the open window. After she interviewed Brother Jerome, he had taken her on a tour of the school, stopping by Ootie's kitchen for a late lunch.

At no time had my father seemed more charming than when he introduced her to Ootie. This was probably the first time she experienced his Louisiana humor and easy rapport with people from all walks of life, trademarks of his personality. I never met Ootie, but never forgot his name or the role he played in my parents' courtship.

Ootie looked up from his cutting board when footsteps interrupted the chop-chop rhythm of his quiet kitchen. His face was startled for a split second, then lit up with a smile when he realized the intruder was Brother Jerome.

"Ootie, what's for dinner tonight? Fried alligator toes?" my father might have asked.

"No, Brother. This is Wednesday—you know I always cook possum stew on Wednesdays!"

Both men would have been relaxed and smiling when they turned to my mother. Brother Jerome introduced the young reporter from Wisconsin as if she were a foreign dignitary, and she may as well have been. Ootie put down his knife and wiped his dark hand on a kitchen towel before greeting her in the warmest voice.

"Pleasure, Miz Canright. So, you from the North?"

Mother would have enjoyed Ootie's easy way of bringing her in. The Louisiana rules and language for "polite" behavior were as different from Wisconsin's as English is from French.

"Now, don't you print any of Brother Jerome's foolishness in the paper, or they be closin' down this school and my kitchen with it!"

Daddy would have continued the banter because he enjoyed it the way tennis players love lobbing a ball back and forth to each other across a net.

"Then we'll both have to move to Wisconsin where they eat snowballs for supper instead of alligators. Why do you think Miss Canright's so skinny?"

This was not the relationship a girl from Wisconsin had anticipated between a Negro and a white man in the Deep South. Nor was it the relationship she'd have expected between a boss and a worker, in general. Since she arrived in Alexandria and began reporting for the *Town Talk*, she often felt like a correspondent in a foreign land—different weather, houses, foods, plants, and the people in Louisiana spoke with strange accents. On weekends when the town was crawling with soldiers, the foreign atmosphere intensified.

Lunch had already ended when they entered Ootie's kitchen that day, but Ootie asked could he fix them a couple of plates. Candy never ate breakfast, and a Hershey Bar with a cup of coffee constituted her usual lunch. Brother Jerome looked at her with those brown eyes and winsome smile, "Miss Canright, you came all the way out here, we can't let you leave Menard without tasting Ootie's fine cooking.

"Only take me a minute, Miz Canright. Why don't you go sit at that table with the big window, and I'll bring y'all some coffee. You take sugar or cream?"

Before my parents had finished their coffee, Ootie reappeared with steaming plates of pork chops, fried okra with tomatoes, and rice topped with brown gravy.

Mother lingered at Menard long past the time she'd expected. She'd never met anyone like Brother Jerome. He was every bit the "southern gentleman," but his manners seemed more natural than affected, more an extension of a warm nature. Mother was already pondering the words she would use to describe Brother to Marion. She would censor the first words that came to her now—

"handsome" and "sexy." Instead, she would tell how refreshing it had been to be with a mature man for a change, someone certain of who he was and what he was doing. She would praise his foresight in transforming Menard and recount examples of his quick wit and charm.

She wouldn't describe his dreamy eyes or that playful laugh, the dimple in his chin; nor would Candy tell her best friend how she'd felt after lunch when Brother Jerome struck a match to light her cigarette and cupped his hand around hers, their heads so close, they almost touched.

After lunch, after a tour of the athletic field, they had sat on a bench under an oak tree behind Ootie's kitchen. The one-way interview had long ended. Daddy asked her about Wisconsin, how she came to Alexandria, her impressions of Louisiana. Everything she said fascinated him. He didn't know why. He loved looking at her face, its fair and delicate features, her warm and intelligent eyes. He loved listening to her—the sound of her voice, the way she used words, the interest and knowledge she seemed to possess, and her surprising maturity for a woman so young. He knew her article would be good, but he wasn't really thinking about that. He wished she would pull out another cigarette so he could light it for her again. And she did.

By the time Daddy's secretary found him sitting with Miss Canright on that bench under the oak tree, they had both smoked several cigarettes. It was time for Brother Jerome's five o'clock meeting. He smiled when he looked up from his watch and said, "We've kept Miss Canright too long. We better have Ootie drive her back, so she'll write something good about us in the paper."

"Thank you, Brother, but there's a bus that takes me right downtown…"

My father would have stopped her mid-sentence. If he'd had a Rolls Royce he'd have sent her back in that, but it was unthinkable that she should return by bus.

While his secretary went to get Ootie, Daddy strolled back to the front entrance with Mother and waited with her until Ootie pulled up in Menard's black sedan. Daddy opened the back door and offered his hand to help her inside. Perhaps he called her

"Candy" when he said goodbye. Maybe he held her hand an instant longer than necessary before he closed the door.

As a daughter, I could never know the intimate part of my parents' courtship, but I know that most love stories require the convergence of need and circumstance before they can begin. It's often the unseen hand of imagination that weaves shimmering threads into our lives, into our stories. Theirs began that day, as did mine, my sisters', my children's. What assumptions, false or true, were already taking shape in each of their heads as they slept that night?

When I discovered the thrill of "making out," I wondered when my parents had kissed for the first time. I remember a photograph of my mother that I studied many times. She was in high school, sitting on a bench with her boyfriend under Grandma and Grandpa's grape arbor. Bathed in sunshine, with their arms casually draped around each other's shoulders, they smiled into the camera. I knew my mother had "smooched" with the boy in the picture, but it was hard to imagine her doing that with Daddy—a man dressed in a black robe with a silver cross hanging from his neck.

I would never have asked, and doubt even now that I want to know, but a male friend once told me it was impossible my father had not had sex with anyone until he was 38 and married my mother. "My father was Catholic Brother, he took a vow of celibacy," I explained again. "Jane, he was a man."

As a boy in Donaldsonville, and even later with the Brothers, my father had a history of rule-breaking. The Pope may have been infallible, but Daddy never claimed that space, never held a "holier than thou" attitude and truly believed that without the Catholic Church and its sacraments, he would not be strong enough to be a good man. He often referred to his "Latin blood," which I later understood was his euphemism for passion, for libido.

I wonder what my father felt that day in Alexandria as he stood on the curb watching Ootie shift into first, pull out into the street and drive away. I imagine my mother was the first to look away, but halfway down the block, perhaps she turned around. I'm sure my father was still standing at the curb, smiling—and she knew she would see him again.

The very next evening she heard a knock on the door. When she opened it, she found Ootie standing there holding a large, covered plate still warm after the drive from Menard. With a mischievous smile, he handed it to her explaining, "Brother Jerome said to bring you some supper. I hope you like chicken and dumplings, Miz Canright."

Mother was speechless for a moment, but Ootie ended the awkwardness. "Don't worry, Miz Canright, it's *chicken*. I wouldn't let Brother Jerome send you none of them alligator toes!" Mother laughed. "Thank you, Ootie, and thank Brother Jerome, too."

Every night after that, Ootie appeared at Mother's apartment door around 7:00 p.m. with another steaming plate. The portions were large enough to feed three people, so Marion also ate well during my parents' courtship.

When Candy called the first time to thank Brother, he probably said he was fulfilling his Sacred Heart vow to feed the hungry, or perhaps he told her that other version of his "open window" story, that when she walked through the door that day, he thought, "Jesus, God! Somebody better put some meat on this poor girl's bones!"

It wasn't surprising to my sisters and me that Daddy had courted Mother with food. This was his favorite way to show love, and it became mine, too. I love roses, but I can't help feeling that when a man loves a woman, he takes her out to dinner, and when a woman loves her children and friends, she feeds them.

During the courtship, Brother Jerome invited Candy to every Catholic social event on his calendar, but there was always another woman accompanying them, so Mother didn't understand she was on a "date" with Daddy. She claimed to have thought she was the chaperone for Daddy and the other women, who were usually married and closer to his age. Mother also claimed that when Daddy asked her to marry him, she was astonished and caught off guard.

"I said 'yes' because I didn't think he was serious," she said, casually taking a drag from her cigarette. "It was during the war and men were always asking you to marry them."

Aunt Marilyn, ten years old at the time, remembers the letters "Eleanor Jean" sent home from Alexandria. "They were filled with glowing stories about "Brother Jerome." Denials aside, Mother was obviously smitten. How could she not be? Daddy was movie-star handsome—black wavy hair, chiseled square jaw, slender body and smiling eyes. As a teenager, when I studied those pictures of Brother Jerome standing in his long robe alongside the Menard basketball team, I could barely believe he was my daddy.

The same day he proposed to Mother, my father wrote a letter to the Sacred Heart Superior requesting a release from his vows. He continued to write to Brother Superior every day…for months, but Sacred Heart didn't want to lose its rising star, and to Brother Superior, my father was like a son. "I've got to bring him to his senses!" the Superior must have thought as he drafted his next letter, offering to reassign Brother Jerome to that mission post in Oklahoma.

Daddy remained respectful but unyielding, as unwavering in his devotion to Candy as he was to God. In all the future battles I would witness, this was Daddy's style. When the smoke cleared, he had always held his ground. The Superior finally relented and with great sadness, released Daddy from his vows. After he told Mother, she placed a long-distance call to Waukesha to tell her family she was getting married.

When the phone rang on Hartwell Avenue that night, it was the first long distance call Grandma and Grandpa had ever received. Aunt Marilyn remembers being as excited by the novelty of a long-distance voice coming through the telephone receiver as she was about her sister's engagement. Stella and Eldon were relieved that Eleanor Jean hadn't been run over by a drunken soldier, but that doesn't mean they were happy to learn the reason for her call.

"But how can you marry a *monk*?" Stella asked her daughter, "That's like stealing from God!"

"How can you marry a man old enough to be your father?!" Eldon shouted into the receiver. Her father had always hated the Roman Catholic Church, and now a *priest* was stealing his daughter?! "Eleanor Jean, you don't want to ruin your life, burn your bridges forever!"

But my mother had made up her mind. She had said yes and now Conrad—she would have to get used to calling him that—had written to his superior requesting release from his job and his vows. "Daddy, I'm going to marry Conrad" and that was that.

After the engagement, I imagine my parents' private moments became more intimate, that my mother allowed herself to act on an impulse she'd felt that first day at Menard. When Brother Jerome leaned to light her cigarette, she had wanted to touch his face. Now her fingers could trace the square outline of that striking jaw; she could run her fingers through his hair and down the nape of his neck. They had touched each other. There had been a first to every delicious, small step to intimacy.

Candy had been in love a couple of times, but never like this. Never had any man looked at her the way Conrad did; those deep brown eyes, so alive and playful, yet calm and assured. She had seen love swimming in that pool of brown, but she had always looked away. One night, sitting beside him on her apartment steps, she did not look away.

In that long, quiet moment, their eyes had spoken. He slipped his arm around her shoulders and drew her close. The long-awaited forbidden kiss changed everything. The kiss was bound to happen. Something heavy, like a stone or longing, cannot remain suspended. Gravity and love will have their way. That kiss was as irrevocable as a stone tossed into a river, a splash followed by ever-widening circles that travel towards an unknowable destination. It launched a family.

Eleanor Jean "Canni" Canright, age 19
Waukesha, Wisconsin

Undated photograph of Conrad Goette as "Brother Jerome,"
serving Sacred Heart Catholic religious order from age 14 to 38

Jane Goette

Daughter of Depression Marries Boy Santa

My parents were married October 31, 1944, in Saint Joseph's Catholic Church in Waukesha. After the ceremony, they returned to Grandma and Grandpa's house on Hartwell Avenue for a wedding breakfast of scrambled eggs and muffins. The wedding guests were offered orange juice, coffee, and milk. Of all the wedding celebrations my father had ever attended during his thirty-eight years of life (including those held during Prohibition) he'd never before been to one that hadn't served a drop of alcohol.

The joylessness of a celebration without so much as a glass of champagne for a wedding toast reflected the level of enthusiasm the Canrights felt for their daughter's husband. No matter how hard my father tried in all the years that followed, my grandparents remained immune to his kindness, charm, and generosity. In their eyes, this latter quality was not so much an asset as a character flaw. Stella and Eldon Canright valued thriftiness, a language as foreign to my father as Chinese.

While my grandparents worried about how Conrad Goette was going to support their daughter, my father thought only about the honeymoon he had planned for Candy. The day after the wedding, Mother and Daddy boarded a train for Chicago, where my father had booked the honeymoon suite at The Palmer House, Chicago's best hotel. Every night they dined in the finest restaurants in town. Knowing how much my mother loved beef and how little she'd had growing up, Daddy insisted she order the best cuts of steak, and he wouldn't let her look at the prices.

When I was twelve and read *Gone with the Wind*, I thought about Daddy when I reached the part that described Rhett's indulgence of Scarlett on their New Orleans honeymoon. Though Daddy had been a Brother the year *Gone with the Wind* was published, he'd stayed up reading all night, finishing the final pages at sunrise the next day. I imagine him sitting by a window in his long, black robe, closing the book and looking out at black trees etched against a red sky. Did he long for his own strong-willed Scarlett?

When my father chose a life in the brotherhood, he was just a boy, more spirited than spiritual; a lonely, restless boy with an absentee father, a tight-laced stepmother, and a heart still mourning his sister Evelyn's death of pneumonia. The siblings were only a year apart; Conrad, 2 and Evelyn 1, when their mother died of diphtheria. They knew their mother only from stories. My father's childhood, marked by tragedy, was rich in stories—about the Mississippi River, Huckleberry Finn, Oak Alley Plantation, his mother's wild brothers, racing their horses down that historic alley of oaks, straight through the front hall of the big house and out its back.

Somewhere in this romantic mix, Hans Brinker skated into my father's imagination. One of his teachers at Catholic school in Donaldsonville, a Sacred Heart brother, had told the boys his own stories about ice-skating in New Jersey when he was a Sacred Heart novitiate. It wasn't a Gingerbread House that lured my father into the Brotherhood, but visions of himself as Hans Brinker racing across a frozen pond in New Jersey.

The same romantic heart that longed to ice-skate at age fourteen must have longed for other things when my father grew to manhood. He was the grandson of Antoine Sobral, a Portuguese immigrant, and Evelina Gonzales, whose heritage I do not know; Latin blood flowed in his veins. So, in 1943 when my mother crossed the threshold of Brother Jerome's office, unbeknownst to both of them, she entered the inner sanctum of Conrad Goette's heart... where he had been quietly waiting for her.

Like Scarlett O'Hara, Eleanor Jean Canright had also known deprivation. And like Rhett Butler, my father took great pleasure in spoiling her.

Mother had been a child of the Great Depression. During the long Wisconsin winters of her youth, her family's daily diet consisted mostly of potatoes; they never had beef. Long before spring arrived, the potatoes turned gray and soft. One winter the Canrights ran out of money and butter at the same time. Without butter, the potatoes tasted grayer than ever.

Restless and discouraged, Eldon Canright set out on a long walk. The icy wind blowing in from across Pewaukee Lake slapped his face, but it didn't hurt as much as the sting of failure. He trudged through the snow— head down, cold hands thrust deep into his empty pockets. I try to imagine his thoughts as he walked alone in the bitter cold. "Should I write Calla and Blanche for more money?" he may have wondered. His college-educated, older sisters had escaped the lay-offs sweeping the country. "Maybe I should sell the helmet," he might have considered, but just for a moment. Grandpa treasured that German helmet with the spear-point top. He'd found it abandoned on a battlefield in France and carried it with him until the war ended and he was shipped back home. Now the German helmet lay nestled in a box at the bottom of the attic wardrobe just below his WWI uniform next to the tall leather boots he wore in Paris and in the proud photographs his family displayed atop the bookcase back home.

Two miles into his walk, Grandpa spied something sparkling in the ice. Curious as a crow, he squatted down to inspect. There, gleaming through the ice—a fifty cent piece! Grandpa reached in his pocket for his house key and began to chisel, brushing away ice-chips as he dug deeper. He pulled off his mitten and pried the coin from its ice bed with his bare, red fingers. Excited as a pirate with a gold doubloon, Eldon lifted the fifty-cent piece to the dying light. Never had a coin looked more beautiful. He planted it deep in his pocket and hurried toward home, stopping at the corner grocery store minutes before it closed. Stella and the children had just sat down to eat when he burst through the door, triumphantly waving a pound of butter. Steam rose from the potatoes like sighs of relief.

My mother enjoyed the succulent rare beef, the posh lobby of their big city hotel, the plays they saw on the Chicago stage, and whatever else was happening upstairs at the Palmer Hotel during their honeymoon in November of 1944, but after a while she began to experience a bitter aftertaste, some feeling she recognized but could not identify. Her appetite vanished. She didn't want to be spoiled anymore; she wanted to know what was next.

So she asked her mature, 38-year-old husband about his plans, the new job, and where they would be living after the honeymoon. Only then did Conrad tell Candy he didn't actually have a job yet. The ease of his Chicago spending had led my young, naïve, smitten mother to assume his financial security. In fact, my father was rapidly depleting the only savings he possessed.

But that night in Chicago my mother did not share my father's optimism about the future. Her parents had been right, Conrad was crazy. She had made the biggest mistake of her life. Grief stricken, my mother threw herself on the bed and began to cry. She realized she had done exactly what her father had warned against, "burned her bridges," and now she was trapped. Marion and her other girlfriends would continue their lives and marry responsible men, while Mother had doomed herself to the same insecure life she'd wanted to escape. Why hadn't she taken the opportunity Aunt Blanche had offered? Why on earth had she married this man? It was obvious now that she didn't really know him. "Oh, my God, my life is ruined!" she thought, as her quiet tears turned to sobs.

My father sat on the edge of the bed for a long time, patting her and imploring, "Candy, please don't cry, Darling." Then he put on his shoes and slipped out of the room. He returned two hours later, his arms filled with gifts—a dozen long-stemmed red roses, a box of Fannie Farmer chocolates, *The New Yorker*, *Commonweal*, *The Atlantic Monthly*, *Harper's* (all my mother's favorite magazines). The pleading look on his face, the shower of gifts spilling onto the bed—it was so endearing, Mother couldn't help but laugh. Conrad told her to wash her face; he was taking her out for a Porterhouse steak!

Just as I understand my mother's hatred of boiled potatoes, I understand my father's impulse to shower largesse was also rooted in childhood experiences. Because my sisters and I grew up in the same town as our daddy, we heard many more stories about his boyhood than we heard about our mother's early life. The old-timers in Donaldsonville regaled us with tales about our father's notorious past. From what they remembered, Conrad Goette was a spoiled little rich boy, and a bad one at that.

When Daddy was about nine or ten, he got a BB gun for Christmas. A few days later, he started using the streetlights of Donaldsonville for target practice. Within a week he'd shot out half the lights in town. Instinctively, the police chief seemed to know who had done the deed. One January afternoon when the school bell rang, the Chief was waiting outside for Daddy.

"Conrad, I want you to come up to the jailhouse with me," the Chief said, giving the young miscreant a stern look. Daddy didn't even wonder why. When they reached the office, the Chief told Daddy to sit down in the chair across from his desk. "Did you shoot out those lights?"

Daddy was bad, but he was no liar. "Yes, Chief, I did it."

The Chief looked him hard in the eye, tilted his chair and said: "Well, Conrad, I've added up the cost of those lights and you can either pay for 'em, or I can ax your daddy for the money. What'll it be?"

There went Daddy's allowance for the next ten months—no more pocket money for fire crackers, stink bombs, ice-cream sodas or silent movies at the Grand. For close to a year, the town of Donaldsonville enjoyed an unprecedented period of peace and tranquility. Each week, Daddy showed up at the jail house to empty his pockets on the Chief's desk. Slowly but surely, the debt got whittled down. On the last day, Daddy appeared at the Chief's door and handed him his week's allowance and final payment. The Chief motioned him inside. Again they sat across the desk from each other.

"Conrad," he said, "you think you've learned something?"

"Yes, Chief," replied a greatly humbled Conrad Goette.

"Well, I think so, too." With that, the Chief reached into a drawer, pulled out a heavy brown paper bag and handed it to Daddy. That bag held ten months of allowance.

What Daddy did next was typical of a lifelong pattern of behavior. He walked through town with that bag of money, gathered up every kid he knew, and took them all out for ice-cream sodas. I think it took him about three weeks to spend the money in the brown paper bag. During that time period, the town of Donaldsonville had its very own Boy Santa Claus.

Until he left Sacred Heart and married, Conrad Goette had never experienced financial worry, material deprivation, or the average realities that might have tempered his Santa Claus impulse. In fact, until age 38, he'd never had to look for a job or a place to live. Marriage changed his life but not his nature or basic habits.

After the honeymoon, Conrad and Candy Goette moved to Baton Rouge where Daddy got a job as an insurance salesman. The house my parents rented during their first year of marriage belonged to a navy man. When he wrote to tell them of his planned return, Mother was already pregnant with Ann. Though my parents searched every day, housing in Baton Rouge was scarce with the war about to end. On December 1, the day the navy man returned, my parents had to move in with friends while they continued their house search. They still hadn't found a home eleven days later when my sister Ann was born.

Thirty years later when Mother worked for *The Plaquemine Post,* she wrote a feature story based on her memory of that time:

"Sitting in my room at the Lady of the Lake Hospital, I listened to another new mother croon to her newborn about 'going home,' and I shed copious tears over my own homeless newborn.

Then one day, like an angel of mercy, came Mrs. Maurin. Sweeping aside all protests (weakly uttered) she insisted that the three of us move in with her and her family in Bayou Goula."

Daddy's cousins, Irma and Lee Maurin, had come to the rescue. While my parents lived with the Maurins, they spoiled Mother and doted on Ann. Irma fixed Candy thick malted milks and homemade cookies. While Mother napped and read, Irma rocked Ann and planned dinner. Mother's days in Bayou Goula were peaceful and quiet except for one, the day fire engines roared past Irma's house, arousing the reporter's curiosity in my mother. She put down her book and rushed outside to investigate. Mother recounts this memory in her essay:

"A fire one day at an elegant old mansion up the road brought out the entire populace of Bayou Goula, and me with them. Young and old lined the road and levee to watch while furniture was brought out of the burning home. Firemen sprayed the roof of the next house. That was the only excitement that punctuated a quiet and uneventful January."

Daddy continued to search for work outside Baton Rouge. A month later, he found a job in Bunkie, a small town near Alexandria. His younger cousin, Earl Rabelais, had just opened a business selling refrigerators. Earl was as gifted in the business area as Conrad was "challenged." He had anticipated the post-war boom in household refrigerators and had bought as many as the nearest factory could sell him. When Earl called daddy about the job, those fridges—or "ice-boxes" as Daddy called them—were selling like hotcakes in Bunkie. Earl needed another salesman. As the son of Sidonius Goette, Conrad had a great fondness and respect for refrigeration.

While Mother had loved her "pleasant interlude" in Bayou Goula, she was ready to have a home of her own and bake her own cookies. It didn't take long for my parents to pack all their worldly possessions in the back of their car the morning of their departure from Bayou Goula. Irma cried as she handed baby Ann to Candy in the front seat, kissed her goodbye, and closed the car door. She and Lee stood waving in the driveway as Daddy turned onto the road and steered his family toward their next home.

Before they left bayou country to head north toward Bunkie, Daddy decided to take a short detour to visit his old home in Donaldsonville. My mother didn't like detours. She was a hurry-up-and-get-there kind of person, but on this day, she felt so happy and hopeful, she enjoyed a rare reprieve from her anxiety and agreed.

One road led to another, and soon Conrad and Candy were following Bayou LaFourche into Donaldsonville. Dolphie Netter, whom my father had known from the day of his birth, happened to be driving down Railroad Avenue with his North Carolina bride. In the 1940's, as it would still be twenty years later, "goin' ridin'" up and down Railroad Avenue was the main amusement on a Sunday afternoon in Donaldsonville.

Dolphie noticed an unfamiliar car driving slowly down the "Avenue." When he got close enough to look inside, he thought he recognized my father, though he hadn't seen him in years, not since his own mother's funeral. Adolph Netter and Sidonius Goette had both been prominent businessmen in Donaldsonville. Their families were friends.

Daddy remembered the day Dolphie was born, in the *first* Netter house—the one that bordered Crescent Park. Later, "Mr. Adolph" moved his family to the home I knew as "the Netters," the one on Lessard Street with the two (until a hurricane uprooted one) palm trees out front. On the day of Dolphie's birth, Daddy and his gang had been playing baseball in the park when a black woman came out onto the front porch to shoo them away.

"Miz Netter 'bout to give birth in here! Y'all go play someplace else!"

Dolphie remembered Conrad only as a Brother, but he'd heard the news about Daddy's sudden departure to marry a Yankee girl. I suppose everyone in Donaldsonville had talked about it. Throughout his adult life, Dolphie's occupation was banking, but those of us who knew him well knew that his true callings were medicine and sleuthing.

On the day that Dolphie spotted my parents on Railroad Avenue, he turned his Oldsmobile around and followed them.

"If that car stops in front of the Bel House," Dolphie told Connie, "then I know it's Conrad Goette."

The car stopped. That afternoon Candy Goette met Connie Netter, the woman who became her best friend five years later when our family moved to Donaldsonville. During most of the Donaldsonville years, "Candy and Connie" were names linked together in our community in the same way as "Lucy and Ethel." My mother and "Miss Connie," both outsiders, were best friends for many years.

From the Bel House that summer of 1946, Mother and Daddy followed Dolphie and Connie back to the Netter's house on Lessard Street. While the husbands talked about their beloved, dead parents, Candy and Connie traded stories about their all-too-alive mothers. Both these young brides had left home to escape their mothers and had landed in Louisiana. They shared a taste for strong coffee, unfiltered cigarettes, and irreverent humor.

Connie hated Donaldsonville and was thinking of going back to North Carolina—with or without Dolphie. Mother hoped she would be happier in her new home than Connie was in hers.

Bel House, Conrad Goette's boyhood home, was the only historical house not destroyed by Union bombardment of 1862. It faces the Mississippi River near its intersection with Bayou LaFourche.

From age 13-37, Josephine Sobral's home was Oak Alley Plantation until she married Sidonius Goette of Donaldsonville.

Sidonius Goette, two-term mayor and prominent businessman in Donaldsonville

Donaldsonville Ice Company
with Anheiser Busch delivery wagon

When the Civil War ended, the Mississippi River and North-South railways could be used for commercial rather than war purposes. German immigrants like Anheiser, Busch, and Goette were more American than Confederate. They were enterprising merchants with no stake in the Confederate cause. Motivated by post-war opportunities, Adolphus Busch quickly began building his beer empire in St. Louis. His first step was a giant leap forward in refrigeration through ice-packing, which made it possible to transport perishables like beer and produce long distances. Sidonius Goette, fellow German, progressive thinker, and close friend to Adolphus, served as distributer of Anheiser Busch in the lower Mississippi region and president of Donaldsonville Ice Company.

Born on a Bayou

The Bunkie years turned out to be some of the happiest of my mother's life. The Rabelais men and their wives felt like old friends from the day my parents arrived, and even though Daddy was as bad at selling refrigerators as he had been at selling insurance, Earl's business was doing so well, even Daddy couldn't hurt it. Later, Earl would say, "Conrad offered to lower the price on a refrigerator while the customer was reaching for his pen to sign!" Although he laughed each time he told a story, I'm sure Earl must have been as relieved as my father when the assistant principal position opened at Bunkie High School.

In addition to the Rabelais network of cousins, my parents formed other friendships, but none more treasured than with Jimmy and Frances Knoll. It began the day Mother went to Dr. Knoll's clinic for a pregnancy test.

When Jimmy went home that night, he told his wife, "Frances, you've got to meet this new woman in town because I can tell you're going to be good friends," and he was right.

The delivery room of Jimmy Knoll's clinic extended over Bayou St. John, so I was literally "born on a bayou." Unfortunately, I arrived the day after Christmas. My parents had just returned from a party when Mother went into labor. I had chosen an inconvenient time to be born, a day no one feels like celebrating, not even the birthday girl.

As if anticipating the long-term consequences of my bad birthday, Daddy gave me the grandest christening party Bunkie had ever known. Mother and Daddy's friends continued to talk about it for decades later. Every time we visited, someone would tell me "Jane, you had the best christening party!" It was as if in that one night, they'd used up all the "happy" my birthday had in it.

A sprinkling of snow dusted the town the night of my christening party. Because snow was almost as rare in Bunkie as in Donaldsonville, my parents' friends arrived in jovial spirits. There was magic in that crisp, cold air. The holiday season had ended, but thanks to Conrad Goette, the liquor store experienced an unexpected surge in sales.

As each couple arrived for the party, they deposited their babies and toddlers next door at Earl and Mary Virginia's apartment. Since the war had ended and the Baby Boom had begun, there were a lot of them, but Mary Virginia was prepared. She hired a black woman with enough experience to have run a daycare center single-handedly. For one night, my parents' friends had the luxury of forgetting they had children. They drank too much, smoked too much, and said things people remembered for the rest of their lives, like the question Earl asked a friend, "How did an ugly son-of-a-bitch like you get to marry a beautiful woman like…?" Everyone in Bunkie had wondered the same thing, but only alcohol could pry loose a question like that. The crowd held its breath until the "ugly son-of-a-bitch" laughed, slapped Earl on the back and replied, "That's for me to know and you to find out!"

Two years later, Jimmy Knoll delivered his second Goette baby. My sister Kay Kay was born a few months after Dr. Knoll had delivered his own daughter, little Martha Frances. All Mother and Daddy's friends had boys in their families, and Jimmy had correctly predicted the sex of each child. Early in my mother's pregnancy, Jimmy had told her, "This one's going to be a boy, Candy." Mother wasn't happy about having another baby so soon after Ann and me, but at least she thought this one would be a different sex. As the months passed, she began to anticipate her little boy's arrival with unexpected joy. She even knit a blue blanket so she wouldn't have to carry him home from the clinic in a hand-me-down pink one.

In later years, I would hear Mother tell Connie the worst part of childbirth was the indignity of lying with your feet in stirrups while a little audience stared down at your naked bottom and talked to you as if you were a child. She remembered the faces of Jimmy's two nurses that November day at the Knoll Clinic. They knew Mother was expecting a son this time, and they kept saying, "Honey, push a little harder; you can do it! Don't you want to see your little boy?"

With the last push they had squealed, "Here he comes!" Jimmy cupped the baby's head in one hand, caught its bottom with his other, and raised the baby by… her little feet. Mother said she knew by the silence in the room this baby was another girl. She was disappointed and tired and she wept. Poor Kay Kay has heard this story her whole life, but she was the most beautiful of Candy and Conrad's four babies. I'm certain my mother's disappointment was short lived when Jimmy handed Kay Kay to her and she saw those long-lashed eyes blinking up at her.

All Mother and Daddy's friends had kids our ages. Perhaps people were eager to resume the lives that war had interrupted, or maybe their generation felt an urge to create life in the aftermath of so much death. Everyone was having babies.

Although Daddy was much older than his cousins, they were all in the same boat now. On a recent visit to Bunkie, Earl Rabelais's widow, Mary Virginia, told my sisters and me, "None of us had any money when Candy and Conrad lived in Bunkie. Of course, we all realized this except your daddy." She laughed, "Conrad was poor; he just didn't know it!"

Mother was never lonely during the Bunkie years and she never felt like an outsider. Friends and children floated through each other's houses as naturally as a summer breeze. The families helped each other out—finding jobs, lending furniture, sharing food, taking care of kids. Mother and her women friends had a study group. When they weren't changing diapers or fixing peanut butter and jelly sandwiches, they talked about books and religion. They drank coffee and smoked cigarettes together and told each other irreverent stories about their in-laws and husbands. Mother was happy in Bunkie.

After their brief reunion in front of the Bel House, Dolphie and Daddy stayed in touch. In the spring of 1951, Dolphie called Daddy in Bunkie to tell him there was an opening for the principal's job in Donaldsonville. He was sure Daddy would get the job if he applied for it. At that time, the principal's job in Donaldsonville paid five thousand dollars a year. That was a higher salary than either of my mother's rich aunts had earned when they were supporting her family in Pewaukee.

"My God, Conrad, how are we ever going to spend all that money?!" gasped the Daughter of Depression.

Mary Kay, Jane, Ann on front steps, Donaldsonville, Louisiana

A Fairy Boat Across the Mississippi

Little wisps of the three years I lived in Bunkie are windows into my first reality, that strange land where all our stories begin, a land with no fixed geography, no history or science—only magic— some good and some bad. Each adult lived there once—the Madison Avenue executive and the Norwegian nurse, the nomad and the glass blower. Whether born Chinese or American, on the ice or in the desert, we live for a while in a world as small as Adam and Eve's. For the first few years of our lives, we all carry the same brief passport.

Like Adam and Eve, once we leave that original world, we can never return. Though our exit isn't dramatic or sudden, it's just as final. Most of us don't even realize we've gone someplace else until the day we try to play pirates or make a mud pie and we can't remember how to do it. Images and feelings flicker on the periphery of consciousness, but we can't hold them. They slip through our fingers like shadows.

Though my suitcase was small, when we left Bunkie I took a few of those wispy memories with me—like the day I ran down the sidewalk and fell. When I opened my eyes, I saw red—a bush filled with scarlet blossoms, long, menacing stamens protruding from the cups like tiny arms, reaching. Alive and dangerous, the flowers had hurt me. Though I didn't yet speak the language or know the point of "telling," I understood the meaning of "red." Blood on the sidewalk, a rip in my pants, and two hands lifting me. From that day on, when I walked down the sidewalk holding my mother's pale hand, I made sure she was between the bush and me. She looked puzzled each time I abruptly switched to her other side.

One Bunkie day, I stood in my baby bed and watched my father hang a birdhouse outside the window. The branch was close to the glass. The birds had a house now, and soon they would move in. I couldn't wait to see them, especially the baby bird.

On another afternoon when all the doors and windows were opened, the sky turned dark at naptime. A terrible, angry clatter erupted just above the house, so loud it rattled the windows. I was

---

frightened and too worried to sleep, but Ann wasn't. "It's just the devil and his wife having a fight in the sky. They're throwing chairs," she explained. I looked up at the ceiling and wondered how many chairs they would break. I knew it wasn't right to break chairs, and now I understood why people hated the Devil.

When naptime ended, Mother lifted me from my bed. I grabbed my teddy bear and ran to the front porch to watch the rain pour down. The sound was sweet music after the terrible noise the Devils had made. A curtain of rain spilled from the rainspout. Though I loved Teddy, and my parents didn't understand, when I saw that little waterfall and the puddle below, I had to throw my bear in. If I hadn't, I would have jumped from the porch myself.

Ricky Rabelais was my age and the first friend I had. I don't remember when or how or what we played, but I remember loving him. I sat in my mother's lap while she drank coffee at Mary Virginia's kitchen table. Perhaps I was pouting because I wanted the tutu Ricky wore. It belonged to Claire Lucille, but that day Ricky's mother let him wear it. Ricky wouldn't even let me have the powder puff hat that went with the tutu. As I sat frowning and bored, sharp screams from outside punctured the drone of grown-up talk.

"Ricky is stuck in the doghouse," Mary Virginia said. I went to the window to look. I saw the bottoms of his feet protruding from the little door. Ricky was my only friend, and now he was stuck in the doghouse and could never come out again to eat or play or sleep in his own bed. Poor Ricky!

When Daddy got the job in Donaldsonville, he explained to my sister that we would be moving to a town on the banks of the "Mighty Mississip'," and after we moved, we would cross that great river back and forth many times each year. It was true. Until the Sunshine Bridge opened in 1964, ferry boats were the mode of transportation as integral to life in Donaldsonville as the subway is to New Yorkers. At age five, my sister Ann could not wait to ride the "Fairy" boat.

I don't remember the actual day we moved into our River Road house, but I remember the next day. I ventured down the back porch steps alone. The grass and weeds of the neglected yard stood taller than my bangs and seemed a mysterious jungle. I don't think I went farther than a few feet from the steps because I was afraid of getting lost. I felt something wonderful but dangerous hiding in the grass luring me forward, but something stopped me. It was as if some force stronger than fear was pulling me back to my house. Perhaps it was the premonition of the life I was about to begin on the River Road, the neighbors I would come to know, or perhaps it was the force of the Mississippi River entering my blood stream—major artery of a continent—with all its history and lore; Mark Twain's river and my daddy's and soon it would be mine, too.

Poetry is the language best suited for me to share the earliest memories I have of my new home in an old house on the River Road. Aside from images and sounds, I have but one specific memory of that first month: My mother is sitting in the bathtub. I am standing beside the tub watching as she soaps the washcloth and begins sliding it from under her lifted chin, down her shoulder and front side of her left arm. She raises her arm and moves the washcloth in the opposite direction from wrist to armpit, across her breasts, then in circles around her big belly. She looks up at me, smiles, and hands me the washcloth, "Jane, will you wash my back. I can't reach it." I think it is because of the baby in her belly. My father has told Ann and me we should help our mother. I feel important.

Jane, Ann, Conrad, Gretchen, Kay Kay, River Road, Spring 1952

A Bend in the River

I was three when my family moved—
not across continents, countries or states—
Bunkie to Donaldsonville,
a move as big as any other.
My old life melted quick as ice-cream,
and like a sweet potato in a Mason jar,
I sprouted new roots overnight.

This home, on a river road.
Pasture and sugarcane fields out back
and strange noises in the night:
metallic clunks on the roof—
"Pecans," my mother said.
Deep bellows from the pasture—
"Cows."
Ghostly moans from the river—
"Fog horns to guide the boats."
In the morning I ventured alone
down the back steps of the house
into a forest of weeds
waving and calling to me.
Every single thing—plant, animal, shadow
--alive and as real as I
in that time without fences.
I stopped in the grass, listening,
sensing that other world—
green arms that touched and tickled.

Animal eyes inviting me,
all speaking a language I understood.
Whispered secrets—a grassy path,
a Fairy trail leading someplace far.
Magic lay shining down the path.
Air, sweet as sugar
cicadas singing,
their voices light as their bones,
rising and falling in waves of grass.
They beckoned me to follow them.
But I stopped—
I didn't want to wander, not now.
I turned and ran back to the house.
Other voices called to me:
St. Amico and nuns with wings on their heads,
hurricanes, hobo dogs and haunted houses
poetry, politics, and three sisters.
Our story was about to begin on the River Road.
The Mississippi was calling me home.

Captain Jim

The longest days of my life were the ones spent on the River Road before I started school. I realize now that time must have felt as dreary and interminable for my mother as it did for me. We Goettes had left Bunkie and crossed a "Fairy" boat expecting a beautiful life lay on the other side. "Daughter of Depression" had moved to the idyllic town whose virtues her husband had extolled as long as she'd known him: an opera house, a thriving market, concerts on the courthouse lawn, warm and friendly people. He would be making more money than my mother could imagine spending. How could she not be happy? Why wasn't I?

After we moved from Bunkie, the only children I ever saw were my sisters. Kay Kay and Gretchen were too little to be playmates, and Ann left home every morning with Daddy to spend the whole long day in the big world of school. It seemed as far away and out of reach as China. I had two more years to wait before I could become a schoolgirl like Ann. At age three and a half I knew only that I had been left behind. Did Mother feel that way, too? From the front steps of our house, we watched Daddy and Ann leave each morning; I would be back on the steps waiting for them every afternoon.

Life in Bunkie had been full of children and nice mothers; we had spilled in and out of each other's houses every day. There were no families like the Rabelais and Knolls on the rural River Road. There were fewer houses with a lot more land between them, a levee in front and only pastures and fields behind. There weren't other streets or intersections, not blocks in a grid pattern like there are in towns. I lived in an old house on a long, lonely ribbon of road that followed the Mississippi all the way down to New Orleans. I could sit watching from the front steps an entire morning and not see a single person walk past our River Road house.

Not until I was an adult did I realize how terribly lonely and bored my mother must have felt after we left Bunkie. She spent her days changing diapers, making grocery lists, feeding children, napping, and, like me, waiting for that green Chevy to pull back into the driveway at 4:00 p.m.

When they returned home, Daddy and Ann brought stories from the outside world. We were hungry for them. Ann talked about little girls with ponytails; some had curls; there were blonde girls and brunettes, girls with freckles, short girls and tall ones. Inside the classroom they played with a big dollhouse and at recess, they rode on a merry-go-round. Ann talked about a lunchroom with long tables filled with children. At school there were blackboards and chalk, reading circles and recess.

At home there were little sisters who wore diapers and took naps and a mother who was always too busy for me. And when Mother ordered me to go outside and play, I heard only the voices of crickets, an occasional "moo" from one of Mrs. Abadie's cows, the distant barking of dogs down the road. I wanted a friend; I wanted a story of my own. If only there could be a war with soldiers galloping across the levee, a lost elephant who wandered into our yard, a riverboat captain who...

The first time I told Daddy about Captain Jim's visits, he put down the *Times Picayune* and humored me by listening and seeming to want to hear more about this man who came every day to visit Mother and me. Most days after he was home a while and Mother disappeared to the kitchen to start dinner, Daddy would relax, slouch in his chair, put his feet on one end of the ottoman, and pat the other—his non-verbal invitation for me to sit. "Well, Topper, did you see Captain Jim today?" I needed no further encouragement to plop down with a brain already spinning a new story.

I was playing in the front yard one day when I heard a riverboat bell. I looked up and saw someone coming over the crest of the levee. When I waved, he waved back and came down to visit. Captain Jim was a very handsome man, I told my father. He had a nice beard, but it wasn't long or gray. When I invited him inside to have a cup of coffee with mother, he took off his captain's hat and let me wear it while we all sat at the kitchen table. He put cream and sugar in my coffee.

"Your mother liked him, too, I suppose?" Daddy asked.

"Sure she did, and he liked her a lot. He wanted Mother to go for a ride on his riverboat, but she had to take care of Kay Kay and Gretchen, and bake a pie, so I went instead," I told Daddy, along with many other details of Captain Jim's friendliness to both Mother and me.

Every day after that, when Daddy came home, we sat together in the living room talking about Captain Jim, who always had to leave right before Daddy and Ann returned from school. Too bad they never got to meet him, but I would tell Daddy all about it—how Captain Jim parked his boat across the levee and came down to drink coffee with Mother and me. Afterwards, when he had to get back to his captain job, Mother would let me go along to help him. She kissed us goodbye, then we headed across the levee to the ramp leading to the deck of Captain Jim's boat.

In the long afternoons while Mother and my little sisters napped, I traveled up and down the Mississippi. Sometimes when there weren't too many barges, Captain Jim sat me on his lap and let me turn the big steering wheel. When I wasn't steering, I had other important jobs to do, like look through a spyglass to make sure nothing was coming around the bend. If I saw pirates, I rang the big bell to warn Captain Jim to go faster. At three o'clock, he turned his boat around and steered it back to our part of the Mississippi. Daddy and Ann would be coming home soon; I needed to get back. After I walked the plank to the shore and waved goodbye, Captain Jim would give his fog horn two quick tugs and churn away. I climbed the levee, over the crest and down the other side to sit on the front steps, where I waited for that green Chevy to appear.

I don't remember whether it was Daddy or me who tired of Captain Jim, but he sailed away one day and never returned.

Jane Goette

Courtesy of Oak Alley Foundation

Oak Alley view from River Road

Oak Alley, a Child's Mirage

One Sunday afternoon when I was a little girl, my father said he was taking us for a drive to see Oak Alley. It didn't mean anything to me. I knew nothing of the world or my family's history, I was simply excited to see anything novel: an elephant, a haunted house, a pagoda, Oak Alley. It seemed an endless journey down the long, winding road from our house on the River Road to Oak Alley with nothing to see on the left side but an endless reel of levee. The view on the right was not much better—stretches of pasture punctuated with brief sprinkles of houses, black people sitting on porches so tired they leaned, an occasional country store with faded images of Coca-Cola, cigarette brands like Phillip Morris (smiling boy under a funny hat,) Jax Beer. Behind all this, sugarcane fields, another endless reel like the levee. Every mile or so, a cow or two; sometimes a dog sitting under a tree.

Finally, my father's cheerful voice over his shoulder, "Okay girls, we're here!" He slowed the Chevy and pulled onto a strip of grass between the levee ditch and the black top. There were few cars on the River Road in those days; my parents didn't bother telling us to look before crossing. That's not why I reached for my father's hand. I had studied his face as we got out of the car. It had that church expression, serious, faraway. I didn't understand but respected whatever it meant.

It's hard to explain the deserted place I observed that Sunday afternoon. My Oak Alley in the 1950s was nothing like the one you may have visited decades later after it became a tourist attraction. I remember a haunting quiet, the quivering heat, the complete silence broken only by the slap of shoes crossing the road. The occasional car that passed along that stretch of River Road might very well have driven past Oak Alley and not even looked—not because it wasn't beautiful but because it was a forgotten place. Not only were there no buses or cars or public entrance, there were no signs of life of any kind--just a Sleeping Beauty of a place in the heat of a long summer's nap from which it might never awake.

We stepped through the tall weeds on the other side of the road. Daddy led his family to the front of the wrought iron fence that lined the plantation. At first it had seemed there was nothing to see but trees until Daddy took my hands and placed them on the bars of the fence. "Look," he said, and I did . I stopped breathing in that instant, as if I were falling out a window into a cloud . I stared through those bars onto a dreamscape more beautiful than anything I'd seen in a fairytale. Fantastical, unreal, like the world trapped inside a snow globe . A long, shaded alleyway cast in a green glow, and at the end where the trees grew smaller and closer together, a pink, columned mansion like a sailboat at the edge of the far horizon .

In the Louisiana of my childhood, shade was a coveted resource for *all* mammals, dogs and children alike. We had no air-conditioning, no one did, but our house didn't even have fans. On Sunday afternoons, my parents ordered my sisters and me outside, "Go play," they said, while they took long naps in the heat of the afternoon. We didn't argue or disobey, just whined heavily as we slunk down the porch stairs at the back of the house to kill time under the house or wander down the road to the irrigation ditch where there was water to wade in, turtles and lizards to catch. Waiting for my parents' naps to end felt long as a prison sentence.

I think Oak Alley's trees must have been at their peak when I first saw them long before the chemical plants came and climate change birthed monster storms. Or perhaps memory is always a rose-colored glass. Fourteen equally spaced trees on opposing sides of the Big House extended all the way to the edge of the River Road. Twenty-eight massive Live Oaks with branches and limbs stretching out across a wide alley; long, laced fingers weaving an unbroken, dense, green canopy, creating a long tunnel that sucked cool air from the river, an alley bathed in fairy light. Glowing, stunning, still the most beautiful place I've ever seen.

I wish I could rewind that memory and freeze time just at that moment —I would edit out the history that came before and after, wash away Oak Alley's sins and tragedies, render it clean as a baptized baby, and save that shining, quiet, quivering beauty seen long ago on a summer's day.

River Road Neighbors

For most Americans, the word "neighborhood" conjures images of houses neatly arranged in a large grid of criss-crossing, tree-lined streets. In a stereotypical 1950-60's neighborhood, a mother goes across the street to borrow a cup of sugar from a neighbor; a child rides her bike around the block to visit a friend. Where I lived, there were no streets or little squares inside bigger squares. My neighborhood defied mathematics; it was more an idea than a logical plan.

Ours was one of a sprinkling of houses scattered along a country road that curved like a ribbon. There were no streets, only one road, the Old River Road that hugged the levee and followed the Mississippi River south to the Gulf of Mexico. Along this road houses grew farther apart as you left one little community and drew closer again as you approached the next. The important places, Baton Rouge and New Orleans, were on the east bank of the Mississippi; we lived on the west surrounded by miles of sugarcane fields. Across the river from Baton Rouge on our side, towns ran south in this order—Port Allen, Plaquemine, White Castle, Donaldsonville, St. James, Vacherie.

My family lived on the outskirts of Donaldsonville, the largest town on the west bank, with a population of around 10,000. Railroad Avenue was the main street of the downtown which dead-ended at Donaldsonville's other main street, Mississippi. Mississippi Street bordered the levee and became the River Road as it exited the town.

Louisiana bookshops and libraries hold rich collections that document the fascinating history of the Old River Road; however, the River Road of my childhood was just a short piece of that historic ribbon of concrete and asphalt. My neighborhood began at the southern end of Donaldsonville, just past the Harps' house, and continued two miles or so, winding around a couple of curves to about the second haunted house, the one right past the Truxillos'. All the human drama I could imagine or handle existed in that two-mile stretch. It was enough.

When I sat on the levee looking at our old house perched on its brick pillars, I sort of loved it, the way you'd love a homely old grandmother with elegant lace hankies but worn shoes. The house had a touch of class and a romantic sense of faded glory. People driving down the River Road may have turned their heads to look at it, not understanding exactly what made them look. Perhaps it was its peculiar ruined beauty, a combination of majesty and melancholy. Our house was like that homely aunt who'd once had money but had fallen on hard times. Like such an aunt, our house was loved, neglected, and somewhat embarrassing.

Many old houses on the River Road were built high off the ground. Ours rested on evenly spaced rows of brick pillars about six feet tall. A sidewalk ran perpendicular from the road leading up to the house. It formed a "V" just as it reached a large lagustrum bush directly in front of our house. To the left and right of the lagustrum, symmetrical cement staircases fanned outward in a graceful curve leading from the ground to a wide landing. From the landing, another set of wide steps forged the rest of the way up to a screened porch which ran the width of the house.

The stairs were the most unique feature of our house. They were graceful like a half-opened Japanese fan, but the effect was more than ornamental. The stairs opened outward from the body of the house, like a pair of arms reaching for a hug. It seemed that anyone looking at the house from the levee could easily see this was a house with a heart.

A long, shell-filled driveway ran along the left side of the house, bordered by a row of tall pecan trees, the bane of my childhood existence. On autumn mornings when my father backed the car out of the garage to drive to six o'clock mass in town, he couldn't stand the thought of smashing hundreds of pecans— though thousands more remained. My September school days began early with Daddy rousing my sisters and me from our beds. He handed us Easter baskets and sent us outside in our nightgowns to clear the driveway. We stood watching as he backed out in the soft light of dawn. Each time a wheel struck a pecan, the crunch and crack rattled Daddy worse than a fingernail on a chalkboard. He would shoot us a look that lacked the piety of someone headed to church when he didn't even have to go.

To the right of the house, another large pecan tree stood in the grassy yard between us and Miss Jambois's bushes. A big producer, in good years that one tree alone spilled so many nuts into the yard, I could plop down in the grass and scoop up handfuls of pecans in a matter of minutes. It took no time at all to fill an Easter basket and get released from pecan duty to run off and play.

My neighborhood didn't have a park, but a child didn't need one where we lived. Right across the road we had the levee, and on its other side, the batcher (a Louisiana term used for the land between the foot of the levee and the Mississippi River), with its trees and scattered ponds. Behind our house an old, dilapidated shed stood nestled into the corner between our back yard and the barbed wire fence that bordered Mrs. Abadie's cow pasture. Beyond the pastures flowed waves and waves of sugarcane fields. They seemed endless, but I knew they ended at The Great Swamp.

Jane Goette

War and Dogs at the Persons'

In childhood, the River Road neighborhood in which we played began at the curve in the road heading south out of town. The Persons' house, the first with accessible children, was in the center of the curve tucked back from the road. This rambling, two-story white house was filled with little boys. The family was known for its proliferation of male children and for its two Great Danes—the meanest dogs on the River Road.

Though I have always had strong pacifist leanings, my fondest memories with the Person boys are from playing war. Although it seemed beneath me to play with a bunch of little kids, especially boys, I couldn't resist the temptation when the Person boys called a war. I overlooked their failings, lowered my friendship standards and enlisted in their army at a moment's notice. As soon as I got word of war, I jumped on my bike and rode down to the Persons' as fast as I could pedal.

From the River Road no one could have guessed the big secret hiding behind the Persons' house—a large field filled with Army jeeps and trucks. They looked exactly like the ones driven by American G.I.'s in the movies that played at the Grand. All this belonged to Mrs. Person's daddy, Tubby Ewing, who also owned the Ford dealership in town.

Row upon row of old Army vehicles sat silent in the scorching Louisiana sun. Wavy heat rose from their metal hoods. Except for the buzz of insects or a cow mooing in the distance, it was quiet as a cemetery back there. I wondered what stories the trucks and jeeps would tell if they could speak. Who were the soldiers who'd ridden in them, and where were they now? Had these brave young men returned home to their families, or were they lying buried in some foreign field, some "Flanders Field" in Europe? Could any of them have met a stranger fate than these jeeps and trucks whose days had ended in Tubby Ewing's field, a bizarre variation of a used-car lot?

"We can play in 'em. Paw Paw don't care as long as we close 'em up so the cats don't pee in 'em."

I ran up and down the long, hot rows, trying to choose my jeep. I was like the little old man in *Millions of Cats*, thinking each one was better than the last. Finally I settled upon an Army-green jeep that looked newer than the others. It was perfect except for a small rip in the front seat. I studied it carefully to make sure there was no blood. It may have been unpatriotic, but I didn't want to sit on the same seat as a dead person.

Choosing my jeep was easier than getting into it. Those metal boxes were hot as ovens. The door handle burned my hand. I stretched my shirt over the handle, using it like a pot holder to open the door. A wave of scorching heat poured over my face stinging my eyes. After both doors were opened, I waited for what seemed as long as a war to stick my head inside. It wasn't long enough. When I ventured inside, trying hard not to let my skin touch the upholstery, the seat burned my thighs. It hurt to breathe, the way it must hurt a beached fish trying to inhale something not meant for its body. For a fleeting moment, I sensed the suffering that had taken place here, encased in this tiny, metal world. Voices interrupted my morbid thoughts. "Hey, look at me! Come see this!" The moment passed like a long sigh.

Soon my own voice joined the chorus: "Hey, look at me! I'm driving a hundred miles an hour!" For awhile each of us had our own vehicle to drive. When this got boring, we paired up and played war. David and Stevie fought over Kay Kay; I ended up with a choice between Gretchen and Mikey. I picked Gretchen because I could count on her to be dramatic. Mikey would have made machine gun noises and thrown grenades out the window. I needed another girl, even a baby sister, to play a good story.

"Let's pretend you were a German nurse and I talked you into coming over to the American side, and now the Nazis are trying to catch us," I began.

"Yeah, and I'm your little sister and I help you give shots."

"Gretchen, how could you be my little sister if I'm an American and you're a German? That doesn't make sense."

It took us awhile to get our story straight. I opened the door and helped Gretchen climb into the passenger side of my jeep. Soon, we were speeding along a country road in France, escaping the Nazis.

Enemy planes rained bullets down upon us; I drove faster and faster, desperate to reach the border. Gretchen was the bleeding German nurse who'd been shot by a Nazi who hated her for coming over to our side. I was rushing her to the nearest Red Cross tent hospital. Gretchen died lots of times on the way, flopping dramatically to the edge of the seat, her blond pigtails dangling out the window. I tried to coach her to say something patriotic or really sad before she died, but she usually messed up her lines or said something silly.

***

The true danger at the Persons', however, was not the Nazis or the Japanese but two vicious Great Danes named "Patches" and "Nig." In the late fifties in the South, it was not uncommon for white people to name their black dogs "Nigger." This racist term seemed perfectly acceptable to those Person boys. They thought it was a great name since "Nig" was black as the ace of spades. My sisters and I were relieved the Persons used this nickname because we hated the other word. It would have been easier for us to utter the mysterious and forbidden "F" word than to say the cruel and ugly "N" word. For our mother, it was worse than any swear word.

Nig embodied the racism that generated his name; he hated black people with a passion. Unfortunately, most of the people too poor to own cars were black; therefore, they were about the only people you saw walking up and down the River Road, and even that was rare. There weren't many cars or trucks either except during the late fall when sugarcane trucks rattled by all day long. When black people neared the Persons' house, they crossed the road and walked on the levee until they were well past Nig's territory.

Nig's partner in crime, "Patches," had but one good eye. The other one was cloudy gray, a perfect accessory to his mottled gray body. Like all dogs out in the country, this blood-thirsty duo ran free. They hated children almost as much as they hated blacks. They struck terror into the hearts of every child unlucky enough to have to ride past their house on a bicycle. This was the unfortunate fate of the four Goette girls. If we were lucky, Patches and Nig were sleeping out back and ignored the scent of fear our bodies released like an alarm bell each time we approached the Persons' house.

Sometimes just when I thought I was in the clear, that belly-deep bark would suddenly rise from under the porch or from a distant corner of the yard. With racing heart and feet I prayed as hard as I pedaled, "Please don't let them bite me; I'll put a nickel in the Poor Box instead of buying a Shoesole at Maurin's after mass, and ..." Then I felt hot breath on my ankles; my socks dampened with warm dog slobber. Nig was on one side of my bike and Patches on the other in what appeared to be a perfectly coordinated attack. I sometimes wondered if they had been hiding in the bushes all morning, strategizing. I imagined it this way: Nig would propose: "Let's wait 'til she gets past the driveway; she'll think she's in the clear," and Patches would reply, "Good thinkin', Nig. We'll launch our surprise attack—it's my favorite."

"Okay, Patches, you take her left foot. I'll get the right one."

Patches, with a dreamy look in his one good eye, replies, "Don't you just love the taste of a little girl's ankle socks?"

Nig, with foamy slobber dribbling down his chin, agrees, "Oh, yes, and very good they are, little girl's ankle socks!"

We were sorry when the Person family moved to another town in North Louisiana, though a cloud of fear lifted for children on bikes, small animals, and black people walking on the River Road. A year or two after they moved, they stopped in to visit us on a trip back to Donaldsonville to see Paw Paw Tubby.

"We have some bad news for y'all," David said shaking his head mournfully. "Someone poisoned Patches. Can you believe someone could be so mean?!"

BIG Miss Landry

Returning from town, if I made it past the Persons', the next house on my way home was *Big* Miss Landry's. Like its owner, it was fairly big, with faded, chipping paint and a sagging front porch that ran the length of the house. Big Miss Landry wore glasses, and her hair was parted in the middle and pulled back in a wrap-around braid. I didn't know her any better than to wave hello if she was on the porch when I passed.

In later years I remember a short, dark-haired woman came to live with Big Miss Landry, a woman who became pregnant and stayed that way. I never passed her porch without seeing the woman—I think her name was "Sis"—dressed in those unmistakable, 1950's two-piece maternity outfits. After a couple of years, I began to wonder what was holding up the baby. This was one of those unsolved childhood mysteries, the kind that get lodged in the back corners of memory's dusty bins. Did the baby die? Had Sis really been pregnant? Was it wishful thinking on her part that she wore those clothes? Perhaps she was just poor and had to wear what had been given to her. Childhood mysteries like this one are rarely solved. We don't know the questions to ask when we're young, and forty years later—there's no one left to answer them.

Big Miss Landry's house bordered the Lane. The Lane was a gravel road that intersected the paved River Road and ran west toward the sugarcane fields. It was an early and very small subdivision. All the houses were brand new but small and modest. There was a row of five or six houses on each side of the Lane. Mrs. Torres and her youngest daughter, Brenda, lived on the left side of the Lane. Gretchen and Brenda became friends after they started first grade and Mother went to work at Lemann's department store as its women's clothing buyer. Mrs. Torres, a widow, worked as Lemanns' seamstress. She soon became my mother's personal tailor. "Torres," as Mother called her, enjoyed the challenge of complicated Vogue patterns, the kind my mother liked. My Mother never had the money to indulge her taste for high fashion, but thanks to Mrs. Torres, she wore outfits rarely found in department stores—

even at Maison Blanche or Godchaux's in New Orleans. Though she lived in Donaldsonville, Louisiana, Candy Goette dressed like a New Yorker. My sisters and I felt proud of our mother's stylishness, but no one felt prouder than Mrs. Torres. With Mother's Audrey Hepburn figure and vogue dresses, she became *the* Donaldsonville trend setter for many years. Mrs. Torres had made that possible.

River Road Gang of Girls

May and Ivy Dugas bought a small lot at the very end of The Lane, built a two-bedroom house, and moved their ever-growing family to the River Road shortly before Myra and I started first grade, a time when a child my own age seemed as rare as a talking monkey.

They were a large family with children whose ages matched each of my sisters and me. When Mother first told me a family was moving near us that had a child Ann's age, one my age, one Kay Kay's and one Gretchen's, I couldn't believe our good fortune. I would have been thrilled to have one child of any age as a neighbor—even a boy—and now we would have a house full of girls (and boys) right down the road. There is no comparable analogy to express my wonder at having real, live children land on my planet.

Ann got Michael, but my little sisters and I each had a Dugas girl of our own. Throughout childhood on the River Road, my little sisters and the Dugas girls were my constant companions. Together we had many make-believe careers—teachers, nuns, nurses, missionaries, explorers...

On a typical Saturday morning, the Dugas girls had to finish their chores before Miss May would let them "go play at the Goettes'." Unless it was raining, our mother would tell us to play outside. As soon as she saw Myra, Cathy and Donna running up the sidewalk, before they even knocked on the door, Mother would tell us, "Just because those girls cleaned their mama's house doesn't mean they can come make a mess of mine. You girls go play outside now." And so we did… almost all the time.

One of our favorite games was playing bakery. We worked long hours concocting gorgeous mud pies and other delectable pastries in our back yard or under the house. We created our own recipe for gourmet mud, smooth as silk. First, we sifted dirt through a piece of screening we found lying under the house. Next, we added water, slowly mixing, stirring, and smashing the bumps to smooth out the mud. When it was just the right consistency, we rolled out biscuits and cakes with cardboard toilet paper holders, our rolling pins.

The Goette-Dugas Bakery's greatest achievement was a three-tiered wedding cake decorated with tiny lagustrum blossoms and bordered with little white seashells from our driveway. We spent a long time sorting through the shells and blossoms we collected, placing them in little piles based on size, shape and color. Before our confection was ready for decoration we first had to perfect the cake—no easy task when the basic ingredients were mud and water. We went up and down the porch steps carrying cans of water from the bathroom, trying not to slop too much of it along the way back down. We scooped the water out with our hands, splashing it across the surface of each mud tier, smoothing it out with the palms of our hands until it was slick and shiny. It gleamed like chocolate, but we knew from experience it would turn ugly gray after it dried.

Since we had already sorted and organized our decorations, we were prepared to choose the best ones to arrange around the top and sides of the tiers so they could stick before the mud dried. First, we rinsed our hands to make sure we did not stain our decorations. Then, quickly but gently, we pressed little white flowers and shells across the tops and sides of each tier. Since the top tier was the centerpiece of the cake, we gave its design our greatest scrutiny and care, placing slightly larger (but the whitest and least broken) shells in an overlapping circle at the center. The piece de resistance was the beautiful sprig of lagustrum blossoms we stuck into the center of the shell circle. When we finished, we scooted around the cake on our bottoms so we could view it from all sides. This was the best work we'd ever done.

"I'm tellin' you—this looks like a real weddin' cake!" Myra exclaimed with pride.

"*Mais, yeh,*" Cathy whispered. We stood together in silent wonder gawking at our work of art. We'd spent a whole morning making this cake, but it truly was splendid. I wished Maurin's Bakery could see it. I imagined the expression on Mr. Maurin's face as he exclaimed, "Why, this cake is more beautiful than anything we've ever baked! You kids didn't do this yourselves?!"

We just couldn't bear to let our cake go to waste. Since we couldn't eat it, we did the next best thing—we held a wedding to go with the cake. This time, Kay Kay wanted to be the bride, (we dispensed with the priest) and Cathy played the groom. On this occasion, the wedding was simply a prop to accompany the true star of this show—the cake.

This had been a childhood day that began like so many others, but it had changed. Myra, Cathy, Donna, Kay Kay, Gretchen and I knew we had done something wonderful; we all felt it. What is the name for such a moment? Is it art? Imagination? Magic? There it was, a mud wedding cake sitting on a cardboard box on the dirt floor under our house. Above our heads, water pipes ran the length of the house. Crumbling asbestos insulation and black cobwebs dangled from the pipes like crystals from a chandelier. A dusty tricycle lay on its side. Nearby, a broken lawn mower stood between two pillars, with Ann's two-wheeler propped on the next pillar down. But…like the flick of a Fairy Godmother's wand, The Cake had transformed everything. We could imagine ourselves in fancy dresses in a fancy ballroom with fancy people. I was not a barefoot girl playing in the mud under my house; I was somebody.

There was no joy in the bakery business after that day; we knew we could never top what we'd done, so we changed careers. We turned to theater.

We had the perfect stage at the side of our yard. Old railroad ties had been stacked against the bushes, four layers high with shorter rows that served as steps to the top of our stage. The area behind the bushes constituted "back stage." Gretchen and Donna, Kay Kay and Cathy, Myra and I comprised the theatre troupe. We did it all—made up the story, coached each other in acting, directed one another through passionate bossing and criticizing, made costumes from whatever happened to be in the laundry hamper, created props from junk found under the house, and then we performed whatever story we agreed upon. The audience usually consisted of our dog Hilda.

Our favorite productions were inspired by "Queen for a Day," a popular T.V. show in the late fifties. I had seen it a few times at the Dugas's house since my mother wouldn't let us get a television.

Although the stories on "Queen for a Day" were supposedly true, they seemed more dramatic than fiction, and I adored them. Contestants competed for the sympathies of the audience. Each told a heartbreaking story, usually about a crippled husband or a dying child whose last wish was to have a little bicycle.

Only one of these tragic figures could be chosen queen. I listened to their hard luck stories and felt sorry for everyone. At the end of the program, the audience voted by applause, which was measured by a scientific machine with a needle. The title, Queen for a Day, was bestowed on the most dramatically pathetic of them all. It helped a woman's chances if she could boo-hoo a lot and also if she were pretty. This winning combination often sent that applause needle off the scale.

Although the winner might have asked for a hearing aid for her husband or a pair of crutches for her little boy, Jack Bailey usually gave her a nice new stove or refrigerator to augment her humble request. Then a fancy lady came out and put a crown on the luckiest of these unlucky women. The audience clapped and the queen cried some more. Everyone in the real audience felt good about it.

When we play-acted the stories in the backyard, our audience did not appreciate all that emotion. Hilda hated to see us cry. The louder we cried, the more disturbed she became, interrupting the dramatic crescendo of our productions by whining and licking us until we stopped.

For our backyard dramas we emulated the stories we'd seen on Queen for a Day, always striving to create a better one with a unique twist. My personal favorite was my own story told as the wife of a brave Army pilot flying across Europe to spy on the communists. My husband's airplane crashed into the Iron Curtain over there in Russia and now he needed a wheelchair. I knew I had come up with a winning combination: heroism, patriotism, anti-communism, a tragic injury, a broken-hearted wife. Who could resist it—the crown was mine.

When we grew tired of the stage, we returned to our favorite play place of all, an old dilapidated tin shed that stood behind our house near the fence separating our yard from Mrs. Abadie's cow pasture. I can't imagine any child's playhouse providing as much fun as our shed. In temperate weather, we climbed up and played on the roof. For Louisiana children, anything higher than a rain barrel was exotic and exhilarating. The shed was a rooftop in Paris; it was a missionary camp high in the Andes. From the top of the shed I could almost see all the way to the Great Swamp.

Since we didn't have a T.V., I used our shed to lure town kids out to the country to play at my old house. One time I invited a little blond-haired girl to come over after school. Peggy was new to our town. She sported blond curls and wore frilly dresses. My mother would never buy me that kind of dress, the gaudy style for which I longed. The fanciest I ever got was maybe a little embroidered pear on a plain, white collar, and Peggy's dresses looked like birthday cakes. As if these were not reasons enough to be fascinated by her, Peggy was also a Protestant. I had never met one before.

Things went really well that first and last afternoon of my friendship with Peggy. We played paper dolls for a while and then we headed outside to the shed. Peggy loved it. She tapped her shoes across the tin roof and twirled around in her flouncy skirt. I swear she looked just like a blonde Shirley Temple. When her mother came to pick her up, I stood on the sidewalk waving as their car backed onto the River Road, and then I raced up the steps and headed to the kitchen to bask in the glory of my social success, but my Mother stood by the stove frowning at me.

"Poor Archie," she said. "That Peggy is a regular little Rhoda!" (Child psychopath from Book of the Month Club 1950's novel, *The Bad Seed*.)

From our kitchen window, Mother happened to be looking and saw Peggy throw our cat off the roof. I hadn't seen her do it; Peggy said Archie had jumped. Mother never let me invite that little girl again, but I didn't want to anyway. The Dugas girls didn't wear frilly dresses and were just barefoot country kids like my sisters and me, but not one of them would ever have done what Peggy did. I wondered why she had done such a mean thing to a little cat that hadn't done anything to her, and Peggy's face had been smiling when she lied to me about Archie. How could she do that? Was it because she was a Protestant?

Most of the time our band of River Road girls played inside the shed. We turned it into a church, a hospital, a school, a store, a house...and then one day while playing Little House on the Prairie, we set it on fire. It had been a bone-chilling, bleak January afternoon. We'd been playing outside in our thin jackets for at least an hour, long enough to feel cold and miserable when I came up with the idea of building a fireplace. "It'll be just like the Ingalls' cabin," I said.

The Dugas girls helped my sisters and me drag a sheet of tin from under the house to the shed. Then we scurried around the yard gathering sticks and twigs and got some newspaper from the porch to help start the fire. We felt so proud when we got the matches, lit the fire and saw it begin to take. We stood around it, warming our hands and complimenting each other on our genius. After a while, Myra noticed smoke pouring from the sides of the tin. "Is it supposed to do that?" she asked. A sickening fear washed over me as I lifted the edge of the tin with my shoe and saw it wasn't just our sticks that were burning.

Because the fireplace had been my idea and I was older than Kay Kay and Gretchen, I knew I was in big trouble if we didn't put out the fire before Mother and Daddy got up from their Sunday nap.

Dugas and Goette girls raced back and forth from the shed to the kitchen and back again carrying milk bottles filled with water, trying not to bump into each other or make any noise. On my third trip, Mother sauntered into the kitchen yawning and reached for the coffee pot. Kay Kay and I froze in our tracks, milk bottles in each hand, panic and guilt written on our faces. There was no point lying. All Mother had to do was look out the kitchen window to see smoke billowing from the shed's windows.

Perhaps it was our frightened faces or the aftermath of a pleasant nap, but instead of fussing at us, Mother helped us. She immediately started filling bottles and called to the other kids from the porch window, "Come. Hurry!" While we doused the fire, she filled more milk bottles. Each time we reached the top porch step, she was standing there to take our empties and hand us full bottles. This made our fire-fighting brigade much more efficient, and soon the smoldering floorboards of the shed had been transformed into a wet, black hole.

Once the fire was out, the enormity of what we had done enveloped us, heavier than a cloud of smoke. We didn't wonder if we'd get punished, only about the nature and severity of it. Myra, Cathy and Donna felt certain our mother would call theirs and they wouldn't be able to play with us anymore. I wondered if I'd get spanked with a hairbrush or a ping-pong paddle before being grounded for the next year of my life.

Our little troop of firefighters shuffled up the back stairs and entered the kitchen, hearts filled with dread. I was afraid to look at my mother, but when I did, she was smiling and holding a plate of brownies. "Here girls, have a brownie," she said.

We had set the shed on fire, but instead of spankings, we got brownies. This moment of unexpected kindness from my mother was as rare as it was dear. At that moment, I loved her so much I felt like crying. Sometimes, there was just no figuring out a parent's reasoning or behavior. That day had a happy ending, except for the big hole at the center of the shed's floor, an uncomfortable reminder of my stupidity and the limitations of imagination.

Donna, Myra, Cathy Dugas; Jane, Gretchen,
Kay Kay Goette on backyard stage, 1955

Jane Goette

Mrs. Lanois, the Reluctant Witch

It seemed to me that families on the River Road either had too many children or none at all. At the highest end of the scale were the Schexneiders, a family with thirteen children. They lived too far down the River Road to be usable neighbors. The Person family with six children, and the Goettes with four, were average-sized families for our community in the late 1950's.

Some of our neighbors on the River Road were childless, and fairytales had taught me that childless women were either sad and longing for children, or evil and determined to steal them. Sometimes childless women stole children and locked them up in towers, like in the story of *Rapunzel*, but even more dangerous was the type of witch who tricked children so she could catch them and eat them for dinner. Rapunzel's situation was dreadful enough, but poor *Hansel and Gretel* nearly ended up in an oven.

One of the rare, childless couples on the River Road lived in the next house down from Big Miss Landry. The Lane divided their two properties. While Big Miss Landry's house was old-fashioned, the Lanois' house was the epitome of modernity—an orange brick ranch with a big picture window in front and a treeless yard. Because Mr. and Mrs. Lanois had an air-conditioner and no kids, we rarely saw them outside their house.

One day when I'd gone over to the Dugas's to watch "Queen for a Day," Michael Dugas told Myra and me that Mrs. Lanois never came out of her house except at night because she was a witch. He said she caught every child she could get and turned them into Sauce Piquante in her big Dutch Oven. I didn't really believe him, but his stories made me long to get a glimpse of the mysterious Mrs. Lanois.

Myra and I made a plan. We would go to the Lanois house, ring the doorbell, and hide when Mrs. Lanois came to answer. We didn't want to get caught, so we ran to the side of her yard and hid behind a bush. The problem was, though we could hear her calling out, "Who's there?" we couldn't see her. From the first time we heard Mrs. Lanois' timid voice, we knew she wasn't a witch. Still, it was thrilling to crouch in the bushes with Myra, the two of us listening and shaking with silent, nervous giggles. The feeling was a kind of intoxication—two little girls, high on the power of pulling one over on a grown-up. After that first time, we were hooked.

On the third day, Mrs. Lanois caught a glimpse of us and called our mothers. My mother said I must go to the Lanois's house, ring the bell, and apologize to Mrs. Lanois. Mother said I had been rude and unkind. This mission required far more courage than the previous one, and the little courage I possessed quickly melted into terror.

Feeling ashamed and knowing I probably deserved to be turned into Sauce Piquante, I sat outside our front porch steps trying to work up the nerve to head down the sidewalk. I had butterflies in my stomach and whenever I got nervous—like at Confession—I had to pee. It was scary kneeling inside the dark wooden box at Ascension Catholic Church waiting for Father McNamara to slide the little wooden grate open on my side. This confession to a real person, not God's representative, felt even more threatening.

On one of my trips back inside to the bathroom, Mother saw me, and asked,

"Well, did you go to Mrs. Lanois's house?"

I shook my head and headed down the hall toward the front door. When I went out, I didn't let myself sit down on the steps this time; it would be too hard to rise again and get my feet moving down the sidewalk. My banishment would not end until I apologized to Mrs. Lanois.

At Ascension Catholic, every time I went to confession, I uttered the words, "I am truly sorry for these and all my sins" but I didn't really feel it. I knew I would sin again—sass my mama and daddy, fight with "my brothers and sisters," tell lies—but this time I was truly sorry. Longing for redemption, I climbed Mrs. Lanois's steps and pressed her doorbell. I jiggled nervously waiting the eternity it took for her to answer the door. I wanted to run away but knew I couldn't this time. When this ordinary, plain-faced housewife opened the door she seemed shy and almost as nervous as I. I blurted out my apology.

"That's all right, Jane. Y'all just scared me. It could have been a nigger man, and I was all by myself." As always, I was jarred to hear someone respectable and seemingly nice use the "N" word, but in this particular moment, that judgment was suspended as an overwhelming sense of relief washed over me. Mrs. Lanois wasn't mad. She had accepted my apology; I had been absolved of my sin.

When I returned home and Mother asked me how it had gone, she rolled her eyes when I told her what Mrs. Lanois had said.

"Why is it that every white woman in the state of Louisiana—fat or skinny, old or young—thinks every Negro man is dying to get himself killed just for the chance to kiss her?!"

I thought about what Mother said. It did seem a strange thing that so many people worried about white women getting raped by colored men. I wasn't exactly sure what "raped" meant, but I knew it had something to do with kissing. And if white people weren't worrying about rape, they worried about getting robbed or murdered. I also noticed the people who worried most about "those thieving darkies" seemed to be those people least likely to possess anything that anybody would want to steal.

While I knew only a few black people, mostly maids and handymen, they all seemed pretty nice. Oliver was the only black person I knew who stole. All you had to do was drive over to his house and ask him to give back your rake or barbeque fork or whatever it was he'd taken when he came to do your yard work. He might grumble a little bit, but in the end, he always returned what he claimed he hadn't stolen.

I thought about Oliver, and Mrs. Lanois, and me. I guess we were all sinners in one way or another. "Thou shalt not steal" was one of the Ten Commandments, so Oliver's sin was pretty well defined. But what about mine, being mean and rude? And what about Mrs. Lanois'? It seemed like it ought to be a sin to hate a person just because they had darker skin than yours. Monsignier Gubler and Father McNamara never talked about this in church, but Mother and Daddy did. It didn't seem to me like Oliver or Mrs. Lanois were bad people. Oliver was poor, and Mrs. Lanois was scared. I guess neither of them had been taught any better.

Jane Goette

Little Miss Landry

The next house after the Lanois's was a lovely, wooden shotgun cottage painted white. "Shotguns" are houses in which the rooms are lined up front to back so you could fire a shot through the front door and have it go straight through the house and out the back door. Perhaps this style was popular in Louisiana because it allowed greater ventilation to cool down the house in summer. This particular shotgun was prettier than most, with its wrap-around porch and gingerbread trim. Crepe Myrtle trees encircled the yard except for one side where a beautiful flower garden grew in the morning sun. It was a little house and this is where Little Miss Landry lived. She was a tiny, precious woman who would have looked like a child if it weren't for her very large breasts. We thought Little Miss Landry was adorable. Everything about her was charming—her wavy auburn hair, her cute little shoes—and she always smelled like she'd just stepped out of a bubble bath.

Little Miss Landry's husband was Big Miss Landry's son, a riverboat captain we rarely saw since he only came home at night. He had black wavy hair and towered above his diminutive wife. The Landrys didn't have their first child until my sister Gretchen started first grade. In that era, married women stayed home even when there were no children to care for. Little Miss Landry must have had a lot of time on her hands.

My sisters and I loved her. She was one of those rare grown-ups who truly liked children. Little Miss Landry seemed genuinely pleased when my sisters and I came to visit, almost as if a grown-up had come to call. She was especially fond of Gretchen. Once Kay Kay started school, lonely little Gretchen began calling on Little Miss Landry every day. Never once was she turned away or greeted with less respect than Miss Landry would have shown to an adult visitor. In turn, Gretchen always held up her end of the conversation, entertaining Miss Landry with daily news reports from our home—"Ann lost a tooth last night." "Hilda vomited." "Mama bought us a box of Sugar Pops." "Daddy saw a rat climbing up the pecan sack on the back porch." Little Miss Landry treated

Gretchen like another grown-up lady. While I was stuck in Miss Morrow's third grade class adding and subtracting figures, Gretchen was in Miss Landry's kitchen eating animal crackers and vanilla wafers. It hardly seemed fair.

Little Miss Landry soon had the baby she had longed for. And then another, but she never stopped caring about "the Goette girls," especially Gretchen. In the spring of 2011, my sister and I had a reunion in New Orleans with our grown-up children. We rented a car and drove to Donaldsonville to revisit our memories and remaining friends. We drove the kids down the River Road, pointing out the houses of our old neighbors along the way from town to our house. Little Miss Landry's house was one of the few that still matched our memories—freshly painted wrap-around porch, flowers surrounding the house, a tree heavy with figs leaning over the drive.

We pulled into her driveway, not knowing if we would find her at home and wondering if she would still recognize us after so many years, especially Gretchen. At 5' 8", my baby sister grew to be the tallest of the Goettes. All through her parenting years in Italy, Gretchen's children, Eleanor and Raimondo, had heard stories about Miss Landry's kindness to their mother when she was a little girl. As we filed onto Miss Landry's porch, El and Rai stood behind their mother, protectively, understanding the importance of this surprise reunion. Miss Landry was in her nineties now. Would she remember their mother? Gretchen knocked; we stood behind her, all of us feeling a bit nervous.

The door opened. When she saw my sister, Miss Landry gasped. With one hand on her heart and the other reaching up for my sister's face, she cried, "Gretchen! My baby, my first baby!"

The Jambois Family

Our most unusual neighbors were the Jambois family. Their Cypress cabin was situated between our house and Little Miss Landry's. Lacking in-door plumbing or modern appliances, the Jambois's way of life seemed from a previous century. They cooked on a big cast-iron stove fueled by wood sticks. Out back the Jambois had a woodpile and a big tree stump where the brothers chopped wood for their cookstove. Ann and I slept on a roll-away in the den situated on the Jambois side of our house. We heard T-Leg or Harpo chopping wood in the early mornings. A little farther back from the woodpile was the family's outhouse; Ann and I smelled that, too.

Sometimes it seemed to me the Jambois family had stepped out of one of my favorite strips in the Sunday funny papers, Dogpatch. Norma (pronounced Nor-mah, with the accent on the second syllable), was the Mammy Yokum of the family, a small, wrinkled woman with thin white hair parted in the middle and pulled to the back of her head in a tight little bun the size of a ping pong ball.

Although all the members of that strange household were brothers and sisters, Norma seemed like the mother. Timmie was the only sister—with whom Norma shared a bed—and the rest of their siblings were brothers. A-leex-say (everyone called him T-Leg because he had one leg shorter than the other), was Norma's baby brother. With his wrinkled face and gray-flecked hair, it was hard to imagine he could be anybody's baby brother.

T-Leg sometimes worked as a painter but mostly he spent his days walking back and forth to town where he purchased one bottle of Mogen David wine at a time from the bar end of Lala's Restaurant. After T-Leg returned home, he would sit drinking his wine at the kitchen table until the bottle was finished. When it was gone, he put on his painter's cap and headed back to town for the next bottle. By late afternoon on the return from his last trip to town, T-Leg would be weaving his way down the River Road, one hand clutching his brown paper bag and the other holding onto a long stick. T-Leg used that stick like a boat paddle to steer himself down the winding sidewalk that led from town, following the curves of the river south to where the houses grew farther apart, and the land, more rural. Every now and then he got off course and fell into the ditch at the side of the road. As long as I remember, this was T-Leg's Monday through Saturday ritual.

No harm came to T-Leg until years later when a group of teenage boys discovered the sadistic pleasure of tormenting an old drunk. T-Leg became the target of a cruel and dangerous game. The boys started to follow him in their car, then suddenly they'd rev the engine pretending they were going to run him down. They would speed up and aim the car straight at him. Scared to death, T-Leg ran as fast as he could, often tripping and falling in the process. The teens laughed, honked the horn and called him names.

T-Leg started walking on the levee instead of the sidewalk, but the boys drove their cars up the levee and continued their torment. Norma told Daddy that T-Leg was so terrified, even the Mogen David couldn't stop his hands from shaking anymore. Finally, T-Leg abandoned his trips to town altogether. He no longer set foot outside the house—and then he died. It broke Norma's heart.

Charlie (pronounced Chaw-lee, with the accent on the second syllable) was an elder brother, white-haired and speechless. He also wore a painter's cap, and he smoked a pipe. People in town called him "Harpo" after the mute Marx brother, but he was "Mr. Charlie" to us. From morning until evening Charlie paced the length of the sidewalk in front of the Jambois's house. He walked slowly, smoking his pipe and watching the occasional car drive by. He seemed a self-appointed sentinel watching lest a troop of Yankee soldiers or Russians or some other threat should suddenly appear over the crest of the levee. Would such an extraordinary event provoke speech at last?

Another person lived in the Jambois house, but he was bed-ridden. I don't know if he was an elder brother or some other relative, but Norma had no use for him. Stubborn and obstinate, his tenacious hold on life outraged Norma. She frequently complained to my mother, "That ole man—he won't die for nothin'!" as if his sole reason for continuing to breathe was simply to spite Norma. I pictured him sitting up in bed with his arms folded across his chest, a defiant look in his eyes, a deep and provocative frown upon his face. But "that ole' man" did eventually die. When he passed from the earth, his death caused barely a ripple. It was Timmie's death, the beloved sister, which sent Norma running over to our house in her nightgown.

The story Norma told of waking up that rainy morning in bed with her sister is one that has become Goette legend. Thirty years later, whenever we awake to rain, my sisters and I find ourselves back on the River Road, remembering Norma and Timmie. Whether we say it aloud or merely think it, the words are always the same— "It's rainin', Timmie."

Early that fall morning when she appeared breathless, barefoot, and crying at our door, Norma told my parents she had awakened early to a soft rain thrumming against the window of her bedroom. Like every other day of her life, she had turned to her sister to comment on the weather.

"Timmie, it's rainin," she said quietly. Timmie did not respond. I imagine Norma looked around the sparse room, at the little statue of Virgin Mary on the nightstand. Perhaps she noticed the stain patterns in the bare plastered wall, how green they looked in the early light of a rainy morn. She wondered if the boys had chopped wood for the stove; she hadn't heard the *whoomp, whoomp* of the ax. The glass panes were fogging up as she watched trails of raindrops slide down the window. She touched Timmie's hand and found it cold. It really was time to get up and light the stove. She spoke again to her sister:

"Timmie, it's rainin'!" Norma said more loudly than before. Still, there was no response. Norma reached over to touch Timmie's shoulder, repeating yet again, the news of the day. As if she were speaking to a child, she said the words gently this time, "It's rainin', Timmie." Norma's heart beat faster now as she leaned over to look into her sister's eyes. Timmie's eyes were opened, but they did not register the worry on Norma's face. Nor did they see how quickly concern changed to terror and panic as Norma realized her only sister was dead. How could this be?!

Norma and Timmie had shared a bed for sixty-five years. For sixty-five years the sisters said the rosary together each night, on their knees on the bare cypress floor of their bedroom. They picked

Japanese plums from their tree in April and made fig preserves every July. During hurricanes, they held each other all through the night. When wild winds rocked their small house, rattled the windows, roared down the chimney, Norma clung to her sister. Timmie was her anchor. She was Norma's newspaper, helpmate, her mirror and best friend in all the world—she was her sister. And now she was gone.

Norma jumped out of bed, screamed and pulled at her hair. She couldn't stand to be in the house with her dead sister. She didn't pause to dress or put in her teeth before she shot out of the house. Seconds later Norma was pounding on our door, standing barefoot, wearing only a rain-dappled nightgown and tear-stained, distraught face. Grief and toothlessness made her words difficult to understand. She threw her arms around my mother and poured out her heart—(bad choice; she should have gone to Little Miss Landry)

"Miss Goette, I ax you—how would you feel if you woke up in the morning and your sister was lying next to you, dead in the bed?!"

Norma's question left my mother as speechless as Mr. Charlie. Mother was never good at expressing her softest feelings nor in knowing how to respond when others expressed theirs. She could write the most touching, sensitive sympathy letters, but she would do anything to avoid having to express such sentiments in person. On the morning of Timmie's death, my mother offered Norma a cup of coffee; it was the only thing she could think to do. Daddy called the doctor. After Norma finished her coffee, he put his arm around her little shoulders, walked her back home and sat with her until Doctor LeBlanc arrived.

In the years after Timmie's death, Norma developed a close friendship with a woman named Miss Pooh. Miss Pooh lived in town and only visited once or twice a week. In our climate, a walk from Donaldsonville to our stretch of the River Road was considered a long one. Though Miss Pooh was no substitute for Timmie, Norma was grateful for the female companionship and news from the outside world, things she could not get from her brothers.

Norma Jambois had never been as far away from home as Baton Rouge, thirty miles upriver from Donaldsonville. The Jambois didn't have a television, a radio or a daily newspaper. Still, some news did drift their way from time to time, enough to create quite a few anxieties in their home. Mostly, Norma worried about communists, murderers, and atheists. Many afternoons she sat on her porch with Miss Pooh, saying the rosary. Regardless of the season or the weather, Miss Pooh wore a black dress, black stockings and black old-lady shoes. I suspect that most of Norma's news of the outside world came from dear Miss Pooh.

One memorable piece of news Norma passed on to my mother was a story Miss Pooh had read in some paper, not the ones we got, about a woman who had been having stomach problems for months. The doctors couldn't find anything wrong with her, but she knew there was something. She suspected it might be some dirty fish she'd eaten that was poisoning her system or maybe a tumor. Determined to find out, she stood over her kitchen sink, slit open her abdomen and washed her intestines under the faucet to get them clean. My mother exclaimed, "My God, she was crazy!"

This was not the appropriate response for Norma, who countered, "Crazy?? I call that brave, me!!"

As strange as the Jambois family seemed to the outside world, they were our neighbors and we cared for them. I guess you couldn't live close enough to hear each other's fights, to smell each other's cooking—or in our case, to smell your neighbor's shit—and not feel a certain level of intimacy. As silent as they often were, we never doubted they felt the same way about us. Whenever Norma heard that one of us kids was sick, faster than the winged feet of an F.T.D. Florist, she ran over to our house with a sweet potato plant. The top of the potato was held by a halo of toothpicks just above the rim of a Mason Jar filled with water. Thread-like roots swirled in the water below and a nice little vine spilled over the sides of the jar Norma offered to us in hopes we'd soon get well.

Unbeknownst to us, one year Norma bought candy for Halloween thinking we might come trick-or-treating. We felt terrible when we heard the next day how Norma had waited and waited, but never heard a single child come tramping up her porch steps. "What a shame," Mother said, "poor as they are, Norma spent all that money on Halloween candy." This only compounded our guilt. The following year, after my sisters and I donned our makeshift costumes, we headed straight to the Jambois's house. The kerosene lamps were out, and the old cypress shutters, closed and barred. We had arrived too late, and all the Halloween candy we ate that night could not erase the bitter taste of regret.

Gretchen, Pierre, Kay Kay, Joe on Jambois'
abandoned porch, 1970

Mrs. Abadie, Big Red Hen

The next house after ours, Mrs. Abadie's, seemed large and grand, especially when compared with the Jambois'. The Abadie house was set far back from the road, as if it were trying to be as removed from its River Road neighbors as possible. The Abadies owned a large pasture that extended behind their yard, our yard, and all the way up to the border of the Lane. The pasture was as deep as it was wide and ran along the backs of the houses along the southern side of Down the Lane.

One of my earliest memories after moving from Bunkie to the River Road occurred in the Abadie's yard. I was three years old. Perhaps my mother was napping; I just know I was alone in our yard when I heard voices next door and wandered toward them. As I peeked through the Abadie's bushes I saw a man grab a chicken by its neck and throw it on a wide tree stump. In his other hand he held an ax. As he raised that hand, the sun glinted on the blade, like a mirror reflecting light. Whack! His arm came down chopping off the chicken's head, sending spurts of bright, red blood like sunbeams from the ax. The headless chicken flopped down from the stump and began running in crazy patterns. The man and the woman laughed. Terrified, thinking the headless chicken was running toward me, I turned and ran home to my mother feeling guilty and ashamed—like someone who's witnessed an atrocity.

Besides chickens, the Abadies had cows, which they kept in the pasture behind our house. In later years when my sisters and I were week-end world explorers, our first obstacle was getting across the Abadie's pasture without having the cows chase us. We had seen scores of westerns at the Grand Theatre in which some hapless cowboy got in the path of a stampede of cattle and was trampled to death. Those wide-eyed cows standing in Mrs. Abadie's pasture looked peaceful enough munching grass, swishing their tails to chase away flies, but we knew how easily they could be transformed into thundering giants capable of trampling little children to death. All it required was an uppity dog who decided to have a go at a creature twenty times its size. Our dogs, the Hobo kind, seemed always to be of that nature.

In childhood we had the feeling Mrs. Abadie didn't quite approve of us. Once when we were running around the house in our underpanties during a thunderstorm, she called our house to tattletale. Little did she know she had awakened our daddy from his Saturday afternoon nap and that bothered him a whole lot more than his daughters playing in a thunderstorm. Daddy had to pretend to be grateful to her for alerting him to our dangerous behavior. He went to the back porch and called to us in a stern voice, "You kids come inside right this minute!" When we reached the top of the porch stairs, he was waiting for us with big bathroom towels, and he was smiling. "You kids want some cocoa?"

The few times I actually encountered Mrs. Abadie, she seemed stiff and formal. Once she walked past our house on the sidewalk when I was playing in the front yard. I said hello to her but she didn't respond, nor did she smile. I assumed she thought we were bad children, too noisy and rambunctious for her refined taste. Perhaps her own children and grandchildren were perfect. I thought this until the day I overheard her grandson, Floyd, who was my age, singing to her out in her driveway next door. He was singing quite loudly the lyrics to a popular song at the time. I think it was Ernie K. Doe, but I'm sure of the words: "You talk too much; you worry me to death. You just taaaaaalk, you talk, too much!" I was shocked. Even a bad girl like me who ran around in her underpanties in thunderstorms would never be that disrespectful to *my* grandmother!

Relations with Mrs. Abadie improved after Ann, Kay Kay and I left home and Daddy took up gardening. He planted tomatoes and peppers along the fence between our yard and hers. When his tomatoes ripened, he sent Gretchen over to Mrs. Abadie's house with a little bag of tomatoes. The next day Mrs. Abadie came up to the fence when Daddy was out tending his garden. She thanked him and handed him a bag of fresh eggs from her chickens. After that, there were frequent little chats at the fence and exchanges of small gifts.

Our childhood neighborhood started at the Persons' house and ended at the Abadies', but as we grew older, our adventures extended far beyond that boundary. In our bicycling days we frequented the irrigation ditches and haunted houses farther down the road and then later, when we could drive the family car, we traveled down the Old River Road to New Orleans and up the Mississippi to Baton Rouge… and beyond. Just as the Mississippi River had once taken Huckleberry Finn, it would take us, too.

Jane Goette

Donaldsonville Elementary School facing Railroad Avenue

*Third grade class photo 1955. Jane is in middle of
first row in the white collar, eyes shut.*

Starting School

I'd waited my whole life to start first grade, but when I finally crossed the threshold of the red brick building with a hundred steps, it was too big, too noisy, too scary, and I longed to be back on the River Road with Mother, Kay Kay, and Gretchen.

Mother did not accompany me to my first day of school. It was Daddy who held my hand and walked me to my classroom. He couldn't stay long because the high school needed him even more than I. Daddy patted my shiny bangs, smiled, and told me to "Knock 'em dead, Topper!" Then he quickly threaded his way through the crowd of mothers and disappeared down the stairs.

Suddenly alone in a sea of mothers and children, I stood exactly where Daddy had left me, a few feet from the heavy wooden door with glass window panes. I had never heard so many voices all at once, nor felt such an avalanche of charged energy. I didn't like it. If I moved my feet even one step from where Daddy had planted me, I might get washed away into the crowd and never be found.

"Mama, when's the bell gonna ring?" asked a wiggly boy whose elbow kept poking me in the ribs. Daddy and Ann mentioned "the bell" frequently—the bell to start school, the three o'clock bell (I didn't know how to tell time), lunch bells and recess bells—bells, bells, bells. Like that scary poem in Mother's black book? I hoped the school bells would sound like the only kind I knew—church bells, which I liked.

I had waited so long to come to this place with its bells, chalkboards, see-saws, and pretty girls with ponytails, but I felt like an orphan standing outside Miss Meduse's classroom waiting for the bell to ring. Would Miss Meduse be nice? Ann said the kids called her "Miss Meduse, the big, fat goose," but Daddy said she was a good teacher. Mother had rolled her eyes. I pictured Mother Goose from nursery rhyme books. This was a comforting imagine in this noisy moment when all I wanted was to be home again on the quiet River Road. Suddenly, a deafening clang jolted my bones. The door flew open, and I was swept inside on a human wave.

As the mothers helped their children find the right desks, Miss Meduse took my hand and led me to mine. She threaded the room talking to parents. I watched the children, especially the little girls with ponytails or curls. So many of them! Only I had short, straight hair, but my new school dress was pretty.

After the mothers trickled out the door, the room grew quiet. Miss Meduse went up and down the rows of desks giving each of us a piece of paper and a pencil. When she reached my desk, she smiled and winked at me. I quivered with pride and confidence. I was still smiling when she started her instructions:

"Boys and girls, I want you to write your name on your paper and then write the alphabet for me."

"The *what*?!!" I thought. I'd never heard of the alphabet. I had come to school expecting to learn reading, writing and arithmetic, but what was this alphabet business? When I looked around the room, all the children's heads were bent over their papers. To my amazement and horror, I was the only one who didn't know what to do.

I looked at the boy to my right and noticed he kept looking up at the little train that ran high on the walls around our classroom. After each time he looked up, he bent his head down and wrote. The little train circling the blackboard must be the alphabet. I tried to draw boxes hooked together like the ones on the wall. I could see each box contained a different squiggle or shape like the ones that filled our books at home. I tried my best to copy them.

Long before I started school, mother had read me Winnie the Pooh and tons of poems with big words. There were various poems I could recite from *A Child's Garden of Verses* and some of Mother's favorites, like "Poor Floyd Ireson with his hard heart, tarred and feathered and carried in a cart by the women of Marblehead!" Every Sunday, Daddy and I read *Joe Palooka* and *Lil' Abner* from the funny papers. I could read lots of the words in the strips. Daddy said I was smart and reading would be a cinch for me in first grade. Our River Road neighbor, Miss Jambois, had taught me the "Our Father" and the "Hail Mary" before I started school. The afternoon I recited those meaningless words to her, she thought I was a genius. Now it turned out, I was the stupidest kid in my class.

My mother had bought me a pair of saddle oxfords, a box of crayons and a light blue bookbag, but she'd sent me to school completely unprepared. How had my parents forgotten something as important as the alphabet? I didn't even know "the alphabet" and "the ABCs" were the same thing. I'd heard the ABC song with its "eleminnowpee," but I didn't know those lyrics nearly as well as the ones to "Little Sir Echo," "The Wild Man from Borneo" or "I Want a Big Fat Mama I Can tell my Troubles to." I certainly didn't know the ABC's had anything to do with reading.

The morning dragged on, and I waited for lunchtime, hoping I might see my sister, but I didn't. The teacher had told us to be sure to go to the bathroom before we came back to the classroom after lunch. I didn't know which bathroom was for boys and which for girls, so I didn't go. Even though I felt the urge, I would wait until I was home.

I don't remember a thing about that afternoon except watching the clock, wishing I knew how to tell time, and waiting to go home. I jiggled and wiggled at my desk, praying for the bell to ring, hating myself for not trying harder to figure out which bathroom was the girls'. Though I was in agony, I was too shy to raise my hand and ask the teacher to let me go to the bathroom. She might get mad at me. Even if she didn't, how would I find it now? I might get lost in this big school and never find my way back home. I wiggled back and forth in my desk harder and harder as my eyeballs began to float. The little boy behind me poked my back.

"Stop that!" he whispered.

Suddenly, the long-awaited Brrrrrrrrrrring!! of the bell screamed in my ears, startling me. A gush between my legs as hot as the shame I felt. I didn't know the alphabet, couldn't tell time and wet my pants like a baby on the first day of school. I waited until the last child reached the door, then I grabbed my new book satchel and rushed out the door, through the crowd to the stairs outside. As I ran to the sidewalk searching for Daddy's green Chevy, I spotted Ann opening the front car door. For once, I felt relieved to be alone in the back.

Jane Goette

"How was it, Topper?" my father asked cheerfully.

"Fine," I said, as I smoothed my bangs, running my fingers down past my eyes. He shifted into first and headed up Railroad Avenue to Mississippi Street and the River Road. I sat perched on the outer edge of the backseat so I wouldn't leave a wet spot and Daddy couldn't see me in the mirror. With one hand against the back of Ann's seat and the other brushing my bangs, I kept my balance the whole way home.

***

Though that first day was by far the worst, I do not have fond memories from my first year in school. Despite not knowing the alphabet, I quickly learned to read, but that turned out to be a disadvantage. In reading circle each child got to read only one page before the next child's turn. My turn went far too quickly. I waited and waited while other children struggled through each word, frustration being the only expression in their story-reading voices. They murdered the stories, which weren't very interesting anyway. The tall, wide windows at Donaldsonville Elementary School were my salvation. Though my body was tied to a small brown chair in a reading circle, my mind escaped out the windows. I flew to China, went down that hole I'd dug in the back yard while Mother was napping; I landed in my little rickshaw which took me through golden, pagoda-lined streets where little girls with bangs just like mine waved to me from the windows.

When I was inside the classroom I was bored but safe. I couldn't wait for recess, but it was a dangerous world out there on the playground. Having a father who was the principal of all the public schools in Donaldsonville automatically put my family on the town map. Ann reveled in her small-town notoriety, but I was shy and didn't particularly want to be noticed. I loved my daddy and bristled with pride when people referred to me as "the principal's daughter," but I also got harassed by other kids: "You think you're so smart just 'cuz your daddy's the principal!"

"No, I don't!" I'd protest, suddenly longing for the safety of anonymity. My preference for low-profile existence was equaled by my big sister's appetite for the limelight. Ann started school the year we moved to Donaldsonville, the year Daddy became the principal. A 38-pound first grader, my sister threw her weight around the playground like a sumo wrestler. Hands on hips, she'd march her skinny self up to boys twice her size commanding them to "Get off my daddy's see-saw!"

Inside the classroom Ann locked horns with Brenda Hood, whose mama was on the school board. It was a classic turf battle. Ann was determined to show that it was she, the principal's daughter, not Brenda, the school board member's daughter, who would run this elementary school.

As our big sisters moved on to third grade, Jeanie Hood and I started first grade, innocently reviving the old rivalry between Ann and Brenda. Although I suspect the battle had little to do with Jeanie or me, Ann claims she *had* to fight Brenda to defend my honor. A gauntlet had been thrown, a rumor that Brenda had told her sister Jeanie not to play with Jane Goette. Whether loyalty or ego motivated Ann's battle, the end result spelled trouble for Daddy and me.

During the middle of an important scheduling meeting the second week of school, a call came from the elementary school. Ordinarily Mrs. Prado saved these phone messages until a meeting had ended, but the elementary school needed Mr. Goette to get over there quickly.

Usually there had to be a serious fight—knocked out teeth, broken bones, or lots of blood—before the elementary teachers interrupted Daddy at the high school. They could handle the usual fights, but this one had put them in a quandary. Daddy grabbed his keys and hurried out to his car.

As soon as the bell for recess had rung that morning, Ann and Brenda started cornering kids as they spilled out on the playground: "Who do you like more, me or her?" I imagine my charismatic sister was as persuasive as LBJ button-holing congressmen in the hallways of the Capitol. Word spread through the playground that Ann Goette and Brenda Hood were going to have a fight.

After a respectable audience had assembled, they went at each other, no holds barred. Ann pulled Brenda's hair; Brenda scratched Ann's arms; they kicked and bit and slapped each other until Miss

Gimbroni pushed her way through the crowd to break up the fight. Expecting a couple of ragamuffin boys, she was momentarily speechless to find Mr. Goette and Mrs. Hood's daughters the stars of this altercation. What was the world coming to?!

The general consensus was that Ann had beat Brenda in the fight, but Daddy wasn't any happier about it than Mrs. Hood. He still didn't have tenure in this new job, and it didn't help his chances any to alienate an influential school board member. By the end of that school year, for once my parents were in agreement about school. Come fall, Ann and I would both be starting at St. Vincent's, the Catholic elementary school in Donaldsonville. Transfers between public and Catholic schools became a revolving door for the Goette girls.

The last to enter that turnstile was my baby sister Gretchen. When Gretchen relates her memories of pre-school life on the River Road, I realize hers were even lonelier than my own. How could they not have been? She was the only child left at home. Mother's day could be broken up with a visit from Connie Netter. She could read her *New Yorker* magazine, a "Book of the Month Club" novel, take an afternoon nap. Gretchen had no one to play with and knew enough to try to stay out of Mother's hair. On some level she understood our mother was depressed. She didn't want to make it worse.

The summer before Gretchen started school, Bubba Lemann approached Mother about working part-time at Lemann's Department Store. Dolphie had put the idea in Bubba's head: "Candy Goette is the best dressed woman in Donaldsonville. She's got an eye for fashion. Bubs, you want to continue losing business to Maison Blanche and Godchaux's? You know as well as I do all the fashionable ladies in this town drive all the way to New Orleans to buy their clothes every year. You get Candy in your store and let *her* pick out the clothes; she'll bring 'em in to Lemann's."

It was the 1950's, so of course Bubba had asked my father first, though they both knew Daddy would defer to whatever "Candy" wanted. Mother was excited. So were we kids. We didn't know any married women who worked outside the home unless they were widows or black women. The fact that Gretchen was starting school and the job was only part-time provided socially acceptable "cover" for my mother to do what she had longed for—return to work.

It was a great idea, not only for Lemann's but also for our family. My mother had never been happy as a housewife. The brief years in Bunkie were an exception because she lived in town amongst a wonderful network of friends who kept life stimulating. Perhaps she'd have been less bored in Donaldsonville if our family had lived in town instead of out in the country, but there would have been a trade-off. As the principal's wife Mother would have been expected to attend more functions, socialize with school people, subject herself to scrutiny and bear the burden of small talk in the service of her husband's career.

Candy Goette, for all her spunk and modernity, was still the daughter of Eldon and Stella, less than adequate role models of social grace, hospitality, or diplomatic discourse. My father was the one with the charm, Mother reasoned; he had spent his boyhood in Donaldsonville. He knew the ways, spoke the language, and was accepted in a way she considered as unappealing as it was unrealistic. The job at Lemann's was a godsend; a first step back into the working world. It was a department store, not a newspaper, but a welcomed reprieve from years alone on the River Road with preschool children. Suddenly we had a different mother. And we liked her better.

Hilda (Goette dog), Kay Kay, Jane with Nancy Netter on lap, Jacinta Sobral "Aunt Lulu," Gretchen in roller skates, Ann sitting on arm of sofa bed, 1959

Aunt Lulu, Daddy's Oldest Living Relative

I have no idea of the date of my first visit to Oak Alley, only that it is linked to another journey soon after that down the River Road to an equally memorable experience, meeting my father's Oldest-Living-Relative. Jacinta "Lulu" Sobral was my dead grandmother's baby sister,. Again, it felt adventurous to travel beyond my family's one-mile stretch of River Road. Any family trip triggered excitement enough to send me racing to find whatever shoes—sandals or "tennies"—my mother had designated. Whether they pinched my toes or floated on my feet didn't matter the least, I was going someplace.

Fantasies of what I might see spun images I still remember: a lady in a pretty pink dress walks briskly across a town street; the white pocketbook crooked at her elbow matches her high-heels; a little girl exactly my age with a blonde ponytail skipping beside a fast-walking mother like my own. In the flash of a momentary passage of an unknown character across a car window's stage, my hungry eyes absorbed minute details of physical feature, attire, and expression. Beneath its cap of short-cropped hair, my mind sizzled with flash fiction. It was a gumbo pot, and I, the chef whose eyes searched the world for spicy, foreign ingredients.

And so, this trip across the mighty Mississip' to meet my father's aunt is one I have never forgotten. In the first few years in Donaldsonville, the number of physically present human beings in my world was as limited as its geography. Except for my parents' friends, Connie and Dolphie, Mr. Graffeo, who delivered the groceries, Miss Jambois, the next-door neighbor who taught me the "Our Father," and Sally May, our once-a-week black maid, I knew no one outside my home. Within the great big world of Donaldsonville, the Goette girls didn't have a single relative besides our parents and each other. Today we would meet this unknown relative from the olden days.

I knew very little about the bigger concept of family, just as I knew little about history, just that the two were tied up, and my mother's family had fought in this long-ago Silver War on Abraham

Lincoln's side and my father's family had fought on the wrong side, but Daddy thought they'd made a mistake. I knew that history and family were important to both Mama and Daddy. Mama had a sister and brothers and parents. All poor Daddy had was this olden-day aunt we were about to meet. Maybe it was because his relatives got killed in the Silver War or because Daddy was already old by the time I was born. It all seemed kind of sad, especially after Daddy explained that Aunt Lulu was deaf and almost blind. I had seen a picture of Helen Keller in a magazine. Despite being deaf and blind, she was famous and had a lot of important friends. Aunt Lulu lived all by herself. Daddy said we would be important to her.

At the time I met Jacinta "Lulu" Sobral, my grandmother's baby sister, it had been 50 years since she'd lived at Oak Alley Plantation. For her, nothing happened after Oak Alley was sold. It's as if Aunt Lulu's story stopped there and then, and in its wake, a deafening silence descended. She now lived in a small cypress house in a sleepy river town called Convent. She lived next door to the Catholic Church and took care of the Rectory for the parish priest.

It was August-hot the day we crossed the Mississippi on the ferry boat at Donaldsonville to make our first visit to Aunt Lulu. We drove over the levee and waited in a line of cars until it was our turn to reach the little booth at the river's edge where a man counted the number of people in our car and told Daddy what we had to pay to cross the river. They exchanged coins and smiles, then he waved us forward. Now we were close enough that I could see that the gravel road ended with nothing solid and stable between it and the boat's deck.

With a jilting bump, I felt the car lurch forward through the gravel cross onto the iron boat-ramp. The chains holding the boat to the dock groaned each time a car entered or exited the ramp, shifting the distribution of weight at that end of the boat. It seemed a balancing act, like a see-saw but far more dangerous. My body stiffened as our car climbed that precariously narrow metal ramp. In that brief eternity, our lives crossed the threshold of disaster. The wheels might go over the edge and plunge the car into the roiling depths of the muddy Mississippi. I closed my eyes and waited. When I opened them again Daddy was steering the car to the right end of the ferry obeying the arm directions given by the man in charge. We rounded the curve of the boat. Daddy pulled close beside another Chevy, both car's bumpers touching the rail.

We had made it; our car didn't fall into the river. Only then did I look out across the wide, sun-sparkled Mississippi. "Come on, kids. We might see Huck Finn's raft floating down the river!" and that seemed true to me. As I peered through the boat railing, river wind in my hair, the Mississippi River seemed to shine with possibilities. Thus began my lifelong love of rivers.

I'm not sure what I'd expected, but when we reached the other side, the road to Aunt Lulu's house looked exactly like our River Road, only more desolate. It must have been the thickest part of summer that day, a time when people stay indoors and everyplace seems deserted. Even the dogs and cats are lethargic, napping under porch steps or in any patch of shade they can find. There seemed nothing to see but the levee, clumps of trees sagging in the heat, and a never-ending ribbon of wavy asphalt. With the windows opened wide, dust flew into our eyes, but if we closed them even halfway, we couldn't breathe in the stuffy, sticky world of the backseat.

My eyes felt heavy by the time Daddy slowed the car and pulled onto the grassy strip between the road and the ditch. We scrambled out of the car, jumped across the ditch, and waited for Daddy to take Gretchen from Mama's arms before helping her climb out while he held the car door open. Daddy led our way across the sidewalk to the steps of a wooden shotgun raised, like all River Road houses, a few feet above the ground. Weathered steps led up to an open porch framed by posts. A cypress swing hung from its ceiling, supported by two rusting chains. I knew even before I tried it, the swing would make a mournful, high-pitched screech, a sound as alarming as it was sad. Though I can't explain it, Aunt Lulu's porch swing told me something about this person I'd not yet met, something truer and sadder than all the adult words that swirled around me: "old," "relative," "Oak Alley," "Catholic," "deaf."

Aunt Lulu's house was surrounded by oak trees thick with Spanish Moss--the gray, grizzled beards of all the old men in the world, hanging in the trees to frighten little children. Everything about Aunt Lulu's place scared and depressed me. The moss-laden trees leaned toward the house as if with time they might slowly swallow our aunt's small house. Who would notice?

In this unearthly quiet place I could almost hear the heat—the charged crackle of air so hot it stung my eyes and sent black dots floating across my path. I wished we could get back in the car and head home. It seemed as if we'd crossed more than a river to reach Aunt Lulu's; her River Road was stuck in the olden days and felt as foreign as Mexico or Japan but far less interesting.

We crowded onto the porch, then Daddy banged very hard on the front door. "So she can feel the vibrations," he explained. Mother bent toward the top porch step, put out her half-smoked cigarette, and reached for Gretchen's hand to pull her away from its edge and toward the door. I held on to a little piece of Daddy's pants as the door opened and an old lady stepped out to greet us. Her mouth opened in a wide smile as she gasped, "Conrad!" (too loudly).

From my vantage point, I saw the roof of her mouth, bright orange, like waxy Halloween candy. She smelled of talcum powder, candy mints and something else I can only describe as an "old lady" smell. I stared up at her in horror and fascination. Hairs, stiff as hairbrush bristles, poked from her ears and a few places on her face. The color and texture of her hair was frighteningly similar to the Spanish Moss that hung from her trees. Aunt Lulu's was pulled back in a crooked bun. Her eyes were cloudy, as if cobwebs had grown inside them. She had an uneven coat of light face powder with dense patches swathed across her large nose and one cheek. Purple, ropey veins shone through her thick stockings, visible above the clunky, tie-up, heeled shoes that all old ladies in Louisiana wore at that time. There was nothing pretty or feminine about Aunt Lulu except her navy blue, polka dotted dress.

Once we were inside, my father pushed my sisters and me up close to Aunt Lulu so she could touch us, one by one. Although her eyes didn't really seem to see me, she said I looked like Josie, my father's mother. With one hand she held my face, while the other slid down my back and across my rump.

"Jane's just like Josie; she's going to have big hips. Does she have her disposition, Conrad?" Daddy shrugged his shoulders as he smiled down at me, and I bristled with pride.

As my sisters took their turns with Aunt Lulu, I studied her living room, starting with the crucifix on the wall behind her. Jesus's agony was rendered in vivid detail; his eyes rolled back and bright red drops of blood dripped from his hands, feet and side. Our crucifix at home was plain wooden, not nearly so interesting, but it had the same palm branch wedged behind it, all brown now with its tips curled like the toes of elf shoes.

The other prominent fixture on the wall was a large, gold-framed painting of Oak Alley. I recognized it right away, for it was the prettiest place I'd ever seen. The long alley of oaks in front gave it the quality of a fantasy world, a place where a beautiful princess might live. It was difficult to imagine Aunt Lulu there.

To the right of Oak Alley stood a large, stuffed chair where Mother sat holding Gretchen, and beside it, a table with a lamp, a newspaper and a magnifying glass. Black rosary beads lay on top of a bookcase which contained more knick-knacks than books. On one shelf a little porcelain black boy with enormous pink lips held the reins of a horse and smiled up at the white man in the saddle. Next to that was a statue of a saint (I knew by the gold plate behind his head). The saint wore brown robes and sandals and looked poor. I thought he must have had ringworm on the crown of his head, for he was bald on top with bangs up front, just like mine. Sweet little birds sat on his shoulders and one, perched in the outstretched palm of his hand. Next to the saint, Aunt Lulu had a glass candy dish filled with gum drops, the kind I'd seen decorating the witch's gingerbread house in *Hansel and Gretel*. I wanted one badly.

Aunt Lulu served Mother and Daddy coffee as dark as the oil Mr. Sam put in our car down at the Esso. She offered my sisters and me ice-cream, a rare and treasured treat. She pulled aluminum ice-cube trays out of the freezer compartment of her refrigerator. Instead of ice, they held white, cloudy cubes which were more crystallized than creamy and had a slightly metallic taste. She served it to us in plastic bowls and handed us each three vanilla wafers to go with it. Aunt Lulu's ice-cream was certainly different, and I didn't much like it. Mother noticed me studying my bowl, taking mice nibbles out of my cookies and she shot me a glance of disapproval. I shut my eyes and started eating.

Across the room, Aunt Lulu talked loudly as she held on to my daddy's hand. Her mouth looked funny when she talked. Her tongue sort of stuck to the roof of her mouth between words making a little clicking sound, and she seemed to open her mouth extra wide, like she was trying to get it unstuck. I didn't pay much attention to what she was telling Daddy, but it seemed like she was either talking about her "Papa" or "the good Lawd."

Over the years we lived in Donaldsonville, my parents would take us on lots of Sunday trips to visit their grown-up friends or Daddy's cousins. Those afternoon visiting expeditions seemed as long as they were boring. At the first signs of restlessness, we were told to run outside and play. In the middle of a summer's afternoon in South Louisiana, no one in her right mind would run, and rarely did a child play anyplace outside unless it was in water. Mother would say, "Quit sitting like bumps on a log! For heaven's sake, you kids need to get out in the fresh air, run around, and have some fun."

On that first visit to meet our great Aunt Lulu, I wished I could trade places with cute baby Gretchen who never got forced outside to have fun. I wanted to be a bump on a log inside that strange house where I could sit on a smooth wooden floor that didn't prickle my bare thighs; where fans moved the heavy air before it could climb on my head and weigh me down; where my parents' voices, the whoosh of the fans, the drone of the ice-box were the background sounds of safety.

After our eviction, Ann, Kay Kay and I sat like bumps on a log along the wooden fence in Aunt Lulu's backyard with nothing to do but watch the Spanish Moss that hung from her oak tree. It seemed alive and a bit ominous, as if all the witches had hung their hair on the branches and gone inside Aunt Lulu's tree to wait for Halloween. If I hadn't been so bored I would never have touched it, but once I did, I liked playing with it. It hung low enough for us to pull handfuls down. My sisters and I made beards out of it and boas and wigs. A teacher at school had told Ann lots of country people slept on mattresses stuffed with Spanish Moss.

"That's so scary," Kay Kay commented. Ann and I agreed; we wondered whether Aunt Lulu's mattress was stuffed with moss. Probably. We moved on to our favorite pastime, figuring out how we could make a million dollars. Since Spanish Moss grew on most trees in Louisiana, it would be the crop from which we would build our fortunes. We could pull down all we wanted and then sell it. The trick was to figure out how it could be used. We agreed that moss mattresses was a dumb idea. I liked Ann's idea best.

"We could make Easter baskets for old people and fill them with Spanish Moss instead of that fake green grass."

"Yeah," I agreed, "and we could put stuff in the baskets that old people like. You know, stuff like prunes and preserves and weird candy made out of orange rinds."

"No matter how old I get, I'll never eat that; I'm gonna still love chocolate and cookies and pies and ice-cream and..." Kay Kay always got off the track. She wasn't much help to Ann and me with our million-dollar schemes.

The afternoon dragged on with muffled voices occasionally drifting out into the yard. Aunt Lulu's voice rang loudest— "Papa...this," and "Papa...that." It seemed queer for an old woman to be talking so much about her daddy.

Feeling irritated and bored as fence posts, my sisters and I would usually have started to fight. By late afternoon, however, we were too hot and miserable to muster the effort. Somewhere in the distance, a rooster crowed. A drop of sweat fell from my chin and landed on my collarbone. I pulled my shirt out so I could watch it slide down my chest. Finally, Mother called us to come in to say goodbye to Aunt Lulu. As we left, Aunt Lulu handed Daddy a jar of fig preserves. Behind his back, Kay Kay and I made yuck faces.

I was so happy when we finally made it back across the river to our own River Road and our own house. To complete my sense of joy, Mother got out her Betty Crocker Cookbook and started melting the chocolate for a batch of brownies with pecans. I'd eaten as little of Aunt Lulu's food as I could get away with, and I was suddenly starving. Later, while we sat eating brownies and drinking milk with Mother, Daddy opened his jar of fig preserves and began smearing the sticky, brown lumps on white bread. He alternated bites of this with sips of Jax Beer.

"Candy, isn't it amazing the way the old lady manages to keep up with the news in spite of being practically blind!" Daddy, shook his head with pride that Aunt Lulu still managed to plow through the daily newspaper, reading line by line with her magnifying glass. With Mother's journalism background and affinity for news, he probably expected her to be equally impressed.

But she wasn't. "Your Aunt Lulu may read the news, but her thinking is hardly current. Someone should tell her the Civil War ended and her side lost."

Daddy came to Aunt Lulu's defense. "Candy, you can't expect somebody of her generation to feel about integration the way you do. She's lived in the South her whole life and doesn't understand why things need to change."

Mother would counter that his dear Aunt Lulu was a terrible racist and of course she didn't see why things should change just as long as Negroes were still serving white people.

I knew Mother was right about Aunt Lulu's prejudice, but I could see my daddy was right, too. Why did Mother have to say these things to him? Couldn't she see how much it hurt him?

The pungent odor of fig preserves and the strong smell of chocolate caused flips in my stomach. I didn't feel hungry anymore.

"Kay Kay, you want my brownie?"

"Sure," she responded, popping the rest of her brownie into her mouth as she stretched out her hand.

When I was in fourth or fifth grade, Aunt Lulu moved across the river to our side and rented a little house near Donaldsonville Elementary School. While she had been deaf since suffering a bad case of measles in childhood (or so I had been told), by the time she moved to Donaldsonville, she was almost completely blind. Daddy made Kay Kay and me walk over from the elementary school once a week to have lunch at her house. Gretchen was in first grade at St. Vincent's, and Ann was also in Catholic school that year.

Kay Kay and I met out front after the twelve o'clock bell rang on Wednesdays to make our weekly pilgrimage to Aunt Lulu's for lunch. We had learned a crude sign-language alphabet and could spell out questions for her. Mostly, we asked her to tell us stories about growing up at Oak Alley. She was always delighted to talk about that. It seemed to me that was the only real life she'd ever had, as if she'd been a child at Oak Alley and then, a lonely old lady with false teeth and cataracts.

Kay Kay and I struggled through those lunches, whispering our negative comments only when Aunt Lulu left the room, fearing that neither blindness nor deafness could truly prevent a grown-up from detecting the bad things children said or thought. Although we rushed to rinse our ice-cream bowls in her sink under the guise of being polite, she knew we had not eaten it.

"You don't like my ice cream, do you? Would you like chocolate better? I could get strawberry."

Kay Kay and I were flabbergasted. How had she known we'd been dumping it down the sink? We quickly spelled out our denials and rushed to change the topic from her food to her stories. We loved to listen to Aunt Lulu describe life in the olden days. She seemed so happy in that long ago time with her family, playing "hide and go seek" in upstairs bedrooms, chasing chickens up into the giant oak trees, hanging colored lanterns at Mardi Gras time.

I loved to hear about the big parties at Oak Alley, the preparations made days ahead, the servants running around chasing chickens down from the oak trees to kill, clean and cook them for the party. There would be pandemonium in both kitchens--the cooking kitchen, located away from the big house to protect it from possible fire, and the summer kitchen where things were kept cool. On the day of the party, look-outs called down from the upstairs attic windows as soon as a carriage was spotted in the distance. Dozens of carriages arrived bringing guests, some of whom stayed for days. She beamed with pride recounting details of those parties—what her brothers and sisters did, their friends, their fancy clothes, how many times they danced. I noticed Aunt Lulu always described those parties from the vantage point of an observer rather than a participant.

She told lots of stories about her mischievous brothers. It seemed those boys loved playing tricks almost as much as they loved riding horses. One trick entailed a tall tale her brother told a young servant boy.

"If you feed grits to a chicken, that chicken will lay triple the number of eggs as usual and those eggs will be twice as delicious." He told the boy he would prove it was true. "I'm gonna feed Bessie some grits tonight. You go count her eggs in the morning." He then gathered up the eggs from all the hens and placed them in Bessie's nest. The next morning he hid behind a tree and watched as the boy discovered them and rushed to tell the cooks. Aunt Lulu would laugh and shake her head, certain her brother was the funniest, cleverest boy who'd ever lived. Everything those brothers did amused her to no end. She seemed proud of their antics, like the times they rode horses at break-neck speed right through the center of the house—in the front door and out the back.

As much as Aunt Lulu was amused by her brothers, it was her sisters she admired most. Evelyn was a great beauty who turned the eye of every eligible bachelor up and down the river; she had suitors from as far away as New Orleans. Josie was the clever one in the family, the great organizer, the one with business sense, the one who kept things going.

"Papa couldn't run Oak Alley without Josie. That's why she married so late in life. Your grandfather courted her for years, but Papa just couldn't let her go. Josie loved Sidonius, but Oak Alley was her home and Papa needed her there.

I think it was after your grandfather was elected mayor of Donaldsonville that Josie finally agreed to the wedding. Sidonius was so excited when he heard the election results, he wanted to be the first one to tell Josie the news. Horse and buggy would have taken him too long to get from town all the way out to Oak Alley, so your grandfather took the train and got the conductor to let him off at Oak Alley even though there wasn't a station. Why, they let him off right in the middle of our sugarcane fields!"

Aunt Lulu once told me that my grandfather had used a diamond ring to carve Antoine Sobral's initials on a window of Oak Alley. At the time, I didn't question the logic or the meaning of this gesture, but many years later it would puzzle me. Why did my grandfather scratch his father-in-law's initials, instead of Josie's, into that windowpane? Was it intended as a gesture of respect to Josie's father, acknowledgement that the Sobrals' 24 years at Oak Alley were indelibly etched into its history?

Each time I've visited Oak Alley over the years, I get a thrill seeing that windowpane with my great-grandfather's name carved in my grandfather's hand. It makes the stories more believable; it provides physical evidence that my family once lived in that beautiful house at the end of a stunning, magical alley of magnificent Live Oaks. It was hard to believe that only one generation separated my family's pink overdraft slips and the Sobrals' Mardi Gras parties at Oak Alley. As difficult as it was to imagine my sisters and me living at Oak Alley, it was even harder to picture Aunt Lulu there.

"Papa sold Oak Alley after Josie and Sidonius married. It broke Josie's heart," which I later discovered was far from the truth. The only daughter whose life was locked in the antebellum past was Jacinta "Lulu" Sobral. When Aunt Lulu's story reached the part where Oak Alley was sold, she got a faraway look and grew quiet. I knew the stories were over for that day.

On other days, she talked about Eveline, "the most beautiful woman in the Delta." She had tons of boyfriends before she picked the one she would marry. Her wedding was the biggest, fanciest wedding you ever saw. The governor of Louisiana sent her a beautiful set of crystal water goblets as a wedding gift. For years I admired them behind the glass doors of our china-less, china closet in Donaldsonville. Those glasses went to Italy with my sister Gretchen, who bears the middle name, Evelyn. When Kay Kay's daughter, Evelyn, married, my sister Gretchen gave *her* the goblets.

During all those years of listening to Aunt Lulu's stories, I never once heard her mention a boyfriend, a "gentleman caller," or a single Oak Alley party at which she had danced. From the old family pictures I'd seen, Aunt Lulu was obviously homely even in her prime. Her older, prettier sisters wore beautiful dresses and danced at parties which were the talk of the Delta. Fifty years later Aunt Lulu still told about them. For the rest of her life she clung to the magic of those romantic nights under the oaks and the memories of all the exciting people who came to call—but never for her. It surprised me that she didn't seem to have any resentment, jealousy or bitterness at having been excluded. I know I would have hated my sisters if they were having all the fun, and I was just watching. Aunt Lulu was part of that family, but she felt the pride of an outsider lucky enough to have witnessed their exciting, romantic lives.

After Aunt Lulu moved to Donaldsonville, I didn't like to see her outside her apartment, away from her stories. It embarrassed me to run into her downtown on Railroad Avenue when I was with my friends. If I spotted her across the street looking bewildered and distrustful, obviously in need of a helping hand, I sometimes pretended not to see her. One time, a colored lady took her arm to help her across the street, and Aunt Lulu whacked her with her pocketbook. She thought all black people were out to steal from her and cheat her. Worst of all, she used the "N word" all the time.

Because Aunt Lulu was deaf, she had no volume control when she spoke. She shouted the word "nigger" out in public as easily as if she were speaking in a confidential tone in the privacy of her home. Many times this occurred within easy earshot of some colored person I knew. I'd dig my fingernails into the palms of my hands and wish I could disappear.

Aunt Lulu was the innocent cause of a few of the biggest fights I remember my parents having. My father felt guilty that he didn't do enough for her, and my mother made no attempt to hide her disdain for "poor" Aunt Lulu. One Sunday when my father brought her over for dinner after mass, my mother stood at the stove, swinging her hips irreverently and singing every verse she knew of: "*Don't Bring Lulu*."

"You can bring Rose with the turned-up nose,
but **don't** bring Lulu.
You can bring Grace with the ugly face
but **don't** bring Lulu."

Aunt Lulu sat at the kitchen table smiling while my sisters and I squirmed uncomfortably, teetering between guilt and giggles. It drove my father crazy. I watched his jaw clenching and unclenching. When I registered his disapproval, my mother's song suddenly seemed more mean-spirited than funny. I wished she would stop.

Sunday was the only day of the week we had our main meal at mid-day. When we had company, after dinner we'd move into the living room for coffee and dessert. I took Aunt Lulu's arm and led her to our biggest, softest living room chair, my father's chair in the corner. Mother followed with the dessert tray. After serving Aunt Lulu, Mother turned on the lamp by the couch and picked up a New Yorker magazine.

"Poor Aunt Lulu," my father said, glancing across the room at her. Aunt Lulu sat staring through milky eyes into space, her usual dwelling place regardless of where her body happened to be.

"You're misplacing your sympathy, Conrad. I've heard stories about the awful way Lulu treats her maid. 'Poor maid!' is what I say, for having to put up with your 'poor' Aunt Lulu." Mother said Aunt Lulu could be a real bitch sometimes. This was too much for Daddy.

"Shush, sh, sh!" my father winced, tucking his head down into his shoulders as if acid had just been poured into his ears. He hated cuss words worse than anything, especially when my mother used them. "Candy, she's a lonely old lady," he said in a voice which sounded pleading.

"That's her own fault, Conrad." Mother made this pronouncement as casually as if she were describing defective curtains. Cool as a cucumber, she sat leafing through her New Yorker while my father grew more restless.

He suddenly rose from his chair and glared at my mother. I saw his jaw clenching again, a tell-tale sign of the anger swelling inside my easy-going father. Conflict with my mother was never easy for him. He adored her and thought her the most beautiful, wonderful, intelligent woman on earth. He bragged about her and told us how lucky we'd be if we grew up to be half as beautiful and smart as she was. Still, Mother's rough language always burned his Catholic ears, and he hated it when she dwelled on Aunt Lulu's shortcomings. Her profane language and less than charitable feelings toward his only living relative put him in the uncomfortable position of not liking her.

He remembered all the insults and slights he'd ever received from her Yankee parents, who were far from perfect. He remembered it was he, rather than her parents, who bought Mother's wedding dress and train ticket to Wisconsin and paid all her bills before she left Alexandria and never said a word about it. He remembered the stingy eggs and muffins the Canrights served after their wedding. All the bad feelings were resurrected.

"And what's so damned great about Eldon Canright or Waukesha, Wisconsin?!" my father said in a rare display of hostility towards his disapproving in-laws.

Mother had stopped reading, although she kept her head bent over her magazine. Daddy was restless and had a wild look in his eyes. Finally, Mother looked up from her magazine.

"Oh, Lord, Conrad... let it go," she said in a tired voice.

"I can never please them, Candy, and you know it. You and your Yankee family think you're better than everyone down here!"

As though sensing the stony silence which followed and wanting to start a polite conversation, Aunt Lulu suddenly blurted, "The nigras are taking over everything. They don't even move aside when they pass you on the sidewalk these days."

This less-than-endearing comment was probably her humble attempt at small talk. Daddy got that pained look again while Mother smiled behind her New Yorker. The air in the room was charged with expectation. My sisters and I grew quiet as ghosts. In that moment I feared the simple act of chewing or swallowing might be enough to stir the air, to ignite the explosion waiting to happen. Daddy glanced at Mother, seeming to dare her to say something, seeming to hold her responsible for Aunt Lulu's remark, as if she had willed this imperfection in his only living relative.

This particular Aunt Lulu fight ended like most of my parents' fights. After Daddy drove Aunt Lulu home, he disappeared for the remainder of the afternoon. He must have gone to the Grand Theater to kill a couple of hours watching some World War II or cowboy movie, the usual movies that came to our town. The only time my father ever went to the movies was after he and Mother had had a

- 112 -

fight. Later, he'd slink back in the house as unobtrusively as possible. By the next morning he was his old self again, bringing Mother coffee in bed and giving her first dibs on the morning paper tucked under his arm.

One day we got a call from Aunt Lulu's neighbor to come and take her to the doctor. She had fallen and split open the back of her head. My father and I took her to Dr. Folse. Daddy had a weak stomach and couldn't look at gory things without having to vomit, so I went in with her to help with communication.

Doctor Folse seemed to take pleasure in showing me the huge crescent-shaped split at the back of Aunt Lulu's head. He took an instrument resembling a crochet hook and lifted the flap to show me her skull underneath.

"Look at this, Jane," he said, as he tapped on her skull. Aunt Lulu sat there blinking with a worried expression on her face while Doctor Folse and I peered at her wound like gawkers at a carnival sideshow. Suddenly, a tender feeling welled up inside me for my Aunt Lulu. I took her hand and held it tightly.

I remembered Mother telling me once when Daddy wasn't around, "You know your Aunt Lulu's deafness and blindness were caused by her 'dear' Papa's carousing." She gave a sarcastic tone to the "dear Papa" part. I never heard Aunt Lulu refer to her father in any other way, and "dear Papa" did seem to be the star character in a great many of her stories.

Apparently, when Aunt Lulu had cataract surgery in New Orleans around 1960, the doctor told my parents that her deafness and eye problems may have resulted from exposure to syphilis. She was the youngest Sobral child and by that time, "dear papa" was taking more regular trips to New Orleans. I guess it was more than plantation business that lured him to the Crescent City.

I couldn't wait to tell my sisters. I wondered what other skeletons might be rattling around in the closets of Oak Alley. Mother interrupted my risqué imaginings with her next statement, spoken in a voice surprisingly tender.

"Poor, old thing," Mother said, sounding almost sympathetic to this woman I thought she hated. Mother told me that Aunt Lulu's family hadn't done "right" by her.

"If 'dear Papa' hadn't indulged himself and his sons so much, he might have put some money aside for poor Lulu. He knew she'd never have a husband."

"But Mother," I said, confused, "you're always telling us women shouldn't depend on husbands."

"In Aunt Lulu's day," she responded, "they had no choice. In the South, white males cornered the market on both choice and opportunity."

Like most Liberals, my mother was a habitual champion of the underdog, but I'd assumed Aunt Lulu was an exception because she was a racist and also, Daddy's "oldest living relative." I wondered why Mother kept her tender feelings towards Aunt Lulu a secret from my father, the one for whom they'd have meant the most.

Shortly after Aunt Lulu's accident, she had to move into the old folk's home in our town where she retreated even farther into the world of her past. At the time of her death in 1973, Jacinta "Lulu" Sobral was 87 years old. She had the gift of all those years of 20th century life to grow, to learn, to change. But she never did. If anything, her illusions about life at Oak Alley grew, and her racism deepened. The sale of Oak Alley had been the greatest tragedy of Lulu Sobral's life, just as it had marked my grandmother's long-postponed liberation.

Piggy Bank Bust

Strange as it may seem, I started looking forward to going to college when I was still in elementary school. I was serious enough to have already begun saving money for it, too. The genesis of this early fixation is a mystery to me; I must have taken to heart those grown-up pontifications about "the importance of education," but I think I was also born with a curiosity that would always require fresh fuel. College seemed a fuel tank with no bottom. The thought of running out of anything, including knowledge, scared me. I am a congenital saver and savorer.

I knew I didn't want to end up in the Poor House or stuck in a little shack somewhere on the River Road with no access to free books since the nearest public library was at least an hour away. I was as vulnerable as most children to fairy tales but skeptical about their endings: "They got married and lived happily ever after."

In an era of "Father Knows Best" and "I Love Lucy," husbands were depicted as having superior judgment. They were better suited to head a household and manage family resources than wives. Men were solid, grounded, dependable; women, prone to flights of fancy and foolishness. The most popular T.V. shows depicted husbands and wives that way. Lucy was the impulsive one; Desi, the one who reigned her in, rescuing her from each disaster she created.

This was at odds with what I saw in the Goette family. My father would get the itch to buy a new car, and he would just do it. He didn't discuss it with my mother or ask her opinion. He didn't check their bank account to see if they had the money. He didn't plan ahead, make a budget, or save for this big purchase. One day, we'd hear the crunch of shells in the driveway and see our father sail in behind the wheel of a fancy new car. He was a sucker for bells and whistles: the 2-tone Oldsmobile with a *four* barrel carburetor (for a man with no interest or knowledge of car mechanics); the green Rambler with push-button automatic transmission; a blue Plymouth with a big retractable flashlight in the trunk; the white Buick with blue vinyl interior *and* air-conditioning! Show my father a car with power-steering, power windows, a dashboard with lots of little lights, buttons to push… and you nailed the sale! My mother's most memorable splurges were *the New Yorker* magazine and a $30 pair of shoes she bought on a buying trip for Lemann's in New York.

So, despite the cultural indoctrination of my childhood, I didn't assume that a man would take care of me and make my dreams come true. Perhaps, too, as a middle child and keen observer, I expected to have to look out for myself. I may have loved Snow White and Cinderella, but I *identified* with Puss 'N Boots. I always suspected that like Puss, *I* would have to strap on my boots and set off someday to make my way in the world.

But there was more to it than mere survival; college seemed to offer me a chance to be somebody, have adventures, lead a life that mattered, make a difference in the world. I wanted to be the knight, not the princess. It was this longing for importance that sent me running to my Piggy Bank rather than the candy store each time a nickel fell into my hands. I knew college cost more than a car, so every time my father came home with a new one and my mother cried, I felt like crying, too. How on earth could I expect them to pay for college? The "Puss" in me knew I would have to do the saving.

I don't remember which came first, the resolve to save or the Piggy Bank. The latter arrived one year as a Christmas gift from someone in Bunkie. Ann and I each got one; hers was pink, and mine, blue. Ann pretended her piggy was a horse and galloped his fat body back and forth across the living room couch. When Pink Pig reared on his hind legs, he looked silly, like he was sitting down. I treated my Blue Pig with more respect. I studied the thin slit in his back and the plug hidden under his stomach. Daddy explained the purpose of these strange features, and told me, "When your Piggy Bank gets full—and that'll take a long time—we'll go to the First National and put your money in the *real* bank." I was hooked.

"Imagine *me*," I thought, "just a little girl, walking into Dolphie's bank like a grown-up!" The ladies who worked at the bank might wonder. With puzzled faces, they would turn to their boss, and Dolphie would shake his head "yes," letting them know I was a serious new customer.

In grade school, my allowance was twenty-five cents a week. On Monday morning when Daddy dropped Kay Kay and me off at Donaldsonville Elementary, he gave us each a quarter, allotting us a nickel a day for an after-school treat at Gimbroni's. This little Italian grocery store was located midway between the elementary school and Daddy's office at the high school, a six-block walk that seemed Lincoln-esque to two lazy Louisiana girls. The "long" trek between schools, and the time we killed at Gimbroni's, allowed Daddy to do his paper work, meet with teachers and talk with the bad kids who had to stay after school.

By the time we arrived at Daddy's office, his day was winding down. With his work done, he would look up from his desk and smile when we appeared. His transition from "principal" to "daddy" was completed once he had asked his daughters, "What did you learn in school today?" Our response, always the same, seemed to amuse our father more than concern him. "Nothing." With the daily ritual completed, we could now talk about Gimbroni's.

When the three o'clock bell finally rang at Donaldsonville Elementary School, my sister and I were always hungry. The vision of Gimbroni's faded-green wooden doors gave us the strength to walk all those blocks (probably two) to reach our after-school oasis. Once in a while, a black kid would come in to buy milk or bread, never candy, and we'd look at each other.

The shelves at Gimbroni's held temptations like the ones that lured the lost children in forests to the Witch's Gingerbread House. Like Hansel and Gretel, we wanted to eat every sweet thing we saw on the shelves: jawbreakers, Elmer's Gold Bricks, Necco Wafers, Nutty Buddies, Fifth Avenues, Devil's Dainties, Sugar Daddies— but "wanting" was not enough to get me to step in front of Gimbroni's cash register and pull that quarter from my pocket. Kay Kay's allowance never lasted more than two days. It drove her crazy each time I walked out empty handed. With her mouth full of chocolate, so close I could smell it, we walked side by side those long blocks to the high school. At the end of each school week, I would have another 15 cents saved for my college education.

As soon as I got home on Fridays, I made a beeline for the blue pig who'd waited patiently all week for my loving attention.

Carefully, I lifted him from the top of my chest of drawers and took him to the sofa. I sat cross-legged with my Piggy Bank protected by the Fort Knox my legs formed around him. Only then did I pull the Kleenex wad from my pocket where three nickels safely nested. I unwound the tissue and dropped the silver coins into the cup of my left palm. With my right thumb and index finger, I picked them up, one at a time, as reverentially as a priest taking communion wafers from the chalice. One by one, I pushed them through the slot in Piggy's back, pausing to enjoy the clink each coin made as it disappeared into the dark belly below.

With a flutter of pride, I lifted my piggy bank, certain it felt heavier than it had the week before. One time I looked up and saw Daddy watching me from the doorway. He smiled and shook his head before he continued on his way to the kitchen. Deriving pleasure from saving money was as baffling to our father as it was to Kay Kay.

By fifth grade, I had become the Queen of Delayed Gratification and needed two hands to hold my piggy bank. When people asked me what I was saving for, they laughed when I told them "college," so I stopped telling. My habit of pinching pennies and nickels really got on Kay Kay's nerves, and I suspect the Gimbroni's didn't much like it either. They always seemed happier to see Kay Kay in their store than me. Though I spent ten minutes studying each item on their shelves, they knew in the end I would buy a Rock 'N Roll on Monday and another one on Wednesday, and that would be all the money they'd see from Jane Goette.

A Rock 'N Roll was the biggest treat you could buy with a nickel. It was two, 5 by 8" sheets of gingerbread coated with hard pink icing. Long before we reached the graveyard a block or two past Gimbroni's, the only sign of Kay Kay's candy bar would be her chocolate mustache, but as we entered Daddy's office, I was still nibbling the first third of one sheet of my Rock 'n Roll.

Daddy would smile at Kay Kay and give her braids a tug. "Where's your candy, Sweetheart? You didn't finish it already, did you?" he'd ask in mock disbelief, winking at me across the top of Kay Kay's head. If Daddy had a lot more work to do, he might reach into his pocket and give us another nickel to share at the vending machine in the teacher's lounge. He knew if he gave me a nickel, chances are I'd take it home and stick it in my bank. This wasn't what he intended, and when we were at his school, this couldn't happen.

Having to share a nickel with Kay Kay ensured it would be consumed in some immediate, delicious pleasure. I was grateful for times like this when Daddy saved me from myself. Though the vending machine at DHS couldn't hold a candle to Gimbroni's, it was thrilling to know that what I admired through the little glass window would actually end up in my mouth.

Jane saving her eggs.

Jane Goette

Sonia's Shame

She was dirty, poor, and stupid--a homely girl with sad eyes too large for a child's face. Sonia's eyes seemed world-weary, yet innocent, always searching. She both fascinated and repelled me, and though I often stared at her, I always avoided eye contact.

Sonia's hair reminded me of straw, in color and texture. I doubted she'd ever felt the bristles of a brush through her hair. While most little girls wore short dresses with petticoats, Sonia's dresses hung closer to her ankles than her knees. She never wore bright colors, and her shoes were brown tie-ups, the kind boys wore.

For me, who never went to school without a Kleenex in my pocket or up my sleeve, the worst sight was a kid with a runny nose. Sonia always had one. From top to bottom, nothing about Sonia merited the most coveted adjective for a little girl, "pretty." Most of the time, her expression seemed like a dog waiting to be kicked.

People in our little town said Sonia's family ate raccoons for dinner and didn't have indoor plumbing, that her parents had come from some foreign country like Poland or Czechoslovakia and could barely speak English. Sonia's family was large, but the older kids didn't go to school anymore. Her family lived miles down the River Road, way past our house. She and her brother rode the school bus in from the country every morning and melted back into oblivion when they left after the three o'clock bell.

Sonia was in my 3rd grade class at Donaldsonville Elementary. Not that year nor any other did I see her at a birthday party or at the swimming pool in summertime. She didn't go to the skating rink in fall, nor to the South Louisiana State Fair, which no kid would miss. I never saw Sonia at Saturday's cowboy matinees, which cost ten cents and showed at least two cartoons, like Baby Huey and Road Runner, then long previews of movies you weren't allowed to see, like "Peyton Place," all this before the feature. What a bargain.

Like everybody else, Sonia was Catholic, but I never saw her at church. Missing Mass on Sundays was a mortal sin, so her family had to go *some*where, but where? And where did they shop? I didn't even see Sonia at the grocery. Maybe it was true that they ate raccoons.

When we lined up for recess, Sonia was the girl no one wanted. As Miss Moreau called names I prayed, "anybody but Sonia!" I didn't want to hold her hand. Back in the classroom, Sonia disappeared into the empty spaces at the back of the room. She rarely spoke or raised her hand. Our teacher never chose Sonia to go up to the chalkboard; she wouldn't have known the answer anyway. Memories of Sonia are not from the classroom, but the playground. She stood alone on the fringes of every game, watching. One time when I skipped through the jump-rope without missing, I saw her smile.

The winter of third grade, I became fixated on Sonia's lips. When I noticed tiny flakes of dried skin sprouting along the vertical lines of her lips, I asked why she didn't use Chapstick. I was trying to be helpful, but she looked at me like I was speaking a foreign language. Her lips got worse; lines became cracks. She licked them so much, a pink, chafed circle formed around her mouth.

I hated recess on really cold days. I didn't want to play anything; just wait for the bell to go inside, put my head on my desk, and listen to Mrs. Moreau read the next chapter of our book. Outside,

in a sunny spot near the door with my back against the bricks, I watched kids and waited. Sonia was *always* watching, but I was watching her--those lips, swollen and oozing something other than blood.

I hadn't even noticed the boys playing tag nearby. Then, one of them bumped into Sonia. It was more a brush than a collision, but Sonia screamed and grabbed her mouth. Tears streamed down her cheeks. A teacher came out with the bell and saw her. She dropped the bell and rushed to Sonia. Squatting down, the teacher coaxed Sonia's hands from her mouth. Thick drops of blood had blossomed through the cracks. As the teacher dabbed Sonia's lips with a Kleenex, Sonia kept crying in a strange way.

The accident horrified and fascinated me. I understood the hurt and tears, but not the way Sonia cried—like an old person, not asking or expecting anything. When the boy said he was sorry, she covered her mouth, nodded, and lowered her head.

The Christmas holidays came. Kids waved goodbye shouting, "See you next year!" When we returned after New Year's, Santa Claus had brought us a present—the new boy! That's how it felt to have Don. In a town small as ours, a new kid was as exciting as a hurricane. Every child at Donaldsonville Elementary envied my class; even the older kids.

With his blond hair, rosy cheeks, and twinkly blue eyes, Don looked like a Hummel figurine or an angel on a holy card. All the little girls loved him; so did our teacher. She chose Don for "line leader," and when no other student knew the answer to an arithmetic problem, Mrs. Moreau would hand him the chalk. "Show them, Don," and he always did.

Blondes were a rare sight in our community of French and Italians. In class, I stared at Don's shiny, gold hair. He looked like a child you'd see in *Life Magazine* or a picture book. I imagined him as Hans Brinker whizzing across the ice on silver skates.

In third grade Don Reynolds was our superstar, best-loved child in the whole school. No one had a bad word for him; he was the nicest boy I'd ever met. He smiled at everyone, even Sonia. When he held the door for her, I wasn't the only one who noticed. Mrs. Moreau told Don he was a real gentleman.

I didn't know which house was Don's, but I knew he lived in town. I wasn't sure where Sonia lived; just far down the River Road. I saw Don at the picture show and at Mr. Henry's Barber Shop, but it wasn't until Palm Sunday that I crossed paths with Sonia, right in front of my house!

Every year at 10:00 mass on Palm Sunday, the big church in town celebrated a little-known River Road saint. The miracle St. Amico performed had occurred in a community so small, it was named "Abend" for its location at a sharp bend in the river. If it hadn't been for the yearly St. Amico parade, I'd have thought there were more chickens in Abend than people.

Like most kids, I went to Sunday mass at 8:00 a.m. even on special days. After fasting for communion, I felt starved by the time I got home, changed, and finally had breakfast. As I was taking my last bite of soggy Cheerios, my sister burst into the kitchen shouting, "Hurry up! The St. Amico parade is coming!" I bolted to the front of the house. The drumbeat and horns were unmistakable; the rhythm, neither jazzy nor churchy, just sort of somber and serious.

Mother and Daddy were already on the sidewalk with my sisters, all eyes focused on the approaching procession. I scooted between my parents, and though I would have liked to hold my mother's hand, I was happy enough just to stand beside her. "You know how far these people have walked?" Daddy asked. I shook my head. I knew it was far, and Daddy admired them for it.

Everybody in Abend must have been in the parade. They didn't look like farmers today; every man, woman, and child, dressed in Sunday's best, walking barefoot, carrying their church shoes. The star attraction was St. Amico, riding on a platform high above the marchers' heads. Sweat beads rimmed the slicked-black hairlines of the men who shouldered it. Perspiration ran down their faces into the creases of their necks—soft brown against stiff white collars.

The flowers on St. Amico's platform nearly covered his sandaled feet. Rosaries dangled from his neck, swinging back and forth. Dollar bills plastered the sides of St. Amico's robe. When he reached us, Daddy stepped across the ditch and handed a bill to the man with the ribbon.

And then I saw Sonia. She looked so different I almost didn't recognize her: hair, brushed and held behind her ears with pink butterfly barrettes; a bright yellow dress with pearly white buttons down the front; even without a petticoat, the dress looked perky. Sonia did, too, walking beside a plump, weary-faced woman, smiling, holding hands, both carrying pairs of white heels. As they passed, Sonia smiled at me; she looked so proud. I envied her—the parade, the butterfly barrettes and fancy shoes, holding hands with her mother. But, my mother was a lot prettier.

By late spring that year, I had a favorite playmate at recess. Betsy and I liked pretending to be Fury and Black Beauty. One day as we galloped past Don, he laughed and called out, "Hey, want some candy?" We circled back. "Yes, please!" I think we both loved Don more than each other even before the candy, but how many kids would share their Tootsie Roll? As Don popped the last chunk in his mouth and we stood there chewing, I felt happy. Don Reynolds was my friend.

I hadn't swallowed yet when Don said, "Hurry up." He bent down, and with his candy wrapper, plucked a dried dog turd from the grass. "Doesn't this look like a Tootsie Roll?" I laughed nervously because it seemed sort of naughty what Don was doing. "Watch this," he said, his mouth glistening with chocolate. "Hey, Sonia, you want some Tootsie Roll?!" he shouted. She was across the playground.

Sonia seemed startled by the sound of her own name and didn't move until she was sure he meant her. When Don waved, she came running. Her face blossomed into a radiant smile, just like that day on the River Road in her yellow dress. Don's dimples deepened in a wide expectant grin as he extended his hand. Sonia approached shyly, not once taking her eyes from Don's, not even hesitating before extending her hand, not even looking. Both of them were smiling when Don placed the candy wrapper in Sonia's palm.

She looked down for what seemed an endless moment. When she raised her eyes and looked into ours, her smile was gone. She didn't say a word, but her face—her stunned, questioning eyes. I had to look away. I didn't say anything. Then the bell rang, and we returned to class.

Miss Moreau began reading, but I couldn't concentrate on the story. My mind wandered. I remembered an afternoon long ago: My mother and little sisters were napping. I was outside, alone and bored when I noticed a snail on the sidewalk. I wondered if it was true about salt making snails

melt. This seemed as preposterous as frying eggs on a hot sidewalk—another thing I'd heard about. I slipped up the back steps to the kitchen for the Morton's, then hurried back. I squatted over the snail, carefully sprinkling salt all over it. When this living creature began to shrivel and melt, I ran home frightened and ashamed.

Jane Goette

Back to School Blues

Summer's end was tinged with sadness. No more swimming pool or vacations out of town, not even small ones, just an ocean of school days so vast I couldn't imagine ever reaching the other side. Not even a new pair of shoes and a box of pristine, unbroken crayons could lift that heavy dread. For my sisters and me there was the added tension of not knowing which school we might be attending any given year.

Daddy wanted us in the public schools, not just because it might seem strange for the principal's own family to choose the alternative but because he thought the curriculum was better.

Mother feared the parochialism of the teachers in the public schools, most of whom were Donaldsonville natives with teaching degrees from local colleges. In the Jim Crow South of the 1950's my mother was more concerned that her children might learn racist, conservative ideas than that they might learn conservative religious ones. The nuns had come from an assortment of places beyond our town, and presumably served God rather than the secular establishment of Louisiana. My sisters and I were fodder in our parents' battles about which schools we would attend.

My father didn't like to argue with Mother, and so the year that Kay Kay started first grade, she thought they'd reached an agreement. As summer progressed and we loaded our cereal with figs—Mother and Daddy ate theirs plain with cream—breakfast talk shifted to uniforms and nuns. Mrs. Torres had measured each of us and begun making our navy blue pleated skirts. Mother bought white blouses and saddle shoes from Lemann's to complete our uniforms.

On the first day of school, Mother woke us up with her usual morning chant, "Get up girls, wash your face and hands, brush your teeth and get dressed tout suite!" When we appeared in the kitchen, Mother put down her paper and inspected us with pleasure. Daddy did not look up from his newspaper and seemed strangely subdued as the table buzzed with first day of school excitement. I had been to Catholic school the year before, but that didn't allay my fears. No teacher, classroom, or mix of kids was ever the same. Would this be the year that revealed how stupid I was? Gretchen was sad to be the only sister left behind, but in my nervousness, I wished we could trade places.

Mother put out her cigarette, took another sip of coffee, and then reached for the hairbrush tucked in her apron pocket. She called us over one by one to fix our hair, check that our blouses were tucked in neatly and our shoes, tied. My sisters dreaded our mother's heavy hand with a hair brush, but this time, she was more gentle than usual as she braided Kay Kay's pigtails and tied a navy blue ribbon at the end of each. My short straight hair required no taming, just a "lick and a promise," as Mother called it. How I loved the feeling of hands in my hair, brushbristles across my scalp. If I couldn't have Shirley Temple curls, why wouldn't my mother even let me have a ponytail?

"Don't be ridiculous," Mother would say, "a Buster Brown is perfect for your kind of hair."

My sister, Kay Kay, chose this moment to offer a helpful observation.

"Jane, have you looked in the mirror? Your ears don't have wrinkles in them. They look like they were ironed!" She pushed my short hair back to prove her point, then laughed as I scrambled to cover them. I had never realized this before, and now I was starting third grade. Thus, began a lifelong self-consciousness about my ears.

Daddy put down his newspaper. "Time to go, girls," he said as he stood up, reached for his suit jacket on the back of his chair and put it on. My cereal turned to a hard lump in my stomach. As we scrambled for book bags and a last glance in the mirror, Mother straightened Daddy's tie. She stood on the front porch with Gretchen, waving as we pulled out of the driveway onto the River Road and headed for town.

When we reached the town limits, the River Road turned into Mississippi Street. We passed Ascension Catholic Church, but Daddy didn't turn left. Instead he headed through town and turned left onto Railroad Avenue.

"Daddy, this isn't the way to St. Vincent's," Ann said in a puzzled voice.

"Y'all aren't going to St. Vincent's," Daddy said, not taking his eyes off the road.

My sisters and I exchanged worried looks and grew quiet in the back seat. Daddy pulled up in front of Donaldsonville Elementary and opened the backseat door for us. As he strode down the sidewalk toward the tall steps leading into the building, we three trailed behind, feeling foolish in our Catholic school uniforms.

Whenever Daddy dropped by the elementary, the all-female staff made a big fuss over him. They seemed genuinely pleased to see him, for reasons other than the novelty of a man in a female world. Daddy had impeccable manners, a gentle sense of humor, and he was consistently kind and patient with those teachers. He possessed a gentlemanly charm that women loved and trusted.

As usual, as soon as the teachers saw Daddy, they gathered around him smiling and chattering with the excitement of the first day of school. Ann, Kay Kay and I shuffled uncomfortably waiting just outside their circle. I saw Miss Gimbroni glance over Daddy's shoulder at us standing there in our uniforms. Once he was gone, I'm sure the teachers gossiped about us, but they would never have asked Daddy the question on all their minds. Our classmates were not so diplomatic.

"What y'all doin' in uniforms? This ain't the Catholic school, no! You stupid or somethin'?"

I don't remember much about that day at school except the tension of knowing we would be going home to Mother when it ended. What were we to say to her when she asked about our day? I thought about all the money Mother had spent on our uniforms even though she fretted about being overdrawn at the First National each month. I remembered how pleased she seemed that morning sending us off to our first day at St. Vincent's.

Everything happy about this first day of school collapsed the moment I realized what was happening. While I didn't understand why the school issue was such a loaded one for my parents, I knew that what Daddy was doing was wrong, and that Mother, who cursed and argued about things, would never have put us kids in this kind of situation. I worried about the inevitable fight my parents would have when Mother found out Daddy had enrolled us in public school. But there wasn't a fight. It was worse than that.

After Donaldsonville Elementary dismissed that first day, Daddy picked us up, dropped us off in our River Road driveway, then drove straight back to his office at the high school. Mother and Gretchen stood at the top of the porch stairs smiling, eager to hear all about our first day of school. Ann and I avoided Mother, busying ourselves with changing out of our uniforms into play clothes. We stayed in the closet a long time hanging up our skirts and folding our blouses. Mother and Gretchen didn't seem to notice our uncharacteristic fastidiousness;

their attention was more focused on Kay Kay. This had been her first day of school.

"Who's your teacher, Kay Kay?" Mother asked, as she reached for a cigarette and lit it.

Kay Kay stood on one foot, fingers flicking her long black eyelashes.

"Sister Patricia," Kay Kay said, carefully avoiding Mother's eyes.

"Honey, Sister Patricia teaches second grade, not first. Don't you know your teacher's name?"

"I don't remember, Mama," Kay Kay said in a timid voice, "it was Sister Somebody."

It didn't take long for Mother to get the truth out of us. She turned toward the window with a stunned look, as if she'd been slapped or kicked in the stomach. Then she walked out of the room to my parents' bedroom and closed the door. We could hear her crying. I had never once in my life heard my mother cry, and the sound filled me with dread and terror. I understood that our family's foundation was shaking, as surely as our old house shook when hurricane winds blew. I never worried about our house falling down in storms because my mother never worried, but now my mother was crying. What would happen to us? In the intuitive way that a child understands abstractions like betrayal, I recognized the present danger.

Those after-school hours dragged. Mother did not emerge from the bedroom. I looked at the clock and knew it was approaching dinner time, yet the kitchen was deserted. It seemed an eternity before Daddy finally returned. When he came up the back steps to the porch, we crowded around him.

"Mama's crying," we said in hushed, anxious voices.

Daddy got a pained expression. His jaw tightened as he studied our worried faces.

"Get in the car, girls. We're going to have dinner at the Chance tonight."

Ordinarily, this would have been a thrill for us. Our family never went out to dinner except once every two years when we made the two-day car trip to Wisconsin to visit Mother's family. All I wanted was to be sitting at our own table with my parents and sisters around me. I wouldn't have cared if we'd had calf's liver for dinner, just as long as things could have been back to normal.

We pulled into the Chance parking lot and Daddy honked the horn.

"Why aren't we going inside, Daddy?" Gretchen asked in her innocence. The rest of us knew, although we couldn't have explained it.

"This will be more fun," Daddy said, turning to face Gretchen in the back seat. "This is what the teenagers do when they come to the Chance."

While we waited for our hamburgers and cokes to be brought out to us, another car pulled in and parked beside us. I recognized Mrs. Kahn from school; every kid knew her. I slunk down in my seat hoping somehow Mrs. Kahn and her husband might not notice us and would just head straight inside the Chance. No such luck. Mrs. Kahn saw us right away, smiled and walked over to Daddy's window.

"Hi, Mr. Goette. Y'all had the same idea Herbert and I had for the first day of school." She glanced around the car, smiling at each of us.

"Where's your mama?" she asked, looking straight at me.

I turned red. "She's, she's sick," I stammered, feeling guilty and ashamed for lying to a teacher.

"Candy doesn't like hamburgers," Daddy said, skillfully employing this insignificant truth to hide the larger one he was avoiding.

Our hamburgers arrived and Mrs. Kahn left.

"Your mother's upset now, but she'll get over this. Don't worry, girls. By the time we get home, she'll be feeling a lot better, you'll see."

But it wasn't true. When we returned home Mother was still in the bedroom. She emerged a few minutes later with eyes swollen and red. It scared me to see her like that.

"How could you do this, Conrad?"

Daddy turned from her to tell us to start taking turns bathing and brushing our teeth. When we came out of the bathroom, Mother was gone.

"To Miss Connie's for a visit," Daddy told us, but after I'd lain awake anxiously listening for the car in our driveway for what seemed like hours, she still wasn't back.

Mother did return the next day. I don't know what they said to each other during the next few days, but the tension in our home was palpable. When I was home, I longed to be someplace else; when I was at school, I worried and couldn't wait to be home.

Eventually my parents' conflict was resolved. Ann went to St. Vincent's, while Kay Kay and I stayed at the public school. But the aftermath of this fight lingered, leaving us all feeling a bit shellshocked. For the Goette girls, the back-to-school blues had a whole new meaning. And whatever it was, it lasted for years. The start of each school year carried hope but also the whisper of anxiety, the ghost of a conflict I never understood and still don't.

My Catholic Town

Almost everybody in Donaldsonville was Catholic; the whites went to Ascension and the blacks to St. Catherine's a few blocks away. Protestants were as foreign to us as Buddhists. It came as quite a surprise to later learn that most Americans were Protestants and not one president had been Catholic until John Kennedy, a fact Kay Kay discovered after Daddy gave her a little cardboard presidential trivia wheel he'd received as a free sample. Kay Kay adored gadgets like this. When she lined up the window to a President's name, information about that president would appear in each of the other windows around the wheel—his age, party, years in office, religion, vice-president, etc. It also displayed the President's picture.

Kay Kay played with her cardboard wheel all the time and enjoyed quizzing the rest of the family on presidential trivia. One day in the kitchen, she asked if anyone knew President (rhymes with clutch) "Buch-a-nin's" religion. Confused, Mother responded "Buchanan?"

"No," Kay Kay shot back, so proud that she had stumped our smart mother, "he was Presbyterian!"

For all we knew, there might have been a "buch-a-nin" denomination among the many other unfamiliar protestant churches. The only thing I knew about Protestants was that they had broken away from "the one true church founded by Jesus Christ to save our souls." After they left the Catholics, they couldn't agree on anything and scattered into a confusing array of religious sects— Baptist, Methodist, Episcopalian, Lutheran, Church of Christ, Mormons... How could a person tell them apart? My only exposure to Protestants was via radio, where they ranted and raved about hell and used Jesus's name in every sentence. If they loved Jesus so much, why had they left His church?

Once in high school, my sister Gretchen and I went to visit a Protestant family in Montgomery, Alabama. We'd become friends with their kids during the brief time they'd lived in Donaldsonville while their father oversaw the building of the Sunshine Bridge, which eventually replaced our ferry. On our visit to Montgomery, the McWhorters took Gretchen and me to Sunday service at their church. It was our first time inside a protestant church, and we were surprised by its dull interior: no statues, crucifixes, fonts of holy water; no saints; not even a statue of Blessed Mother. Only the wooden pews indicated this building was intended as a church. I can't recall the sermon, only that the minister frequently invoked the name "Jesus," which seemed too familiar a term to be so overused. My Catholic ears preferred more respectful terms, like "our Lord," or "Christ," or just plain "God."

Sunday service at the Montgomery church seemed more like a social gathering than a religious one. The parishioners talked inside, called out to each other from across pews, chatted with the minister before and after the service. They sang a lot of churchy songs and didn't kneel down even once. The most shocking thing of all was their version of communion; it was as casual as if they were passing around a basket of cookies at a party. The whole thing lacked seriousness. The magic, mystery and drama of the Catholic mass was gone.

My church was dark and cavernous, filled with shadows and strange light that seemed to spill from heaven itself. The air I breathed smelled of incense and holy water. On either side of the altar stood statues of flying angels holding golden candelabras; one angel wore a pink robe and the other, blue. To the right of the communion rail hung a large crucifix, so close I could see the agony on Jesus' face.

Communion was the highlight of the Catholic Mass, the most dramatic moment, serious, and serene. The altar boys rang heavy golden bells at just the moment the priest raised the host above his head and recited the magic, Latin words that changed bread and wine into the body and blood of Christ. At this moment everybody in church bowed their heads, shut their eyes, and prayed silently. No one smiled during communion like they did in Montgomery. During the consecration, I tried to concentrate, to pray, to really feel what I knew I was supposed to feel, but it wasn't easy. I couldn't help staring at others, studying their facial expressions...or their hats or fancy rosaries, some of which sparkled like gems.

Church was filled with things to fascinate a child—statues of saints; stained-glass windows depicting religious scenes; Stations of the Cross; side altars that featured Mary and Joseph; hand-embroidered altar cloths topped by massive flower arrangements and enormous candles, and in the corners of the church, dark wooden confessionals with heavy purple curtains.

I was five years old and terrified the first time I stepped into a confessional box and closed the heavy velvet curtain. It was dark inside except for the faint light that shone on a crucifix. By the time I had children, it already seemed unimaginable that loving parents had allowed their small children to enter a dark box with a very graphic depiction of torture—a man with thorns stuck in his head, nails hammered into his hands and feet, a sword slash in his side dripping blood.

The crucifix scared me; the whispering on the other side of the grated window scared me more; the darkness and solitude scared me most. During the long minutes that I waited, I jiggled and wiggled trying not to wet my pants, trying to remember the words to the Acts of Contrition, trying to rehearse my list of sins:

- Lied (6 times)
- Said curse words (3 times; this number greatly increased with age)
- Sassed my mother and father (12 times)
- Fought with my sisters (150 times) In future years after I'd learned my multiplication table, I would count the number of days since my last confession and multiply it by four or five. If it had been a long time since my last confession, I reduced my multiple to two, figuring God wouldn't quibble about the exact number.
- Coveted my neighbor's goods (I really wanted that ring Myra Dugas's aunt bought her at the Five and Dime)

Suddenly, the grated window slid open, and everything I knew left me. Through the little holes I saw the silhouette of the priest waiting in the shadows to hear my sins, but I couldn't remember a single one. In fact, I'd forgotten everything I'd been practicing for months. My lips were as cold and numb as Jesus's. The priest waited, but to no avail. Finally, he turned his head and looked at me.

Realizing the situation, he gently coached my confession, "Bless me, Father…"

I eventually mastered confession, but never my nervousness. In later years, fear of forgetting sins was replaced by fear of remembering. Because my family was well known in our small town, I was also afraid the priest would recognize me. Once, in eighth grade, Father McNamara ended his absolution with, "Go in peace, Jane." I was the only Jane in Donaldsonville.

Whenever Catholics in Ascension Parish had a serious sin to confess, they sought a different church—maybe Smoke Bend or Belle Rose, but if the sin was really bad, they'd take the ferry across the river and drive sixty miles to New Orleans to make confession at the big Jesuit church downtown where anonymity was assured.

Before Vatican II changed things, it was imperative for Catholics to wipe their souls clean before Easter Sunday. In Donaldsonville, on Easter Saturday all four confessionals ran full speed all afternoon and into the night. Sometimes there'd be four confessionals in operation at the same time and long lines snaking through the church for each one of them. I don't know where we found the extra priests at Easter, but we certainly needed them. Confession before Easter was the most important one of the year, unless you'd committed a mortal sin, in which case you had better go immediately. If you got hit by a car or struck by lightning, there was no saving you.

My mother's relationship with the Catholic Church was always a mystery and remains so today, long after her death. Despite having been raised Catholic, there were long periods in which she did not even attend *Sunday* mass, a mortal sin at the time. During other periods of our shared lives, Mother attended mass regularly and went off to Grand Coteau's week-long Catholic retreat for women. She read progressive Catholic journals like *Commonweal*, and I think she even prayed at night in her bedroom, but never spoke about spiritual matters.

My mother was quite open and vocal about her criticisms of Catholic hierarchy and local church leaders but extremely private with her inner, more personal thoughts. It was clear to me that faith was always a struggle for her. I would describe my mother as an idealistic skeptic with strong romantic leanings, an innate sense of moral justice, and a questioning mind. It's easy to see why these characteristics conflicted with a Catholic Church in league with the other Louisiana institutions of the day that perpetuated discrimination against Blacks.

The periods in which Mother didn't go to mass at all had good and bad sides. When my sisters and I returned from mass with Daddy, as soon as we opened the front door we would smell bacon and eggs, coffee, hot cocoa, and Mother's streusel-filled coffeecake. Because Catholics had to fast before mass if they were going to Communion, we were starved by the time we got home and dying to replace the bad-breath taste of a communion wafer. You couldn't chew it up and swallow it because we believed it was the "body of Christ," which meant you'd be chewing god, and you didn't need the Sisters to tell you *that* was a sin. The wafer seemed designed to stick to the roof of your mouth. Despite my tongue's best efforts, I could never pry it loose enough to just swallow and get it over with.

The bad parts of these "out" phases were my parents' fights. Daddy would beg my mother to return to church. The more adamantly he insisted, the more adamant Mother was in her refusal. It drove my father crazy. He didn't understand it. During his whole Catholic life, he seemed not to have experienced a moment's doubt about his faith, while my mother, even in her religious phases, viewed Catholic sacraments and rituals as symbolic traditions. To my father, the sacraments were real. Bread and wine turned into the body and blood of Christ, uniting us with God. My father once told me, "Without the grace of the sacraments, I would be nothing. The lowliest of the low. The sacraments give me the strength to be a good person." He believed this with all his heart.

When I was a child in Donaldsonville, missing mass on Sunday was still considered a mortal sin. It pained my father that the person he loved most in this world committed a mortal sin every Sunday with an ease that confounded him. The sacrament of confession was essential for Candy to be restored to God. Conrad would never leave her behind in this world or the next.

One Easter Saturday after begging her and begging her to go into town and make her confession, he could stand it no longer. I was sitting at the kitchen table, reading the comics. Mother was at the stove, stirring a pot. My parents had been arguing all day about church and after the latest round, Daddy started to leave the room. He stopped suddenly, turned around, and marched toward my mother. He grabbed my mother's arm, spun her around, and scooped her up in his arms the way he would do his children.

"Conrad, have you gone crazy? What the hell do you think you're doing? Put me down!"

"I'm taking you to church and you're going to confession!" Daddy said, as he carried her toward the porch door.

Cool as a cucumber, Mother responded in a calm voice now: "Conrad, you can put me in the car. You can carry me into church. You can open the curtain and throw me into the confessional, but you can't make me confess."

Daddy put her down and left the house. He didn't return until dinnertime. Nothing more was said.

The Catholics in our community came from France, Nova Scotia, Spain, Italy and Germany. The largest group by far, however, was Cajun. They were the descendants of French Catholics in Nova Scotia who were expelled from Canada for refusing to swear allegiance to the British crown. These loyalists got in boats and headed south; most ended up in Louisiana. Perhaps they were drawn this way because New Orleans already had quite a French population, but they didn't settle in the city. They fanned out into the bayous of Louisiana, the small tributaries which form the delta region between the Mississippi River and the Gulf of Mexico in the southern part of the state. Donaldsonville was built along the river at the mouth of Bayou LaFourche, about sixty miles north of New Orleans.

On the Goette side, my grandfather was the son of a German boot maker who'd left Baden-Baden and come to Donaldsonville to make his fortune in the New World. I gather things didn't turn out quite as he'd planned, for my great-grandfather Goette ended his life with suicide. His son, however, fared much better in the New World. Sidonius prospered, became a prominent businessman and mayor of Donaldsonville.

My German Goette grandfather and my Spanish-Portuguese Sobral grandmother were Catholics, as were most of the people who settled in the "Golden Horn," the term used to describe our section of the Mississippi Delta. Sin and repentance seem as much a part of our local heritage as sugar cane and crawfish.

There have always been two main streets in Donaldsonville— Railroad Avenue, which begins at the train station and dead ends at the other main street of our town, which is Mississippi Street. By far, the most impressive, imposing, dominant structure in the town has always been the Ascension Catholic Church on Mississippi Street. It remains a much-respected building and centerpiece of the town. Even now in this new millennium, it is not uncommon to see men of all ages tip their hats (or baseball caps) in respect as they drive past the church. Others will unconsciously raise their right thumbs to their lips and make a little cross as they pass the church.

If you study the building carefully you'll notice a slight change in color of the bricks around the base of the church. Shortly after construction of the church began, a little over a hundred years ago, it suddenly halted. This dramatic interruption was not due to lack of funds, lack of Catholics, or lack of the people's desire for a grand church, but because the whole town was punished for a terrible sin.

***

In the early days of our history, small enclaves of Catholics were spread up and down the Mississippi River from New Orleans to Baton Rouge. They'd have to wait for a priest to come by riverboat to perform their weddings, baptisms, communions and confirmations. In order to get a priest to perform mass on Christmas day, there had to be a large enough congregation of Catholics to justify a stop, and the way Catholic communities communicated this to a priest traveling upriver from New Orleans was by lighting enormous bonfires on top of the levee. The blazing fire was the signal for a boat to stop and deliver the priest to a little community of Catholics. This is the story I was told explaining the origins of the Christmas Eve bonfires on the levee. Of course, the tradition had long outlived its original purpose. When I was a child on the River Road, the appearance of bonfire constructions on top of the levee was as much a harbinger of Christmas as Salvation Army Santas were to city children.

My father was born in 1905, when Donaldsonville was already a thriving river town with a rich sugar cane industry. It had a large outdoor market, lots of stores, an impressive boat landing, streets filled with horses and buggies, my grandfather's ice and soda pop factories and an abundance of Catholics. South Louisiana Catholics baptize their children as soon after their births as they can prepare the big party that follows.

"Except during the excommunication period," my father explained.

"The what?!" I asked in disbelief. "Excommunication" was the scariest word in the Catholic language, reserved for the deadliest of sins, like getting divorced and remarrying. I eagerly awaited his story.

By the end of the 19th century, Donaldsonville had grown large enough to need a church of its own. Lots of money was raised and there were plans to build the grandest church on the west bank of the river anywhere between New Orleans and Baton Rouge. These River Road Catholics wanted to build a church as impressive as St. Louis Cathedral in New Orleans. Boats passing upriver would see its steeple rising above the top of the levee. Passers-by would know this was a community of importance, and no one was more invested in that vision than Father Ceuppens, the pastor of Ascension Parish.

Even before the construction began in 1875, Father Ceuppens and the townspeople began thinking about the interior, the part that really makes it a church. People willingly scrimped, saved and contributed generously to this project even if it meant eating nothing but beans and rice for ten years. They'd seen pictures and heard stories about the grand cathedrals of Europe—the paintings by great artists, the statues, the stained-glass windows, marble steps and golden altars—and they were determined to build and furnish such a church right here on the banks of the Mississippi River. Finally, the time came to dispatch Father Ceuppens to France to buy such treasures for their own little cathedral.

The good Catholics of Ascension Parish accompanied their priest to the Donaldsonville dock and bid him farewell with handshakes and claps on the back. Some held tightly to their rosaries and began to pray as the boat pulled away from the river's bank. "Bon chance, mon pere!" some called out. The next day they went about their business and began the long wait. Days stretched into weeks and weeks into months, but still Father Ceuppens did not return with marble columns, statues, and stain glass windows.

Finally, word came from the port of New Orleans that Father Ceuppens would be on the next day's passenger ship. When the boat rounded the curve and blew its whistle, half the town must have heard it. A crowd gathered on the levee. Small children peeked shyly from behind their mother's skirts, and grown men pushed and jockeyed for position just to get a glimpse of the returning hero and his treasures.

Ceuppens was but a small man dressed in a plain black cassock and starched white collar, carrying a weathered suitcase. No crates and boxes accompanied him. Though the townspeople smiled, shook his hand, and slapped him on the back, Father Ceuppens felt the weight of their disappointment. That disappointment grew with each day the expected barge failed to appear at the Donaldsonville dock.

Today no one knows the names of those who appeared at Father Ceuppen's house one night, banging loudly and smelling of whiskey. When he opened the door, they pulled him out into the street, dragged him several blocks to the base of the levee where a barrel of tar and another of feathers awaited him in the gloomy, moonless night.

"They tarred and feathered him," my father explained, "and rode him out of town on a rail."

"Gosh, just like 'Poor Floyd Ireson!'" I thought, hearing my mother's imitation brogue as she recited from heart

Poor Floyd Ireson, with his hard heart,
 tarred and feathered and carried in a cart
by the women of Marblehead!

Daddy paused, looked at me sadly and continued his story. "Two days later a large freighter docked in Donaldsonville and unloaded huge crates stamped 'Paris, France.' It took all day for the boatmen to unload the heavy boxes and crates—stained glass, marble statues, fine linens. They say when they unboxed the large statue of Blessed Mary, there was a tear in her eye, a real tear."

News about the tar and feathering of Father Ceuppens traveled up and down the river. I don't know how long it took for it to reach Rome, but when it did, the pope took no time at all to reach his decision. The whole town of Donaldsonville was subjected to one of the strongest punishments the church can give, an interdiction, which was like an excommunication that lasted a few years.

Official documents provide no details corroborating my father's story besides references to "bodily harm" having been done to Father Ceuppens after a "forcible eviction from the rectory." Church records *do* show an abrupt suspension of the celebration of the sacraments and a vehement objection from Father Ceuppens to the church's reopening in 1885 based on the fact that he had been "defamed, misjudged and mistreated" by its parishioners.

After I heard Daddy's story, I never passed Ascension Catholic Church without noticing the change of color in its bricks, evidence of the interruption.

***

The pope's lesson sank in. During the 1960's when I was attending Ascension Catholic Church, Monsignor Gubler was our pastor and the town treated him like a king. He seemed to relish the role. Money from the weekly collection baskets was used to finance trips for him to Rome and to the Holy Land. While he was away, he left many duties to a good Catholic lady who lived near the church and used to play the organ at Sunday masses. After returning from his Easter trip to the Holy Land, he presented Jeanne Marie with a gift to show his appreciation. When she opened it, she was surprised to find a larger than life size portrait of...not Jesus or St. Peter, but of the monsignor himself. Embarrassed by the gift, she blurted, "I...I don't know what to say." Monsignor Gubler gave Jeanne Marie an understanding smile, patted her hand and replied, "You deserve it."

HEART OF CONTROVERSY--A drive for funds to construct the "new" Catholic Church, right, ignited the spark which began a church war lasting from 1874 to 1891. A difference in coloring in the bricks is visible at the base of the steeple, indicating a break in construction. At the left is the old church, built in 1840 and demolished in 1911.

Taken from the sesquicentennial edition of the Donaldsonville Chief 1972, edited by Candy Goette

My mother never cared for Monsignor Gubler. She thought it outrageous that our small town had two Catholic churches--the big, grand one for the whites and a smaller, humbler one for the black Catholics. There was also a white Catholic School, St. Vincent's, and a black Catholic School, St. Catherine's, walking distance apart. Though St. Catherine's had no playground or even a swing set, the children could play on a large, grassy lot that stood directly in front of the school. They played the same games River Road children played on the levee and had as much fun at recess as the white kids—until Monsignor Gubler orchestrated the purchase of that lot, which everyone knew belonged to St. Catherine's. Gubler insisted the white boys at Catholic High needed a larger space for afternoon football practice. As compensation for confiscating the land, Gubler offered St. Catherine's additional funds for books. It was already a dirty deal, but Gubler made it worse. Once he obtained authorized control of the land, he erected a completely unnecessary fence, whose only purpose could have been to shut the black children out. St. Catherine's children had no place to play, while the lot sat empty all day long until the white boys came over after school.

That fence was the last straw for Mother. She said, "That fence is a monument to hatefulness," and she never set foot inside Ascension Catholic Church again. From that time on, my mother attended weekly mass at St. Catherine's Church. She was the solitary white attendee until my sisters and I followed shortly after. I loved going to St. Catherine's; it felt more real.

Ann's Horse Nipper

My sister Ann has been an avid reader for as long as I can remember, but when she was ten years old, she became dangerously lost in her books. Zombie like, she walked among us oblivious to her surroundings, deaf to the voices of sisters, parents and teachers, caring only for the book she held in her hands. Ann read in the bathtub and on car rides and under the covers at night with a flashlight. Mostly, she read books about horses. Before leaving elementary school, she'd read Black Beauty, Misty of Chincoteague, The Black Stallion and every other horse book available within a thirty-mile radius. Ann didn't want to play or talk or go to sleep or wake up for school. All she did was read or lie on her back holding imaginary reins as she galloped away into fantasy.

During the period Ann went AWOL, multiplication had sailed over her head, as peripheral and annoying to her consciousness as a mosquito buzzing in the room. Her body had been confined to an oak desk in Sister Josephine's classroom, but Ann's mind had floated out the tall French windows the moment she sat down and reopened the novel hidden inside her assignment book. Sister Josephine warned my parents that if Ann didn't learn the multiplication tables soon, she would fail math for the year.

My parents were worried. They consulted their friend, Dolphie Netter. Although Dolphie was a banker by trade, he was a doctor at heart. He spent far more time reading his Merck's Manuel than the financial pages of the Times Picayune. This medical avocation extended to the mind as well as the body. The first I.Q. test I ever took was administered by Dolphie inside his bank office. He had tested all the Goette girls and most of Bubba and Camille's kids, too. We were Dolphie's guinea pigs. Our parents delivered us like gumdrops to a child with a sweet tooth.

Dr. Netter was more than ready to sign on to Ann's case. After consulting his manuals and reading a few articles, Dolphie concluded the problem lay in Ann's subconscious mind. That being the case, her subconscious mind must be penetrated in order to reach the problem and cure it. He recommended hypnosis.

Jane Goette

As fortune would have it, Ascension Parish Schools had just hired its very first school psychologist. The amiable Perry Davis hit it off with Daddy right away. Although Dr. Davis had been hired to establish a testing program for our parish school system, he was as much a frustrated Dr. Freud as Dolphie was a Dr. Kildare. His true passion was not for testing but for the subconscious mind, and the best key to unlock it was hypnosis. Dr. Davis was as experienced administering hypnosis as Dolphie was in giving I.Q. tests and eager to take on Ann's case.

"Don't worry, Conrad," he said, "I'll get to the bottom of this. Give me a month or two, and Ann's going to put down her books and rejoin the world." He devised a plan that would hinge on the answer to two important questions.

"Is there a particular food that Ann really hates?" Dr. Davis asked my father. Anyone who knew Ann could have answered that one—lima beans! Lima beans put Ann in a bad mood, made her feel like running away from home. She would have been happy to share a can of Campbell's Soup with hoboes around a campfire. She couldn't stand to look at the sickly green legumes. With her fork, Ann slid lima beans under her knife, hoping Mother would think she'd eaten them. Once, she used lima beans to create a little art project on her plate, much too creative to be destroyed by her teeth. If my parents insisted, her last resort was to shut her eyes, put them in her mouth, pretend to chew and swallow, then spit them in her napkin when no one was looking.

Dr. Davis's second question was intended to explore Ann's loves. He felt certain this was tied to those books she lived in.

"You see, Conrad, Ann is living in her books because there's something in them that is pulling her. Her mind is choosing to dwell in that world because it has something she's not getting in this one. We've got to figure out what it is."

The next Saturday morning, Ann was sitting in a big leather reclining chair in Dr. Davis's office. He explained to Ann that hypnosis was like taking a little trip. All she had to do was shut her eyes, relax, listen to his voice and by the time he'd counted backwards from ten, she would be ready to begin. Ann liked Dr.

Davis, and this sounded like fun. She put her head back and closed her eyes.

"Ann, let yourself relax in that chair as if you were floating on a cloud. You're going to feel so relaxed, your eyes will feel a little heavy. It's okay. Let your closed eyes rest like a tired bird in its nest."

After this prelude, he would ask her to count backwards with him and told her she was getting sleepier with each number. Long before he reached ten, Ann was out.

"Easiest person I've ever hypnotized," Dr. Davis told Daddy and Dolphie.

The first few weeks when he hypnotized her, he sent her on great adventures. Although most of them entailed Ann meeting a wild stallion somewhere and being the only human who could ever ride him, she also got to fly airplanes, eat hot fudge sundaes and sit on Clark Gable's lap.

On Saturday mornings to give Mother a break, Daddy would take all four of us with him to the high school. Kay Kay, Gretchen and I watched T.V. in the school auditorium while Ann visited Dr. Davis in another part of the school. Daddy stayed in his office catching up on paperwork until it was time to drive us home for lunch.

Since we didn't have a television at home, watching the Saturday morning shows seemed a real treat... until I learned what Ann was doing. There was no question she was having more fun in her airplane than Sky King and his niece Penny up on the T.V. screen. She rode better horses than the Texas Rangers. And just as "My Little Margie" ended, Ann would prance down the aisle of the auditorium in time for "Fury."

After a few weeks, the sister I knew slowly began to return. She went to play at friends' houses, joined dinner table conversations at home and sometimes went to the cowboy movies with us on Saturday afternoons. Although Ann had no memory of it, Dr. Davis had planted a hypnotic connection between her books and lima beans. Until her obsessive reading was under control, each time Ann opened a novel she tasted lima beans. Dr. Davis had not learned his

Jane Goette

art in Vienna, but Daddy and Dolphie felt certain the great Sigmund Freud could not have done a better job than "Perry."

Ann started paying attention to Sister Josephine's lessons and learned enough multiplication to pass fifth grade math. Daddy was so happy he sent Perry Davis a bottle of Jack Daniels whiskey, and Mother invited him to dinner. No one was surprised when Dr. Davis left Donaldsonville to take an important job at a state psychiatric clinic.

Perhaps if Dr. Davis hadn't moved away the next year, Ann would never have had a real horse of her own. It would have been better for all of us. I'm sure the horses he helped Ann conjure were far superior to the one she finally got.

For months on end Ann nagged, pleaded, bargained and begged for a horse.

"Daddy, I'll die if I don't get a horse! It's all I want. If you let me have one, I'll be so good. I'll study my multiplication table and make my bed and go to mass every day of the week and..."

Daddy finally put down his newspaper and gave Ann an amused look. "Honey, you don't know dada from yaya about taking care of a horse."

"How can you say that? I've read about a million books on horses; I know how to take care of a horse better than anybody!"

"If I can't have a horse," Ann wailed, "I don't want to live anymore."

Mother rolled her eyes and went back to reading the newspaper, but I could tell Ann had gotten to our father.

On Ann's tenth birthday, Daddy appeared in the yard of St. Vincent's Catholic School holding the reins of a horse called "Nipper" for his nasty habit of biting children on the legs as they climbed into his saddle. Word sped through the classrooms faster than a hurricane warning, "There's a man out there with a horse!"

Although Ann could not have guessed that man was our father, she sprang from her desk, pushed her way around the heavy skirts of Sister Angelina and was the first child to burst through the open doorway. Perhaps she was expecting to see Roy Rogers standing there with Trigger, but she was even more pleased to see her old daddy, clad in suit and tie, holding the reins of a cranky horse.

I always imagined that moment in the school yard of St. Vincent's as one of the high points of Ann's life. Being the prom queen some years later must have been peanuts compared to such glory. I imagined her climbing into the saddle with the whole school watching in envy. School girls and nuns alike gasped as she took the reins in her hands, gave a little kick and rode off into the noonday sun—a star, a cowgirl, the embodiment of everyone's dream come true. Crowds of girls and nuns pushed to get a better view. They shaded their eyes against the harsh light of noon and squinted to catch the last glimpse of Ann Goette riding away.

When we were grown up, Ann told me quite a different version of the story. Daddy bought the horse from Frankie Sotile, an active 4-H boy in the public high school where Daddy was principal. When Daddy showed up in the school yard, it was Frankie who helped Ann into the saddle, slapping Nipper's nose each time he turned around to bite her. Frankie handed Ann the reins and backed away to clear the way for her departure. Everyone was watching, all right, but there was no riding off into the noonday sun. Ann kicked Nipper to get going but he stubbornly refused to move. While Ann was poised to show off her horsemanship, Nipper had other ideas. He planted himself as firmly in one spot as if he'd been a statue. The only thing moving on Nipper was his tail, flicking off the flies. For Ann, the moment is remembered as one of complete humiliation.

Frankie Sotile led Nipper home for Ann and staked him out on the levee in front of our house. Each day Ann rushed home, changed her clothes and headed to the levee with sugar cubes in her pockets. My most vivid memories of Ann's horse days are of her sitting on the levee while Nipper lay in the clover, his head resting in her lap. She stroked him, fed him clover and treated him like a house cat, none of which ever really improved his disposition.

Each time Ann attempted to ride Nipper, some disaster befell her. Nipper seemed bent on killing the only person stubborn enough to love the world's meanest horse. Once, he galloped toward a low-hanging tree branch and refused Ann's attempts to veer him away. "Whack!" The tree hit her right in the forehead, knocking her unconscious. When she came to, Nipper was calmly standing atop the levee, nibbling clover. Ann came home with a blinding headache and eyes swollen to thin slits.

The event which finally sent that awful horse packing was actually not his fault. Ann had been riding Nipper on the levee one afternoon. Afterwards, she tied him back to his stake and ran down the levee heading for our house across the road. On her way down, she stepped in a nest of bumble bees which proceeded to swarm her whole body, stinging her. The bees were in her hair and up her shirt. When my mother heard Ann's screams, she was certain Nipper had darted into the road and they'd been hit by a car. Immobilized by grief, our mother was found cowering behind the refrigerator when the crisis was over.

A man was driving his pickup down the River Road. When he heard Ann's screams, he slammed on his brakes and ran up the levee to help her. He ripped off her shirt, used it to bat the bees away from her head and body, then carried my trembling, weeping sister across the road and into our house. Mother came out from behind the refrigerator and calmed down enough to follow his instructions. While she ran to get the box of baking soda, Ann started vomiting. The man said that was to be expected.

I watched with a mixture of fear, sympathy and revulsion. I hardly recognized Ann. Her head seemed twice its normal size. Her bumpy brow stuck out like a little shelf over her eyes which were once again two slits. Her lips were so large they practically touched the tip of her swollen nose. Even her ears were strange; they looked like candle drippings stuck onto the sides of her head. Poor Ann looked like one of those Halloween masks sitting in the display window of Slim's store downtown.

"Is Ann going to stay like this, Mama?" Kay Kay asked anxiously.

"No, she's going to sleep for a couple of days and then she'll start to look like Ann again." I guess my mother was so happy Ann hadn't been killed, it didn't seem to bother her that Ann looked like a monster.

Although this time Nipper really had nothing to do with Ann's being hurt, the incident was the last straw for my mother. She knew the accident she had imagined was still possible. Having experienced Ann's death in her imagination, she wasn't going to take any more chances—"That damned horse has to go!" My father was in complete agreement.

Ann was the only one sorry to see Nipper go. She never gave up on him and to this day, my sister has a strong affinity for mean animals.

Ann on Nipper

Eldon Canright "Grandpa" in WWI Uniform
with unidentified friends, 1917

Grandpa Canright's Attic

Every other summer our family made the long trek to Wisconsin to visit Mother's family. We stayed with her parents in Waukesha because they had room for us. Aunt Marilyn and Uncle Glen lived in West Allis, near enough to visit almost every day. Those bi-annual trips to Wisconsin were important to our mother and to us kids, too. Daddy's parents and sister died long before my parents even met. We didn't have any close blood relatives in Louisiana except Aunt Lulu.

Aunt Marilyn was ten years younger than Mother, wore her long hair in a braid that hung down her back, and dressed in shorts and sandals all summer. She and Uncle Glen did things no one in Louisiana would do. They hiked in the jungles of Yucatan, Mexico, canoed through the wilds of Canada, and went to protest marches against the bomb. Mother's brother, Uncle Maynard, lived two hours away in Twin Lakes. Uncle Maynard owned a pharmacy with a soda fountain and a comic book stand. He and Aunt Florence had a motor boat and sometimes took us speeding across the lakes so fast, I thought I'd fly out. Like Mother, we lived for those Wisconsin summers.

By the summer of 1955, Gretchen had joined her big sisters in the back seat. For two long days we rode scrunched together in a car without air-conditioning, passing through a hundred small towns with sad-eyed dogs and confusing signs nailed to signposts. While our parents stared at their maps in the front seat, I peered out the window into the eyes of each unloved dog, feeling guilty to leave it behind. Mississippi was the longest state.

When we finally arrived at Grandpa and Grandma's, there was the inevitable awkwardness of greeting relatives we rarely saw, yankees who did not behave like Louisiana families. No grown-ups scooped us up in their arms and smothered us with kisses. My mother's parents never quite knew what to do when our green Chevy pulled into their elm tree-lined driveway and their four Louisiana granddaughters spilled out of the car. Two years had stretched between our last visit and this one, an eternity in the life of a child. Our hair and haircuts had changed; teeth had been lost, and sizes were all different now.

Grandma and Grandpa looked the same. My French-Canadian grandmother from Iowa, still thin and nervous, still a brunette with fewer silver threads in her hair than were in my mother's. The backdoor of their house swung open, and white-haired Grandpa Canright strode out to the driveway ahead of Grandma, his confident, hearty voice greeting us with faintly familiar words, "Well, if you aren't a sight for sore eyes! Conrad, you must have taken the long way 'round Robin Hood's barn!" He laughed. We all did.

Everybody was excited, but the moment didn't feel quite right. I kept waiting for something else: A hug, a kiss, a hand touching my hair or cupping my face. No one seemed to know what to do. In this tree-lined driveway at 809 Hartwell Avenue, my father seemed too warm and friendly, my grandparents too cold and strained. My sisters and I shuffled uncomfortably between the two cultures from which our parents had come, those who kiss, and those who don't.

After we got inside, things felt better. When the teapot whistled and the coffee cups clattered, we kids knew we were free to go. Ann headed to the sunporch at the front of the house that faced Hartwell Avenue. Perhaps an older kid would pass by on the sidewalk, then Ann would call out to her. If not, Ann would settle into her latest horse book, while Kay Kay, Gretchen, and I explored the house, each of us lingering before some object that caught our fancy. We peeled away from each other as the house ripened to familiarity, I, waiting for my chance to sneak upstairs alone, past the landing where no one could see where I went.

At the end of the upstairs hall, to the left there was the yellow bathroom with the funny windows and claw-footed tub. The windows were frosted with a pattern I imagined to be snowflakes. On the wall, between the sink and toilet, there was a little wooden door with a white ceramic knob. It reminded me of the window inside the confession box at Ascension Catholic. This one opened out like a door instead of sliding to the side like in the confessional. In the shadowy light at the other side, instead of a priest there was a laundry chute that went all the way down to the basement. If I could have fit, I would have wanted to slide down that chute. I imagined landing in Wonderland like Alice, not a laundry basket. But the door to my land of wonder was never this one.

I turned toward the door that looked like it led to a closet. Though I knew what I would find, I hadn't been to this house in two years, half of Gretchen's life. With a rush of excitement and a twinge of fear, I turned the handle and opened the heavy door that hid a secret staircase, narrow, dark, dusty, and steep. A cloud of air from another world enveloped me that felt familiar and foreign at the same time, comfortable, yet exciting. If that air were put in a bottle and mailed to me a hundred years later, one whiff and I would have been back climbing the stairs to Grandma and Grandpa's attic.

My grandparents' attic smelled like history and memories from another world, which is what it held. I flicked on the light, always the dimmest bulb, just enough to illuminate the first five steps before light from the windows above would make the climb less frightening. I reached the top and stepped into the attic. A tarnished brass bed with a faded thin quilt stood tucked just beneath the eaves of the slanted, beamed ceiling; a large trunk rested on the floor by the foot of the bed. On the far side of the attic there was an armoire where Grandpa's WWI uniform hung. His boots were inside, too, and above the uniform, his helmet, and the German one he found abandoned on a battlefield in France. This one was more ornate, sporting what looked like a spear tip on top. Though I loved to look at it, I would never have touched it without someone else beside me. It had been worn by an enemy, but even worse, it had been worn by a dead person. Stories about war fascinated and terrified me in equal measure.

My mother, who didn't allow Ann and me to see WWII movies, didn't know that in addition to her father's made-up stories about Old King Neptune and the mermaids, he also told us true ones from the war: soldiers with their guts spilling out, steaming onto the cold ground; the German soldier Grandpa came upon in the woods, not yet dead, maggots crawling across his blown-up knee. Grandpa gave him water. The man pressed a wallet into Grandpa's palm and pointed to a picture. Grandpa looked. In the small photograph, the man stood beside a woman and three children. All were smiling.

Grandpa nodded and tried to give the wallet back, but the man shook his head and looked at him. Grandpa understood. After the war, he mailed the wallet to the German address inside, to the dead man's family. Grandpa's experiences in France did not turn him into a pacifist, but they did, me.

I avoided the armoire. I wanted the war to stay shut inside where it could never come out. All those Waukesha weeks, I played with safer mementos Grandpa had brought home from France, like the children's tea sets stored in the trunk, three different sets, all real china. My favorite was the tea set bought in Paris but made in Japan with peaceful scenes from that foreign land, hand-painted in blue against a white background. The cups were large enough to hold real tea, yet small enough to appeal to a child who didn't drink tea yet.

On rainy days during those Waukesha visits, my little sisters and I held fancy tea parties in the attic. Dressed in shorts or playsuits, we sat on our bottoms on the dusty floor taking turns pouring tea into each other's cups from the blue and white china teapot. We addressed each other as "Lady," in our most polite British accents: "Lady Kay Kay, will you attend the duke's ball tomorrow?" to which the Lady might reply, "Oh yes, but my favorite gown is at the cleaners, so I shall have to wear the green one with the ruby buttons."

As much as I loved tea parties with my sisters, sometimes I preferred to be alone, just listening to the music of the rain. It seemed more thrilling than talk of balls. The percussion rhythm, rising and falling, drumming the roof with the force of a bass drum at a symphony's moment of crescendo. Then tapping softly, like the Highway Man at Bess's window, waiting for her in the moonlight of the old inn's yard.

I sat beside the window and watched the rain fall, tilting my head upwards, straining to see where it began in the sky. I could never tell. It was easier to understand the small stories enacted on the glass stage beside me, each droplet born upon the window, whose life would proceed while I watched. I felt a small grief each time one slid too soon off the edge into oblivion. But many times, one droplet would slide into another, happily merge, and journey all the way down the pane, married in the truest sense, disappearing as the one large raindrop they had become before they reached the end of their long window lives.

The drama of rain, the cool glass, the gray and green outside flooded me with feelings I didn't understand, a bittersweet gush of love as strong as it was amorphous, with no object except the world itself with all it mysteries and wonder. I knew, too, that there were places in the world where war was not locked up in an armoire in the corner of an attic. Everything was out there beyond the clouds and this rainy day, including my own adult story waiting for me to grow up.

I yearned to begin that exciting adult life, but I wanted it to be the way I *played* it in the attic. At the end of a long day in the grown-up world of foreign travel and tea parties, after saving people and writing books and getting hungry, I would come down the stairs and there would be a mother and a father waiting for me at the dinner table. I would be a little girl in a family, taking my place in the circle, surrounded by parents, sisters, and grandparents whose voices would rise above the table like steam from summer's sweet, Wisconsin corn.

I ate my summer corn, licked my buttery fingers, and listened to Grandpa Canright. The rain had stopped. Tomorrow he would take us swimming at Lac LaBelle, and though he didn't say it, I knew we would stop for ice-cream on the way home. Meanwhile, those other lives, the ones that had ended and the ones that had not yet begun, lay quietly waiting at the top of the stairs—in the attic, out the window, and beyond the sky I could see.

Full cast of The Little Blue Angel.

DONALDSONVILLE ELEMENTARY
SCHOOL
presents
THE LITTLE BLUE ANGEL
Christmas Operetta
AT ELEMENTARY SCHOOL AUDITORIUM
Wed., Dec. 11 — 9:30 a. m. & 7:30 p. m.
Thurs., Dec. 12—9:30 a. m. & 1:15 p. m
Adm. — Adults 50c
This Ticket Compliments of
M. J. SOTILE CANDY COMPANY

Admission ticket to the operetta.

Mrs. Kahn, my Favorite Teacher

Although my first year at Donaldsonville Elementary had been horrible, the other grades got better. I liked each year's teacher better than the last, but Mrs. Kahn, my fifth-grade teacher, was the best of them all. During fifth grade school became everything I'd ever hoped it would be.

Mrs. Kahn was the only teacher who did art projects with her students in an era long before art became standard fare at public schools. She bought her own supplies and read arts and crafts magazines to select projects for us—ghost puppets and witches for Halloween, pilgrim hats and feathered headbands for Thanksgiving, necklaces and crowns at Mardi Gras and woven baskets for Easter. Though she gave us patterns and easy-to-follow directions, she also encouraged us to experiment and displayed every child's design, no matter how botched the end product. She made us feel like artists.

After lunch recess, Mrs. Kahn's students didn't groan when the bell rang to send us back to class. All year long she read great books to us, like *The Little Princess*, *Tom Sawyer*, and *Heidi*. We surged through the door, scrambled into our seats, eager to find out what would happen next to characters brought to life by Mrs. Kahn's expressive reading. She never had to shush us; we did it to each other so the reading could begin.

Unlike other teachers, Mrs. Kahn told us true stories about her own life and seemed interested in ours. When Perry raised his hand to tell the class he'd found somebody's finger in a jar of peanut butter, she pretended she believed him and said she was glad it hadn't ended up in his sandwich. At the beginning of the year, Perry's stories were always lies, but Mrs. Kahn listened respectfully and frowned if anyone laughed. Eventually, Perry started telling true ones like the time he helped his daddy catch a big turtle behind the levee and how happy his mama was they'd have meat for supper.

For decades, the highlight of Mrs. Kahn's fifth grade was the annual Christmas operetta. Although the other classes got to be in it, Mrs. Kahn chose the play, the cast, the costumes and she directed all the acting. The fifth graders in her class always had the starring roles. The year I had her, Mrs. Kahn selected an operetta everyone said was the best she'd ever done, "The Little Blue Angel."

Donald Rodrigue, as the poor boy who teaches Princess Maria (Jane) the true meaning of Christmas.

After she'd found the script and ordered it, she was as excited for it to arrive as we were. She told us we'd have to work extra hard now to make up for the time we were going to spend on the play. No one minded the shortened recess, the extra pages of arithmetic and the longer homework. Our teacher's enthusiasm was contagious. Even the homeliest, most awkward of children believed they could shine on Mrs. Kahn's stage. One day Mrs. Kahn returned from lunch carrying a big box.

"Here they are!" she announced, breathless from running up the steps. "Boys and girls, put your arithmetic books away—we're going to read the play!"

Wow, this was fun already! She passed out the scripts, then explained how a play differed from other stories. She told us about setting, scene and dialogue. Before we'd even opened our booklets, most of the girls wanted to be the little blue angel. She was featured on the cover—a beautiful girl in a flowing gown, wings and a golden halo above her head. After I read the script, I realized the best part was Princess Maria. The story was really about her, and she had the most lines. Desperate for the part, I took my script home that night and memorized most of her lines. By the time we had auditions, I had *become* Princess Maria.

This lead character was a rich and lonely little princess who had everything, but nothing gave her pleasure. Her life was empty and meaningless until a poor boy showed up on Christmas Eve to teach her the true meaning of Christmas. The boy was supposed to be a stand-in for Jesus. He disappeared just as mysteriously as he'd arrived and then the little blue angel appeared at the top of Princess Maria's Christmas tree and sang a beautiful song to conclude the operetta on a heart-warming note.

Janelle Laughlin was cast in the coveted part of the angel. She deserved it, too. Not only could she sing better than Shirley Temple, Janelle was as beautiful as an angel. When she appeared at the top of the Christmas tree, the audience gasped. They couldn't see the ladder she was standing on behind the tree. The little kids believed she was a real angel. How else could she have risen to the top of that tree?

I got the role of Princess Maria. Daddy said it was because I had such good expression, but Ann told me everyone at Catholic school said it was because I was the principal's daughter. Years later Daddy delighted in telling how I snapped back at Ann, "You tell those snobs at St. Vincent's to come to the play, and they'll see why I got the part!" I imagine I must have fancied myself a young Natalie Wood or Audrey Hepburn, but Daddy thought me Judy Garland. Like the rest of us, he had a tin ear. He was so impressed with the way I sang my one song, *"Things, Things, Things,"* he signed me up for singing lessons with Mrs. Barrios.

Mrs. Kahn's operettas contained parts for every child; there were bakers, soldiers, dolls, elves, ponies. While I had a starring role in fifth grade, the previous year Myra and I had been "Breezes," and Kay Kay and Cathy, "Sunshine Fairies." The wonderful thing about Mrs. Kahn's plays was that every child had a song to sing and a costume to wear on stage. No child who ever had Mrs. Kahn for a teacher ever forgot the thrill of being in one of her operettas. It was the Donaldsonville equivalent of Broadway and my crowning moment of childhood glory.

Mrs. Kahn was that rare breed of teacher who truly made a difference in children's lives. So many of the "best practices" in teaching today were things Mrs. Kahn instinctively knew to do: reading to her class, differentiating to challenge each child without frustrating any of us, providing hands-on experiences, teaching in different modalities. She liked and respected children, and though her class was always fun, she also challenged us to do things we didn't think we could do.

Our town was blessed to have her. She taught hundreds and hundreds of Donaldsonville children, and I don't think there was a single kid she didn't like—rich or poor, fat or skinny, dumb or smart. Because she had none of her own, I was blessed to be one of Mrs. Kahn's children for a year in my life. And a very good year it was.

Fifth-grade teachers Eva Kahn and Polly Dance examine a new library book.

Jane Goette

1957 South Louisiana State Fair

Imagine living in a small town the likes of Sleepy Hollow, but without a headless horseman to keep things lively. Then one night a spaceship lands near the high school on a big empty lot. The extraterrestrials build a fence around the lot so you can't see what they're doing. By the end of the week, just when you're dying of curiosity, they open the gates and reveal this marvelous, wonder-filled, little world. They let you play there for two or three days, then they pack it up and take it away in their spaceship. The people of Sleepy Hollow are so sad, the extraterrestrials promise they'll come back every year...and they do.

In Donaldsonville, Louisiana, each September after the thrill of new crayons had faded, and the pecans started plopping on the roof of our house which meant Daddy would get us up at 6:00 a.m. to clear the driveway before he went to mass, and I'd already broken my New School Year's resolution to practice my multiplication table every night so I'd look smart to the other kids, and I was rapidly growing sick of school and the other kids, and Christmas was still months away... well, when I was a kid in Donaldsonville with a case of the mid-September blues, the only thing that pulled me through was anticipating the South Louisiana State Fair.

Though I lived for those raucous carnivals all through childhood, the most memorable by far was the Fair of 1957 when I was in fifth grade. Images from past fairs melded together with images from fairytales, Mardi Gras, circuses, and tall tales kids would tell each other about freaks. As the event drew nearer, I could think of little else. Even Mrs. Kahn, the best teacher Donaldsonville ever had, could not corral my restless September mind. I sat at my desk trying to focus on those elusive multiplication facts, but my inner ear strained to hear signs of the approaching Fair. The moment the first big truck rumbled down Railroad Avenue, I flew from my desk to peek out our classroom window. I watched enormous, brightly colored trucks and trailers drive past my school on their way across town to the South Louisiana State Fairgrounds.

Jane Goette

For white people, the weekend long Fair opened every year on Friday afternoon. Black people had only one day to enjoy the Fair, and it was on Thursday. It was torture to drive by on that afternoon and hear the unmistakable cacophony of shouts, screams, laughter, carousel music and announcements blaring from the loud speakers. As painful as it was for me at that time to be locked out on Thursday, I can imagine black kids must have felt like Adam and Eve getting kicked out of Paradise come Friday morning.

The white schools dismissed early on opening day of the Fair. The year I was in fifth grade, I watched the clock all morning waiting for the bell to liberate me from Mrs. Kahn's classroom. Tightrope walkers, sword swallowers, bumper cars, mountains of pies, sequined ladies eating cotton candy as fluffy as their hair—all that magic had started across town. The spaceship had landed, and at one o'clock, the gates would open again to let me into that once-a-year world.

This year, Frances Knoll, my mother's best friend, was coming all the way from Bunkie so her daughter, Little Martha Frances, could go to the Fair with my sisters and me. Living in the country, we loved to have company, especially the rare occasion of sleepover guests with children. What a great day this would be—an afternoon at the fair and the Bunkie friends, arriving that night in time for supper.

I couldn't wait to see Martha Frances, a tiny girl smitten by tragedy before she was out of diapers. Her handsome father had died when she was a baby, making her almost the same as an orphan. The only orphans I knew were the ones in books, fascinating characters all, clever and brave, not at all like ordinary children.

It had been ages since we'd visited Bunkie. I pictured Martha Frances a perfect Dickinsonian waif, small and delicate. Perhaps there'd be a smudge of dirt on her cheek. Was it being a half-orphan that had made her so quiet, or was she just shy? I wondered if she'd grown at all since I'd seen her—I hoped not. Though Martha Frances was Kay Kay's age, she was as small and cute as a three-year-old. It would be an exaggeration to compare her to Thumbelina, though I could easily imagine her sleeping inside a large tropical flower or curled up in a pelican's nest. I looked forward to playing with her the way I would a new doll at Christmas.

During the days before the Fair's big opening, every hour or two another truck roared into town past our elementary school on its way to the fairgrounds. Because my classroom faced the avenue, I found every excuse possible to approach the windows. On my third or fourth trip to the pencil sharpener, Mrs. Kahn said, "Jane Goette, sit down. The only thing that needs sharpening in this class is your head."

My father was the principal of both the elementary and the high school in Donaldsonville. His office was on the other side of town at DHS, right across from the fairgrounds. From his descriptions, Mrs. Kahn had it easy compared to the poor high school teachers. How could they teach with all that commotion going on across the street? Students heard hammers clanging, elephants trumpeting and distant curses hurled by the rough men who labored for days in the Louisiana heat to erect tents, stages, rides, avenues of concessions and most amazing of all, the freak show alley. With bearded ladies and three-headed men sitting in tents just across the street, how on earth could a kid sit still in a desk and concentrate on algebra or Louisiana history?

Friday morning after breakfast, Daddy gave my sisters and me each a dollar to take to the Fair. In 1957, that seemed like a fortune. Since all our birthdays fell after the Fair, and Ann still qualified for the 12-and-under "youth" rate, Daddy reasoned we should all get the same amount of spending money. He made a ceremony of his dollar dispensing, lining us up at the door in chronological order.

"Now," Daddy began, "I know Ann will have her dollar spent ten minutes after she gets to the Fair. Kay Kay's going to buy a bunch of candy and come home with sticky hair, and Jane's going to come home with that dollar still in her pocket. Y'all do what you want with your money, but make sure your little sister, Gretchen, gets to do what she wants with hers."

I knew he thought Ann would try to borrow Gretchen's dollar, and I'd try to get her to spend it so I wouldn't have to spend mine, and Kay Kay...well, she'd be so busy eating she wouldn't notice if

Jane Goette

Gretchen fell in a hyena's cage or danced off with the Wild Man from Borneo. Daddy knew us well.

When school dismissed, Kay Kay, Gretchen and I headed to the fairgrounds with the Dugas girls. Though we never saw her, Ann was there, too, with her friends from the Catholic School. From eavesdropping on their phone conversations, I knew this year was different, and those girls were as excited about the boys they'd meet at the fair as they were about the rides. These changed priorities didn't make any sense. There were always boys in town, but the Fair came only once a year. It was too important to get distracted and risk missing something really big. My strategy was to scope out the Fair on Friday afternoon, explore every inch of the fairgrounds and know exactly how to spend my money on Saturday when we returned for the entire day.

Kids were lined up at the door when the bell finally rang Friday afternoon at 1:00. We'd had lunch in the school cafeteria an hour before, but most of it ended up in the garbage can. What kid would eat meatloaf and green beans when she knew cotton candy was waiting across town? Certainly not the Goette and Dugas girls. As soon as we reached the fairgrounds, we charted a course to the concession area to survey the array of sweet, forbidden treats only available to us once a year. I smelled the cotton candy moments before we reached the magic tub that spun endless streams of sticky webs, light as angel's hair.

Two steps beyond, scores of candy apples gleamed like rubies lined upon a shelf. These jeweled wonders beckoned, as tempting as Snow White's apple, and seemed the perfect height for a child to reach. From the tops of their lacquered coats wooden sticks invited small hands to "Take me," … and Kay Kay did.

Gretchen reached in her pocket for Daddy's dollar, but I tugged on her hand. "Wait 'til you've seen everything." Though she took her hand out, her gaze never left Kay Kay's apple. Oblivious to our hungry eyes, Kay Kay gave her full concentration to the arduous task of chipping away at the hard crust of her apple. Little wisps of hair were already glued to her sticky cheeks.

The dusty, buttery aroma of popcorn and roasted peanuts drifted by, offering new temptations. Kay Kay hesitated a moment

- 168 -

but seemed to realize she needed both hands to navigate her way around her candy apple. A little beyond the peanut stand, vendors sold hot dogs, spicy chili, barbecue chicken, ribs, red beans and rice, jambalaya, potato salad and dirty rice. Grown-ups dominated these lines. We walked past them with barely a glance.

To escape the mid-afternoon heat, we headed toward the Food Pavilion at the edge of the fairgrounds closest to the high school. This section was housed in a long, wooden building that ran the length of the entire block. Three years later, the same tornado that flew Billy Hayward from the flagpole at the high school also picked up the South Louisiana State Fair Food Pavilion and tossed it across the street in a jumbled pile of giant pick-up-sticks. Fortunately, the storm hit in April when the building stood as empty and forlorn as if it were already in the process of becoming a ghost.

Until its demise, the Food Pavilion drew some of the best cooks and bakers from across the state of Louisiana. They arrived each autumn with visions of ribbons dancing in their heads, and for most, it didn't take a tornado to blow their dreams away.

The first section of the pavilion was my least favorite. I didn't enjoy looking at pickles and things in jars, but Myra Dugas mined all the humor of which a pickle was capable. She pointed to a jar on the top shelf and laughed. "Look at that one," she said, "It looks like my brother's you-know-what."

Gretchen tugged on my sleeve. "What, Jane? What does it look like?"

"Like Michael's nose," I said, "now, let's go."

We walked past the pickled okra and mirlitons (pronounced "melly-tohn,") a vegetable pear, in search of the dessert tables. The magnetism of sugar lured many pairs of small feet in that direction. Each dessert was accompanied by a label printed in the contestant's best handwriting: Aunt Betty's sweet potato turnovers, passed through the family for generations and submitted by her great niece, Miss Tillie Boudreau of Bayou Goulah; Mrs. Harold Aucoin, Jr.'s Bourbon bread pudding, Mrs. Emile LaSalle's River Road pecan pies, Miss Lucy Belle Falsetto's fig cookies.

Glorious cakes covered in shimmering frosting filled the tables to our left; every conceivable variation of fudge occupied the shelves to our right. I felt proud when Myra said, "Your mama's fudge could win the blue ribbon; Miss Candy makes the best fudge in town!" I secretly resolved to share my fudge with Myra the next time Mother put some in my lunch.

"Let's go back to the concessions," Kay Kay said, "I'm starved!"

I looked, I lusted, I fingered the dollar bill in my pocket, but in the end I was overwhelmed by the choices and bought nothing. Kay Kay and Gretchen bought cotton candy and the Dugas girls, fried donuts dusted with powdered sugar. I stood apart from them, watching each child drift into her own bubble of delicious pleasure. "Tomorrow," I thought, "I'll save my money for tomorrow," but it was killing me.

"Kay Kay, can I have a bite?" I asked, trying to sound casual.

"Get your own," Kay Kay mumbled, lips glistening.

Next we headed for the section of the fairgrounds where the big rides towered above a sea of tent tops. Though Myra and I were the only two big enough to be allowed on any of these rides, we all loved to watch them. The Round-Up was one of our favorites. The man at the entrance took people's tickets and then herded them along a big circular wall. With their heads, backs and heels pressed against the metal wall, the riders faced a crowd of spectators. Once the ticket gate closed, the music started and the Round-Up began to spin. It picked up speed, began to tilt and rose in the air. It spun faster and faster until suddenly, the floor dropped off. A wave of screams washed over us. The Round-Up riders were glued to the wall, with nothing but centrifugal force to prevent them from falling to their deaths.

"I'm going on that one!" Myra bragged.

"Me, too," I said, not to be outdone by Myra Dugas. Though Myra was technically older, I had invented the explorers game we played each weekend. To keep command, I needed the other kids to see me as braver than she. Like the Emperor with his invisible clothes, I wanted others to admire me, but even more, I wanted to become what I pretended to be.

Standing before those towering hunks of steel at the center of the South Louisiana State Fairgrounds, I feigned interest and regret at being still too young to ride them. Secretly, I was terrified of any ride that took me higher than a horse's saddle on a merry-go-round. Kay Kay pointed as the Round-Up reached its zenith.

"How do they stay up there?" she asked, her mouth shiny from the sticky residue of melted sugar.

"I think they use some kind of magnets," I replied with know-it-all authority.

"No, they don't. It's centrepedle force. My brother Michael told me," Myra said, a bit smugly, I thought. Since Michael Dugas was considered a science whiz, I knew better than to challenge Myra's explanation.

I would not have dreamed of going on most of the rides in this section of the fairgrounds, but "The Bullet" was the Tyrannosaurus Rex of all rides. We stood gaping before that diabolical machine, inching closer together. The base of the ride was a fulcrum, with a long metal pipe attached at its center. A metal cage the size of a Volkswagen front seat dangled from each end. It resembled a giant see-saw on a high base, but rather than individual seats at each end, there were small cages holding two people strapped to a little bench inside. When the door shut, the passengers' faces peered through the metal grate window. Once the ride got going, the long bar twirled up and down and around like a baton doing figure-eight's. As if this were not thrill enough, each metal cage was attached in such a way that it could rotate freely in response to motion.

The carnie who ran The Bullet seemed to enjoy stopping the rotation just when a couple of girls were hanging upside down from the top cage. Their screams always brought more spectators. Whether sadism or business acumen motivated his operational technique, the results were the same. Some passengers laughed and shouted; others screamed in terror, and some vomited. This smell commingled with all the others—cotton candy, peanuts, elephant poop, cigarette smoke, engine exhaust, human body odor and the products used to hide it. I felt rather dizzy and steered our group toward the rear of the fairgrounds where the crowds were thinner. And that is how we discovered the man with the ruby slippers.

The route I chose took us through my favorite part of the fairgrounds, freak show alley. My mother had strictly forbidden my sisters and me to ever go into one of those shows. This didn't stop me from studying the provocative pictures that decorated the sides of the tents, hoping for a glance inside each time a tent flap opened. I was dying to see two-headed children, midgets and giants, ladies with beards, sword-swallowers, fire breathers, the fattest man on earth, the "armless wonder," and "Little Egypt," the woman half human/half reptile. "She walks, she talks, she crawls on her belly like a reptile," sang the barker. I felt horrified and fascinated, just like I'd been the day Nan Dupere showed me a cow fetus.

Once when Daddy drove Ann down the River Road to visit Nan at her family's farm, Mrs. Dupere saw me in the backseat and invited me to stay, too. Ann wasn't very happy, but Daddy said I should get to see the farm because it was educational. I was fascinated by all the animals, the barn, the hay, and the rope swing, but Nan said she'd saved the best thing for last. She led us back to the farmhouse and into the bathroom. Once inside, she locked the door and reached for something hidden behind a stack of towels. Nan pulled out a big glass mayonnaise jar. Inside, a tiny cow floated in a sea of formaldehyde.

"You can't tell anyone," Nan whispered.

I pictured myself, shrunken small like Alice in Wonderland, trapped in a jar, begging to get out. There were mysteries in this world no one talked about, just as surely as there were undiscovered lands.

The miniature cow was not the only amazing thing I saw that day at Nan's. While Ann and I stood in the kitchen waiting for Daddy to pick us up, we watched Mrs. Dupere begin the family's dinner. She was heating oil in a deep cast iron frying pan. Next to the stove was a bowl of what I assumed to be chicken legs or wings until Mrs. Dupere told us they were frog legs. I hadn't known that people ate frogs. I watched as she dredged each piece in seasoned flour and tossed them into the sizzling oil. Once they hit the sizzling skillet, the frog legs started jumping around like they were trying to escape. I was terrified, but Mrs. Dupere just laughed.

I was so glad to see Daddy's car pull into the driveway. I opened the door and began to run, turning to shout, "Thank you, Miss

Dupere!" loud enough for Daddy to know I hadn't forgotten my manners.

"Well, Topper," Daddy said, studying my face in his rearview mirror, "how did you like the farm?"

"It was okay," I said without enthusiasm.

"Would you like to go there again sometime?"

"No thank you," I said. "There was animal poop everywhere."

Daddy laughed and often repeated those words as my summation of life on a farm. I didn't want to sound like a baby and tell him how much it scared me to see the legs of dead frogs jumping out of Mrs. Dupere's frying pan, and I had promised Nan not to tell about the miniature cow in the jar.

In equal measure I was drawn to and repelled by strange, inexplicable things. This fascination with the bizarre made me desperate to see the people in the freak shows and afraid at the same time. I wondered if they had families and lives outside the fair. How did the fat lady take a bath? Was Little Egypt's soul human or reptile? As I stood outside the freak show tents, I wanted a peek but was also afraid that if I went inside, one of the freaks would look into my eyes and I would never get out of the tent again.

"Come on, Jane, let's go!" Kay Kay said, tugging on my arm. Myra, Cathy and Gretchen had grown bored, too. Reluctantly, I moved on. We threaded our way through the forest of tall people until we reached a clearing on the outer fringe of the fairgrounds where it was easier to breathe. We sat down to rest on the few wisps of grass remaining after being trampled by hundreds of feet. I was hungry and not too disappointed that it was almost time to walk to Daddy's office.

There wasn't much going on at the back of the fairgrounds except for one small crowd. We walked over to investigate. A man stood in front of the group. In the palms of his hands, he held a darling little pair of high-heeled shoes. Shiny red with diamond clips on the front, they reminded me of Dorothy's ruby slippers from The Wizard of Oz, only these were fancier.

"Anyone here thinks they kin fit in these here lil' shoes, step right up. Place your bets, folks. All the little lady has to do is walk in these shoes, and y'all kin all be winners. That's right, folks; you bet a dollar and if you win, you get your dollar back and a prize of your choice from this shelf right here," he said, pointing to an array of teddy bears, horse statues and Kewpie dolls.

Myra and I looked down at our feet. Just the week before we'd had a big fight over whose feet were larger. Mrs. Kahn had caught us with my right foot and Myra's left sticking out in the aisle between our desks, wrestling for position. Myra's foot was bigger, but I kept trying to inch mine up to gain a wrongful advantage. Being the same age and constant companions, Myra and I competed over everything—from whose older sibling was smarter to whose pencil eraser worked better. Even though my foot was smaller than Myra's, there was no way any one of us, including Gretchen, could have fit into those ruby shoes. Still, Cinderella fantasies filled our heads, and while we weren't quite ready for a handsome prince, a turquoise teddy bear would do just fine.

Reluctantly, we left the fair and headed for the high school to meet Daddy. For my sisters and me, disappointment at having to leave the Fair was offset by the excitement of the Bunkie company, due to arrive at any minute. Once home, we'd barely had time to exchange Fair stories with Ann before Frances Knoll's blue Buick pulled into our driveway.

Frances was a commanding figure with a big, cheerful voice to match. Mother talked about her often, even though we'd moved from Bunkie six years before. Frances' husband, Dr. Knoll, had delivered both Kay Kay and me in his Bunkie Clinic. He would have delivered Gretchen, too, if he hadn't died first, leaving little Martha Frances half an orphan. I watched Frances head up the sidewalk with her arms opened toward my mother. Few people, including my sisters and me, ever dared such bold affection with Mother. I'd expected her to wince or look uncomfortable, but instead, she smiled as Frances wrapped her in a bear hug.

"I declare, Candy Goette, you're just as skinny as the first time I saw you in Bunkie ten years ago!" Little Martha Frances stood behind her mother, holding on to the edge of her skirt and peeking out at us from time to time. Although she was eight, she looked younger than Gretchen. She wore a little pink sunsuit and the tiniest white sandals I'd ever seen.

Suddenly, it hit me! I poked Kay Kay and whispered, "Look at her feet!" There was no question, Martha Frances could walk in those red high heels back at the Fair. As soon as we got her alone, we'd talk her into it.

That night after dinner and baths, all five of us children crowded into beds in the back room of our house. The grown-ups didn't even check on us or seem to care if we went to sleep when we were supposed to. We talked half the night about the Fair—the rides, the circus acts at the Grand Stand, the food, the freak shows, the high school bands from across the river and the man with the ruby slippers.

"Martha Frances," I said, "you should see those little high heels. They sparkle just like Dorothy's in 'The Wizard of Oz.'"

"Only, they're even more beautiful; they have diamonds," Kay Kay added, standing on one foot, twisting her braid.

"Like princess shoes!" Gretchen blurted.

"And you're just the one to fit in them," I said, looking straight into Martha Frances's eyes. "Just think, we could all win whatever prizes we want—teddy bears, dolls, horses (I glanced Ann's way)—all kinds of stuff."

Ann yawned, picked up whatever horse book she was reading at the time and sank into her pillow. So what. Martha Frances was hooked.

Although this was Martha's first fair, she had us to take care of her; we'd make sure she had a good time, and we'd make her try on the shoes. Her eyes lit up when we talked about them, but when we described her starring role in the ruby slipper contest, her enthusiasm turned to terror. She looked down at the floor, bit her lip and shook her head, no. In the end, she was no match for her strong-willed hosts. We coerced, cajoled and flattered her into submission. After all, what child can resist the possibility of achieving some distant glory? I think Little Martha Frances went to sleep that night dreaming her own small dream—a little girl in a pink sunsuit, parading in ruby, high-heeled slippers before a cheering crowd. I went to sleep thinking how envious Myra would be that Martha Frances was mine.

The early hours of Saturday morning seemed endless. We kids were dressed and ready for the fair by 7:00 a.m. but my father wouldn't take us before 10:00, the official opening. After breakfast, we walked down the lane to the Dugas' house to show off Martha Frances, but when Myra opened the door, she hardly looked at Martha.

"Guess what! My Aunt Tootie is taking me to the Fair, just me, and she says she'll take me on any ride I want." Pretty Aunt Tootie was standing behind Myra smiling while she took the bobby pins out of her curlers.

Aunt Tootie was a senior in high school. I couldn't figure out how someone that young could get to be an aunt; it seemed like cheating.

"That's real nice, Myra," I said with a fake smile. "We'll see y'all at the Fair." We waved goodbye and headed back home.

At 10:00 all five of us were sitting in the car waiting when Daddy finally emerged from the house with his keys. We even forgot to fight about where we sat. Daddy dropped us off, told us to have a good time and drove away. We stood frozen for a moment, overwhelmed by the crowds of people streaming into the Fair. We could have been in New York City. In that moment of shared awe, I experienced a brief flicker of hope that Ann might join our trek to the back of the fairgrounds to see the ruby slippers. Two seconds later, she spotted her friend, Goo, ran towards her and never looked back. Just once, I wished she'd choose us. Maybe Ann would be sorry later when she saw her little sisters coming home with a horse statue.

We took Martha Frances all over the fairgrounds, knowing she'd never seen anything this grand in Bunkie. Her small hand felt sweaty in mine and might have slipped out had she not held on so tightly. It was a lot more fun playing big sister to her than to Kay Kay and Gretchen.

We wandered around sight-seeing and negotiating which rides to go on. As we approached the area with the big ones, Gretchen tugged on my arm. "Isn't that Myra?" she said, pointing in the direction of the...the BULLET! I couldn't believe my eyes. Myra and Aunt Tootie were handing their tickets to a man who was opening the door to one of the cages. It seemed impossible that Myra would actually ride the Bullet. Worse yet, she was smiling! Could it be that Myra Dugas outshone me in an area far more important than the size of our feet? Henceforth, would she be the undisputed leader of our River Road pack? In that moment I felt myself shrink in stature, no longer the brave girl I fancied myself to be, instead, more like the nervous figure Don Knotts played on the Steve Allen Show.

"Boy, Myra sure is brave," Kay Kay said in an overawed voice, as the long metal bar carried Myra's little cage up into the sky.

"So what!" I snapped, turning to go before Myra could spot us and start to wave.

We'd retreated a few steps when a blood-curdling scream stopped me in my tracks. I turned to see Myra's panicked face pressed against the metal grate. The tips of her fingers clutched the holes in the window, as if she were trying to climb out. From that high and dangerous place, Myra radiated fear like cold sunshine. She screamed and banged on the grate begging the carnie to stop the ride. From where I stood, my friend looked small and pitiful.

"Let me out! Let me out!" Myra cried in a piercing voice. "Oh, Mister, PLEASE let me out!!" she sobbed.

I prayed the man would stop that ride and let Myra out of her cage. Breathlessly I watched, hating the carnie who seemed to take pleasure in Myra's suffering. Finally, he took the toothpick out of his grinning mouth and reached for the lever to bring Myra and Aunt Tootie safely back to the ground. I felt like running to Myra and hugging her, but instinct told me it was the wrong thing to do. I turned and led our group in the opposite direction.

The scene we'd just witnessed simplified our ride decisions. No one objected when I suggested we buy tickets for the Merry-Go-Round. Though I'd never have admitted it, the Carousel was still my favorite ride. I loved to study the faces and positions of the horses that galloped around that endless circle. Pretending they were real and mine to choose, I walked from horse to horse looking for the best one... until the carnie shouted at me, "Just pick one, kid, or get off!"

Late September was still unbearably hot in Louisiana. By early afternoon, our band of four was tired and sweaty, but we wouldn't leave the Fair until Martha Frances tried on those red high heels, and she knew it. She squeezed my hand tighter as we headed to the back of the fairgrounds. It was more crowded than the day before, but finally we spotted the ruby slipper man. I slipped free of Martha Frances's grasp, weaseled through the crowd to the front, and handed the man my dollar to place our bet. While he collected money from others, Kay Kay, Gretchen and Martha Frances made their way up front and stood beside me. We watched as a young couple led their little girl up center to try on the shoes. The carnie smiled as he maneuvered the little girl around to his right side and crouched down to help her.

"Well, little lady, let's see what we got here. Maybe you're a winner!" he said, as the child turned her head searching for her mom. Because the carnie was between the child and her parents, they couldn't really see what he was doing. The man knelt, lifting one knee to form a resting place for the little girl's foot. As he leaned forward to put the shoe on, he held her ankle with one hand and the shoe in his other. It didn't seem like he was letting her foot go all the way in. I thought I could have done a better job if I'd been the carnie.

"I think if I pushed a little harder…" the girl began, but the man cut her off.

"Well, folks, as y'all kin see, the shoe just don't fit. Is there anybody else who wants a try?"

We looked at Martha Frances, but she was stone silent, hanging her head. She reached for my hand, but I shrugged her off and stepped forward.

"Mister, I think those little shoes will fit Martha Frances," I said in a timid voice, pointing to my small friend. The man seemed not to hear me. He went on talking to the crowd as if I weren't there. Bewildered, I looked at Kay Kay and Gretchen. We three began trying to get his attention. "Mister, Mister!" we cried, more boldly than before. We even pushed Martha Frances toward him so he could see how little her feet were, but he continued to ignore us.

"Mister, let Martha Frances try!" we shouted in our loudest voices. At last we understood—he knew we had a winner.

We couldn't believe a grown man would deliberately cheat children. We were brought up to respect all grown-ups. The bad ones were only in movies and books, not in real life, not in our town. We had given him a whole dollar to purchase a chance, and we'd received nothing in return. The man was a liar and a cheat and who knew…maybe a murderer, too. Suddenly, he seemed far scarier than anyone in the freak show.

I had finally had enough of the Louisiana State Fair. Organ grinder music pounded the air with an insistent, hollow, cheerless tone. A never-ending stream of announcements blared from high placed speakers. I was sick of people shouting; I was sick of the crowds and flashes of color. My eyes hurt as much as my feet.

I looked at the disappointed faces clustered around me. I was the big one, but the strut had drained out of me. "Y'all wanna go home?" I asked, though we had another hour left. They nodded. As we turned to go, Gretchen reached for my other hand. We threaded our way through the dwindling crowd. The sweet aroma of cotton candy had turned as sour as my mood. I didn't feel brave or lucky or anything at all except tired and inexplicably sad.

When we shuffled through the front doors of DHS, we found Daddy in his office working. He looked up surprised to see us but obviously pleased.

"So, did you kids see the Wild Man from Borneo at the Fair?" That was the title of one of the songs Daddy sang to us every Saturday night when he washed our hair. His kind, smiling face filled me with love. I wanted to rush into his arms, but instead I shook my head.

"No, Daddy, he wasn't there today."

"Well, that's a good thing because he would've eaten up all the cotton candy and a couple of children, too." He winked at Martha Frances so she'd know it was a joke.

We didn't go home with teddy bears or horse statues, but the story of our day generated interest and sympathy around the dinner table. Ann said she wished she'd been with us; she'd have made that man let Martha Frances try on the shoes. Mother, Daddy, Frances, and Ann were all extra nice to us that night. After dinner Daddy told us to get in the car. "I'm taking y'all to the Dairy Queen." He said to order anything we wanted. We didn't go out for ice-cream very often, so I didn't want to choose the wrong thing. Should I get a hot fudge sundae, a root beer float or a malted milk? As usual, I was the last to decide.

"Come on, Jane, it's *my* dollar—just spend it." Daddy shook his head and patted my bangs.

We felt like fat, happy rabbits when we went to bed that night, but I had a terrible dream. I was wandering alone at night in freak show alley. The ruby slipper man was standing by a tent. "Wanna see, little girl?" he asked with a strange smile. He pulled open the flap and inside there was a row of jars on a shelf. I saw Martha Frances floating in one. She was as small as a pickle and naked, except for her little red high heels. The man was holding a large pickle in his hands and smiling at me, the kind of smile that makes you shiver.

Special Train Excursion

VIA

The Texas and Pacific Railway

Friday, October 3rd, 1930

$1.00 Round Trip

New Orleans

TO

DONALDSONVILLE

AND RETURN

ACCOUNT

School Day

South Louisiana State Fair

See the Exhibits, Basket Ball Tournament, Physical Training
Contests, Track and Field Meet, Circus and Vaudeville Acts. Also
Big Midway with Side Shows and Concessions.

BAND MUSIC FOR THE GRAND STAND.

ORCHESTRA FOR DANCING.

Teachers and Pupils Admitted to Fairgrounds FREE!

SPECIAL TRAIN SCHEDULE

Leave New Orleans · · · · · · · ·	8:00 a.m., October 3rd	
" Gretna · · · · · · · ·	8:50 a.m.,	" 3rd
" Westwego · · · · · · · ·	9:00 a.m.,	" 3rd
Arrive Donaldsonville · · · · · · ·	10:30 a.m.,	" 3rd

RETURNING

Leave Donaldsonville · · · · · ·	4:45 p.m., October 3rd	
Arrive Westwego · · · · · · · ·	6:15 p.m.,	" 3rd
" Gretna · · · · · · · ·	6:25 p.m.,	" 3rd
" New Orleans · · · · · · · ·	7:15 p.m.,	" 3rd

For further information write the undersigned or handle through
your school.

R. S. VICKERS, Secretary-Manager,

South Louisiana State Fair, Donaldsonville, La.

*Attractions in 1930: Exhibits, Tournaments, Band Music for Grand
Stand, Orchestra for Dancing, Midway, Sideshows, Circus,
Vaudeville Acts…*

Jane Goette

River Road Explorers

In addition to art, literature and theater, Mrs. Kahn introduced her 5th grade students to history. Nothing ignited my imagination like her lessons about the explorers. Theater and art were passing fancies. Whatever arts and crafts I produced that year are long forgotten. I don't even know what became of the beautiful Princess Maria costume after I hung it in the closet. That moment of glory on the stage faded, but Mrs. Kahn left me with two gifts that changed my life—a lifelong taste for discovery and a belief that every child, with the right inspiration, can do amazing things.

Mrs. Kahn's first history lesson was about the Children's Crusade. There was a picture in our textbook depicting a brigade of children in tunics and funny-looking shoes. They walked down a winding road all by themselves, not a grown-up in sight. I wasn't particularly interested in the religious motivation for their grand adventure, but the notion that children could set off on their own and wind up in a history book electrified my imagination.

The next topic that fed my enthusiasm for history was the discovery of the New World. We spent a lot of time reading and talking about those early explorers. Suddenly, history meant adventure, sensation, wonders to behold, glory, the kind of experiences I longed for. What could be more exciting than discovering something no one else had ever seen?

I imagined Columbus's surprise when it finally dawned on him that what he'd found was not India, but a whole new world that no one knew existed. To be the first to see a wild, new land, raging rivers, waterfalls, strange animals, exotic plants—now this was a fantasy I could sink my teeth into. Who would want to be an actress, a tightrope walker or an airplane pilot when you could be an explorer?

Every day after school, especially when I needed company in the bathroom at night, I told my little sisters everything Mrs. Kahn taught us that week about the discovery of the New World. By Friday night, I had convinced them—and myself, too—that undiscovered lands lay somewhere through the sugarcane fields behind our house. If we were brave enough, we would find our own New World. My sisters and I couldn't wait for morning to begin our first exploring expedition with the Dugas girls.

After Mother and Daddy turned out the lights and the house grew quiet, I lay in my sofa bed with visions of maps and medals dancing in my head. I knew we would find something the other explorers had overlooked, not as dramatic as a continent perhaps, but new and wonderful. Even Mrs. Kahn had said it was impossible that everything in the world had already been discovered. Maybe we'd name the new land after her. The Kingdom of Kahn.

In the weeks ahead, I would lead my "men" over the levee, skirting the ponds and willows and water moccasins until we came to the banks of the river where we "discovered" the Mighty Mississip'. We blazed trails through pastures and sugarcane fields up and down the River Road. For months and months we explored every Saturday, until finally…we found a new world we would name "Paradise."

After our Saturday morning cinnamon toast and corn flakes, we packed lunch meat sandwiches and sat around waiting for Myra, Cathy and Donna to arrive. Mae Dugas never let the girls come until they had finished their chores. In my impatience, I sometimes called Myra to ask what was taking them so long, and every week her response was the same, "We're not through buffin' the floors!"

I know our friends had other chores, but nothing required as much time as that buffing. My sisters and I had never heard that word in our house. Sure enough, my few peeks inside Myra's front door showed living room floors shiny and clean enough to lick. After we started playing explorers, Mae's girls started buffing her floors faster than ever.

As soon as Myra, Cathy and Donna arrived, we would study the location and mood of Miz Abadie's cows before planning our route across her pasture. Every Saturday I tried to steer our group a little farther than the week before, or at least in a different direction. Serious explorers had to push ahead toward parts unknown. They had to climb trees along the way to get their bearings, assess the dangers, and eat their bologna sandwiches in the shade.

I fancied myself the captain of the crew since I'd invented the game. With a Christopher Columbus strut and a Buster Brown haircut, I looked the role, too. We were little girls in hand-me-down jeans and old sneakers, scooting under barbed wire fences, crossing sugarcane fields, leaping across irrigation ditches. There was another uninvited, member of our gang, and though she loved us, she often endangered our lives. Our slew-footed, sad-eyed hobo dog, Hilda, drove Miz Abadie's cows crazy.

The first time we discovered this, we were smack in the middle of the pasture. All Miz Abadie's cows ever did was stand in the field eating grass. In all the years we lived next door, I had never seen a single one of those cows run until the day Hilda trailed along behind us. When I heard her barking and looked back, I saw a familiar scene from the cowboy movies—a stampede!

"Run!" I screamed, grabbing Gretchen's hand. How many times had the Goette and Dugas children witnessed the hapless cowboy who falls from his horse and gets trampled to death by a stampeding herd of cattle?! Myra grabbed Donna's hand and no one stopped running 'til we reached the barbed wire, scooted under and collapsed in the ditch on the other side. Hilda idled along, and if it's true a dog can smile, then she wore a satisfied grin. As we lay panting and speechless, she licked us as if to soothe our racing hearts.

Our explorations took us into other pastures besides Mrs. Abadie's, and one Saturday in a pasture farther down the River Road we discovered the best tree I've ever known. It seemed specially designed for the six of us with branches tailored to every girl's size and dexterity. You could practically walk up the thing, the branches started so low on the trunk. From the ground, branches spread horizontally. The next tier up, other branches fanned out in a gradual incline. Even Gretchen and Donna could scramble up that tree in a jiffy.

Each of us claimed a particular branch for our own, which then became our "apartment" when we pretended to be grown-up women in New York. We spent a lot of time calling each other on the telephone and dropping by each other's apartments for coffee. Days and nights passed quickly in that tree, needing only a child's voice to shout "Goodnight!" or "Good morning!" and another to signify the click of a switch or brrrrrrring of the morning bell.

One Saturday, Myra Dugas and I went exploring by ourselves. We had important things to discuss, like how mean our mothers were because they wouldn't let us pierce our ears. As we talked, we walked farther and farther down the River Road. We spotted a little clump of trees off in the distance far from any house or road. To us it looked like unclaimed land. We plopped under a tree and tried to figure out a way to get our ears pierced.

Maybe we could do it ourselves if we had the guts. Of course we had the guts, we were explorers! Before we could talk ourselves out of it, we also became inventors. Myra and I found tiny sticks with pointed ends to use as our surgical instruments. Instruments in hand, we sat face to face. I would do Myra's first earlobe at the same time she did mine. This way, neither of us could chicken out.

We pressed our sticks against earlobe flesh and slowly began to press. As we increased the pressure, we studied each other's faces for signs of pain. The tension mounted. I remembered the nuns had told us to offer up our pain to help the poor souls in Purgatory get to heaven. If you didn't cry but endured pain bravely, you could help pave the way for some poor souls in Purgatory to get out of there and on up to heaven.

Myra and I didn't pierce our ears that day, though we did create deep purple dents in our earlobes. I had to wait until I became a long-haired political hippie in Madison to finally realize my quest for pierced ears and dangly earrings. Though neither of us ever became nuns or saved any poor souls that day, we didn't walk away empty handed. Besides purple welts in our ears, Myra and I came away with renewed faith in our exploring vocation. So what if we were too scared to pierce our ears—we'd found a little undiscovered clump of trees off the River Road and we named this tiny land "Scarepeare".

During the year that we were Saturday explorers, we made one major discovery. We hiked through a couple of miles of sugarcane before we found Paradise. Just when we thought we'd never reach the end of the sugarcane, we emerged into a large clearing. In the middle of this clearing, shining like a cool star, was Paradise. From a distance, it really did look like a separate land, the way countries were often depicted in children's books like Winnie the Pooh. Because of the density of trees, the thick, tangled vines, and the incredible cacophony of birds, we knew it was a wild, undiscovered place. Years later I found out that wooded areas, like Paradise, had been left in the middle of cane fields from the days when all the plowing was done by animals. Paradise provided a cool resting place and its pond, a source of water, for man and animal alike.

Explorers Kay Kay, Jane, Gretchen

When we first spotted Paradise, we knew that our many weeks of exploring had finally paid off. We ran towards those trees with the joy Columbus's men must have felt as their feet touched land after months at sea. Like our exploring predecessors, we didn't know what we might find, but we hastened toward whatever lay waiting. We might find wild animals or pirates, but in this happy moment, there was no fear.

Out in the clearing, the sun beat down on us relentlessly, but the moment we entered the place we would name Paradise, the world turned cool and green. We wandered around, wide-eyed. The ground was spongy, padded with the rot of years of fallen leaves. We took soft steps, and for a little while, we didn't even speak. Words might break the spell.

There was the aura of quiet, respectful wonder. The land around us seemed sacred somehow. Maybe we'd discover an altar overgrown with vines. Under the fallen leaves, perhaps a relic lay hidden, an old clay pot fired in an ancient oven. Or maybe we'd find something so new we would have to study it for days to understand its meaning or use.

Spellbound, we walked on through the trees until, at the very center of Paradise, we discovered a pond. Our new land had everything we needed to live here. We sat down on a log and tried to think like Columbus. Next week we would bring paper and pencil so we could draw a map of our discovery. Without a map or a relic, how could we prove what we'd found? Someone else might come along later and think they had found it first.

We also solemnly promised that we would keep Paradise a secret. It would remain our place only so long as no one else knew about it. I returned home that afternoon wishing I could tell Mrs. Kahn. When I went to bed that night, I lay awake for a long time remembering Paradise and wondering what we might find the next Saturday when we returned to explore our new land.

For many months that year, we made weekly trips to Paradise. "Let's pretend we're in Africa and Myra and I are doctors and Cathy and Kay Kay are missionaries who got attacked by a tiger, and Donna and Gretchen are their two little children who dragged their bleeding bodies to our hospital, and we have to take care of them, but the medicine we need is across the jungle and so I set out alone to get it, and while I trek through the jungle…"

One Saturday, feeling too lazy to hike all the way to Paradise, we returned to the pasture with the greatest tree. It had rained that week, and one ditch we'd crossed many times in the past was filled with water and too wide to jump. I suggested we build a bridge, an idea more appealing than returning home. We scavenged for materials, hauling long sticks and dried cane stalks to lay across the top of the ditch.

It wasn't perfect, but we could help each other across one at a time without getting our shoes completely wet. The rest of the way was easy. We quickly crossed the remaining fields of tall grass and found our tree. In no time we'd climbed up to our various apartments and started to eat our sandwiches. We lounged on branches telephoning each other's apartments. "Brringgg, brringgg."

"Oh, hi, Annette," I might say to Myra, "want to come up to my place for a cup of coffee?"

"Sure," Myra would reply, "just as soon as I put on my lipstick."

After visits to each other's apartments and many cups of coffee, someone would call out "Nighttime!" and cries of "Goodnight!" rang out from branch to branch. Before I'd had time to grow bored with pretend sleeping, a distant shout startled me awake. I bolted upright and stiffened with attention. All of us were sitting now, listening. On all our treks, we'd never seen nor heard anyone besides ourselves. It was a woman's voice we heard now. A moment later, we saw in the distance a dark-haired woman trudging toward us with a large German Shepherd running beside her. Calmly, we watched them approach. The woman was carrying something that rested in the crook of her arm, a long stick or a baton, I thought. She was shouting something that became clear at the same moment I realized the stick was a rifle.

"Get the hell out of here!" she yelled, raising her gun. With the speed and commotion of a tree full of monkeys, we scampered down the branches, spilling onto the ground in rapid succession. A gunshot sounded, and we literally ran for our lives. The woman's dog was barking. I heard her clear, crisp command, "sic 'em, sic 'em!" then, another gunshot.

I didn't think about the other kids or the grapes I'd left behind at the foot of the tree or anything but "dark-haired lady, gun, barking dog, danger, danger, danger. Run, run, run!"

I focused only on reaching the irrigation ditch that separated this pasture from the next. If I could make it to the ditch, I'd be in the clear. The loudest sound of this frantic race came from inside my chest as I gulped air, erasing the distance between me and safety. But then I made the serious mistake of looking back. My little sister, Gretchen had not kept up with us. She was still far behind and running. I saw her stumble and fall face forward into the tall grass. I don't remember making a decision. As with most emergencies, something kicked in that bypassed conscious thought. I was running back for Gretchen whether I wanted to or not. The dog was just ahead of the woman running towards us when I grabbed Gretchen's hand, yanked her off the ground, and ran as fast as I possibly could dragging her along.

With none of our earlier care, we plunged across the ditch not caring if our shoes got wet. We made it past the ditch but didn't stop running until we reached Mrs. Abadie's pasture. We scooted under the barbed wire and collapsed in the soft grass on our side. We were in that shaky state of near hysteria, where it's as easy to cry as it is to giggle and you sort of do both at the same time. We looked at each other, suddenly realizing how dear each person was, like soldiers after a battle. So this is why John Wayne and Audie Murphy loved those guys on the battlefront after hating them the night before. We were elated. We were alive!

For the next hour we hashed and rehashed every millisecond of our close call with death. Remarkably, each child had her own version of the story, what she was doing at the moment the woman appeared, who spotted the gun first, exactly how big the dog was. Funny how that dog kept growing with the retelling. Was it really as big as a Great Dane?

Our first instinct was to run home and begin telling everyone we knew our story. Maybe they'd put the story in *The Donaldsonville Chief.* I imagined my face on the front page. Looking brave and serious, I'd stare into the camera and let the world see what a girl hero looked like.

In the midst of those grandiose revelries, a terrible thought suddenly crossed my mind—what if our parents wouldn't let us go exploring anymore? No more exploring!? No more wandering through the cane fields or back of the levee? Life just wouldn't seem worth living anymore. Was a picture in the *Chief* worth this? I thought not.

With a little reasoning and gentle coaxing, I helped my young companions see it my way. None of us wanted to give up our free and easy lives as explorers. When we hung around our houses, our parents always found work for us to do. May would think of more things to clean and our daddy would make us peel pecans. There's something about an inactive child that sets off an alarm in a parent's head. It drives them crazy to see you lying around even if you're not putting your feet on the couch or whining that you're hungry. No, it was definitely best to stay as far away on Saturdays as possible. With the specter of weekend chores looming in our futures, each of us swore that no outsider would ever drag the truth from us; our lips were sealed. Solemnly, we trudged toward home.

With the terrible weight of our secret on my shoulders, I slunk up the back steps to my house. I hoped my parents would be too busy to notice my sisters and me, or to ask how our morning was. I wondered if they'd be able to see that I was different. My life had been touched by danger and heroism. Did it show? Did I look somehow older? I headed for the bathroom to study my face in the mirror. I frowned into the glass, turned my head from side to side, tilted my chin, and looked into my eyes. After staring, I turned away, the way others might see me. My research was interrupted by an impatient knock at the door. "Jane, are you still in there?"

It was my father. I opened the door. With frank and honest eyes I looked right into his face. My gaze invited…no, dared him to really look at me this time, to see the change. Yes, I was different now. That little girl who only a month ago had been too scared to go off the high dive? Well, she was gone. The challenge of a diving board seemed trivial after having faced death in a cow pasture. All these thoughts flashed through my mind in the instant it took my father to brush past me and into the bathroom.

Kay Kay and Gretchen called me out to the porch. "Did you tell him?" they asked.

"Of course not!" I snapped.

We didn't tell, but it was like having a mosquito bite and trying not to scratch. I can't remember who finally broke down first, but by suppertime, the secret we'd vowed to keep forever had somehow slipped out. The remarkable thing is that nothing happened. Our mother said, "Well, sure sounds like you girls had an interesting day," and Daddy asked us how big the dog was. When we told him, he just smiled and picked up the newspaper.

The year I was in fifth grade remains the most memorable year of my childhood. Maybe it was because some part of me sensed it was drawing to a close. Maybe it was because Mrs. Kahn was such a good teacher, she made the world come alive for me. All I know for sure is that the best memories of my River Road childhood are from those Saturdays exploring the countryside with my sisters, the Dugas girls, and Hilda.

The following year I would get invited to a party where the kids played "spin the bottle." I wasn't ready for that. I was probably the only girl in my class who still played with dolls, although I knew enough to do it in private. I was no more interested in boys than I was in the longitude or latitude of Burma. I was a little girl in patent leather Mary Janes and white ankle socks when that bottle landed on me. Buddy Montero kissed me that night, and I never played dolls again.

Although it would be many years before I got my next kiss, that evening at Bobby Jo Breaux's birthday party marked a change in my life. It ushered in a new period of lying around indoors with my feet on the couch. I wouldn't know how to have fun anymore. I would feel that I'd outgrown the country life and would be restless for the time when I could fly away.

Life was never again quite as satisfying as it was in those days when I could still invent it, my 5th grade year as a world explorer—my best year.

Louie Crochet Loves Mr. Goette

Louie Crochet was born "down the bayou," which meant somewhere in the country along the miles and miles of Bayou LaFourche. When he was a few days old, a tornado struck his home, picked Louie up out of his cradle and carried him far away. If he screamed, no one heard him above the roar of the wind. They found little Louie the next day miles from his home, lying naked on the banks of the bayou. This time, he was screaming for sure. Louie was hungry, and he would stay that way for as long as I knew him.

Louie Crochet was shaped like Humpty Dumpty and wore thick glasses, always smudged. Although I never saw his bare feet, I'd heard he had six toes on each foot, and that wasn't all that was wrong with Louie. He inherited a vision problem that eventually earned him a "legally blind" designation. In addition, Louie and a couple of his siblings were slightly retarded decades before such handicaps were called "challenges." The current term is more fitting for the Louie I knew. Birth had presented him with many challenges—physical, mental, socio-economic, and he worked hard to meet every one.

Louie never advanced beyond the 5th grade at Donaldsonville Elementary. He stayed in the back of Mrs. Kahn's room for quite a few years; he liked it there, and Mrs. Kahn liked Louie. He was a big help—used to crack and peel her pecans every fall, washed her chalkboards, moved heavy furniture and happily ran whatever errands she needed. If a kid from the class got knocked in the head out on the playground, Louie would carry that child in his arms all the way inside to find Mrs. Kahn, who was most likely drinking coffee in the teacher's lounge.

In childhood, I never felt sorry for Louie; I envied him. He enjoyed a special status in our school. He got to carry the notes the teachers sent each other, and they never had to worry that Louie might read them. Louie watched over us at recess and was quick to tell Mrs. Kahn if anyone misbehaved. He'd give her his report right after the bell rang, then she'd smile and give him a treat from the vending machine in the teacher's lounge.

Whenever my daddy came over to the elementary school to check on things, he always stopped by to see Louie. He'd ask Louie how Kay Kay and I were behaving. Louie loved my daddy and he took special care to watch over my sister and me. On one of Daddy's visits, Louie reported with great concern that Kay Kay wasn't drinking her milk. Louie oversaw the dumping of the lunch trays into the big barrels (our left-overs were carted away to feed somebody's pigs each day), and when he shook Kay Kay's milk carton, it was still full! He stood guard and watched Kay Kay and me like a hawk. He fretted so about Kay Kay, who in spite of Louie's daily fussing, continued to dump her milk into the pig barrel.

Louie's exasperation was matched by my sister's obstinance. After grappling with the problem and worrying to death about Kay Kay, he decided it was time to get help from my father. One weekend he walked all the way from town, down the River Road to our house. I heard a knock on the door and was surprised to see Louie Crotchet standing there, wiping sweat from his face with a large handkerchief before getting down to business.

"Tell Mr. Goette it's Louie, come to see him about Kay Kay," he said in his deep, slow voice. I went back to the kitchen where Daddy sat drinking coffee and reading the *Morning Advocate*.

"Louie Crochet's here to see you about Kay Kay," I said, glancing over at Kay Kay who'd eaten all her cheerios, leaving the milk to grow warm in the bowl. She was swinging her legs under the table and flicking her long eyelashes with her fingertips, my sister's usual signs of nervousness. Daddy put down his newspaper, went to the front door and invited Louie to sit down in the living room.

"What brings you out here on a fine Saturday morning, Louie?"

"Mr. Goette, I hate to tell you 'dis, but Kay Kay still ain't drinkin' her milk," Louie said, shaking his head.

"Kay Kay!" my father shouted toward the kitchen, "you better come out here."

Kay Kay appeared at the living room archway, twirling the ends of her braids. When she saw Louie's glare, she glared right back at him.

"Louie tells me you're still throwing your milk away every day. How do you expect to have strong bones if you don't drink your milk?"

Daddy looked serious as he addressed Kay Kay, but his relaxed, slumped posture in his brown reading chair, feet resting on the ottoman, told me this little sermon was more for Louie's benefit than for Kay Kay's. It did, however, set the stage for Louie to deliver his own little sermon.

"Kay Kay, look over dair at your daddy sittin' dair wit 'dem strong boones. If Mr. Goette din't drink his milk when he was a lil' boy like you, he couldn't be sittin' up so strong as he is." Louie reached for his handkerchief and wiped his brow. He was passionate about this milk business, and he had worked up a sweat from his long walk out to our house.

"Thank you, Louie," Daddy said with a smile, "and someday Kay Kay's going to thank you, too." Fat chance, I thought. Then he turned toward Kay Kay and frowned.

"Kay Kay, go to the kitchen and get Louie a nice cold glass of lemonade. Louie, would you like one of Miz Goette's brownies?"

I knew even before Louie nodded his head he'd like several of Miz Goette's brownies. I hoped Kay Kay wouldn't bring the whole plate, for Louie would surely eat them all.

That wasn't Louie's only visit to our house. For years he would appear at our door every Christmas Eve to bring Daddy a gift. It was always a bottle of *Old Spice* aftershave, and Daddy was always surprised and grateful. Louie would come in, eat a few dozen Christmas cookies, then head back down the River Road to town, carrying a fruitcake or big tin of cookies, Daddy's gift to him. Louie would have said that Daddy was his friend, and that was the truth.

Eventually, when Louie reached the legal age to quit school, he had to leave the fifth grade. Mrs. Kahn cried when he left, and Louie cried, too. All the teachers at the elementary school missed him and worried about what would become of poor Louie. To make matters worse, his eyesight was rapidly deteriorating.

Shortly after Louie left school, there was a knock on his door one afternoon. This time it was Daddy paying a visit to Louie's house. Louie was happy to see him and proudly introduced Mr. Goette to his mama.

"Mrs. Crochet, I was wondering if you would let Louie come over to the high school to work for me. We sure could use his help over there." Patting Louie's shoulder, Daddy continued, "Mr. Nub, (the high school janitor whose nickname was acquired years ago when he'd sawed off his thumb), he's a mighty fine man, but he's getting older and he could really use a young assistant like Louie to help him out."

Louie stood tall and proud at Daddy's side. If Mr. Goette needed him, he was ready to serve. And serve, he did. Louie saw me through high school, as well as my sisters Kay Kay and Gretchen who followed after. During all the time my father was principal, Louie was a welcomed guest in his office, and Daddy was rarely too busy to make time to listen to Louie give a report on the condition of the school. He thanked Louie often for the fine job he was doing and genuinely honored his loyal service. Until the day my father retired, Louie was made to feel a respected figure on the Donaldsonville High School campus. That unspoken rule was never broken except during my junior year when Louie's troubles began.

By then, Louie's vision had deteriorated so badly, the only job he could still perform was spearing large pieces of trash out on the grounds or in the football stadium. That long stick also helped him find his way around the DHS campus. Away from school, he used a cane when he walked downtown where the streets were less familiar to him than the school grounds. When he reached a street corner, rarely did he have to wait more than a few minutes before someone came along to help him across. People in town looked out for Louie. He was one of us.

During my junior year, a small clique of boys began to play with Louie, a game he didn't understand or enjoy. Sometimes they grabbed his trash stick and stood around him passing the stick to another boy just as Louie reached for it. "Here it is, Louie," one kid would shout just before he handed it to another. Though I saw the frustration on Louie's face, he kept his cool and waited for the bell to call them back to class.

The teasing became more abusive. They used terms like stupid, moron, and blind son-of-a-bitch. I once saw a boy wad a piece of paper from his notebook and throw it on the grass. "Look, Louie, you missed one," he said, winking at his friends. Those of us who saw these things picked up the papers and glared at the bullies.

The unkindest of all insults ever hurled at Louie was to call him lazy. This, he could not ignore. "Shut up!" he yelled and waved his broom as if to hit the kid who'd said it. Things were getting worse, but no one could stop it. Whenever a by-stander tried to intervene or told these boys their antics weren't funny, the reply hurled back was, "What's the matter? Got no sense of humor?"

Now that Louie had tried to push one of them, perhaps they felt justified in plotting revenge. A couple days later, when the after-lunch bell rang to send juniors and seniors back to class, a few boys lingered behind. They took Louie's broom, shoved him into the bathroom by the gym and jammed the broom in the door handle so Louie couldn't get out. During final period, someone finally heard his cries and freed him.

Louie had been pounding on the bathroom door, sobbing and crying out for "Mr. Goette." The kid who discovered him went to tell my father just as the final bell rang. By the time I reached my locker downstairs, the hallway was buzzing with the big news about Louie and how Mr. Goette had stormed down the crowded hallway madder than anyone had ever seen him. As the hall thinned, I leaned against my locker, bolting to attention each time I heard the far door open.

Finally, I saw them. Daddy had waited for the hallway to empty. With one arm wrapped around Louie's shoulder, he used the other to guide him down the long hall toward the safe harbor at the end where I stood watching. Louie's balled fists swiped at his nose and lifted his glasses enough to rub the tears streaming from his eyes. I followed them through the office door, as Daddy guided Louie to a chair, pulled out his handkerchief and handed it to him, just as he did my sisters and me whenever we cried. I saw no signs of anger now, only tenderness.

"Go get Louie a Coke," he said, reaching into his pocket and handing me some change. When I returned from the teacher's lounge, Daddy was still patting big old Louie whose head now rested against his shoulder. His smudged glasses lay in his lap. I'd never seen Louie without his glasses before. I wondered whether they always looked this squinty without them or if it was because of crying so long. Louie put them back on, blew his nose and reached for the coke.

Kay Kay and Gretchen arrived at the high school a little later, in time to see Daddy driving away with Louie. As we waited for him to return, I told them what had happened. I think Daddy must have stayed awhile at the Crochets' home, or maybe time just feels slower when it's heavy with sadness or worry. Though we had a million questions after Daddy returned, we rode in silence the whole way home.

The next day, Daddy called all the junior boys down to the auditorium. My friend, Bob, told me the room was silent and though Bob's ear itched, he was too afraid to scratch it. I could picture Daddy's jaw jutting out the way it did when he was really mad. He told those boys if anyone ever dared lay a hand on Louie or teased him, he would hear about it. "I don't care who your mama and daddy are, or if you're the star of the football team," he said, glaring into each pair of eyes, "I'm gonna suspend you!"

That's all he said. He didn't ask a single question. A minute or two later, he shouted, "Get back to class!" and stormed out of the auditorium slamming the door behind him. I didn't see anyone so much as tease Louie Crochet after that. He resumed his duties with the same seriousness and passion he'd always shown, like an engineer in the control room working to get those astronauts safely on the moon. No one interrupted Louie's work anymore. A couple of times a high school student would stop to thank him.

My father was promoted to a central office position the year after I graduated. The man who succeeded him as principal didn't particularly like to have Louie hanging around his office. Until Daddy retired from Ascension Parish Schools, he would find reasons to drop by DHS from time to time, to pay a visit to Louie.

The last time I saw Louie Crochet was after my father's retirement and my parents had moved across the river to Baton Rouge. A friend from New York had come along on this trip to visit my family. I wanted to show her my real home, Donaldsonville. We crossed the river on the Sunshine Bridge and drove down the River Road into town. Along the way, I identified places she'd heard featured in the stories I told about growing up in Louisiana.

In the midst of my tour, I spotted Louie Crochet, standing on a street corner, waiting for someone to help him across. He carried a white cane now, but aside from that, he seemed unchanged—same haircut, same Humpty Dumpty figure and smudged glasses. His demeanor was as confident and patient as ever. I parked the car and went to greet him.

"Hi, Louie, do you remember me?" Though Louie was looking straight at my face, I could tell he couldn't see me.

"I'm Jane, Louie...Jane Goette." Louie's puzzled face broke into a smile brighter than Jimmy Davis' sunshine.

"How ya doin', Jane? You like it up there in the North?"

"Yeah, Louie, but it's good to be home." Louie nodded, as if he knew what it meant to miss a home he'd never left. He shuffled and furrowed his brow.

"How ya daddy, doin', Jane?" Louie shook his head and looked down at his brown shoes. "I sure miss Mr. Goette."

"He's fine, Louie, and he misses you, too."

Louie stood quietly, looking down at his shoes. He shook his head again, reached in his pocket, pulled out his handkerchief and blew his nose.

I think it was the handkerchief that did it.

These weren't the feelings I'd anticipated as I drove across the Sunshine Bridge that morning. I was quiet on the drive home, but my friend didn't seem to mind. She leafed through a New Yorker and glanced at the flat landscape sliding past her window. As I listened to the rhythm of tires slapping blacktop, I noticed how the road shot through the cane fields straight as an arrow, straight as my sister grew with all that milk Louie made her drink. "Next time I see Louie," I thought, "I'm going to tell him about Kay Kay's strong 'boons.'" My heavy heart lightened.

Jane Goette

Crossing the Mason-Dixon Line

Of all the biennial trips my family took to Wisconsin, there is one I remember most vividly. A car trip of that distance and in that direction was unusual in the 1950s and early 1960s before interstate highways. The farthest most of my friends had traveled was to Biloxi, Mississippi or Grand Isle on the Louisiana Gulf Coast. My three sisters and I enjoyed the status accorded us in our small town for having been all the way to the North, a place as foreign to Donaldsonville as England.

In preparation for these trips, my father picked up road maps at Sam's Esso Station. Every night after dinner, my parents sat bent over those maps, a cloud of smoke looming above their heads as the ashtray filled. They studied those Esso maps with the same earnestness as early explorers peering before navigational charts. Still, we often ended up lost. Like Columbus's sailors, my sisters and I did not have much confidence in our captain, and neither did our mother.

Poor Daddy. Those Esso maps didn't exactly match the roads we found once we'd set out. It was easy to take a wrong turn in some little Mississippi town or to arrive at a spot on the map in Tennessee to find the road we were supposed to take no longer existed. At such moments my mother would cry and throw up her hands in a paroxysm of despair. "We're lost, Conrad! We'll never get there!" We grew silent in the back seat, praying that somehow our parents would find the way.

Such times were hardest on Kay Kay, who at eight still had a terrible fear of getting lost. Fairytales like *Hansel and Gretel* had left their mark on my little sister, and our Mother's unrestrained pessimism didn't help. Kay Kay couldn't even enjoy a Sunday afternoon drive on the levee.

These family outings were rare, usually occurring around the time Daddy traded in an old car for a newer one. As much as my sister feared straying from home, I adored it. Whenever Daddy called, "Let's go for a ride!" I was the first one inside.

It was exciting to drive along the top of the levee. From its modest summit, the whole flat world around us seemed beautiful and vast. Scenery rolled past in a context greatly altered by a little altitude and a lot of imagination. A mile or two past the second haunted house, the sights grew less familiar. Kay Kay would twist the ends of her braids and turn to stare out the back window, hoping to see our house in the distance.

Meanwhile, I indulged my fantasy of crossing into a foreign continent—Europe, Africa or the Orient. I searched the landscape for tigers and pandas, windmills and towers. Perhaps if I looked hard enough, I might see a Chinese girl, just my age, stepping out of a pagoda. Our Sunday drives were aborted before I discovered any of the foreign treasures that waited just around the next curve of the levee. Kay Kay's anxious voice punctured the bubble of my grand imaginings.

"Daddy, are we lost?"

"Of course not, Sweetheart! How can you get lost on the levee?"

My father's cheerful confidence could not allay Kay Kay's fears. After a few more miles, she would tearfully beg him to turn the car around. Instead of having an adventure, we would have another interminable Sunday afternoon on the River Road. While Mother and Daddy napped, their four daughters were sentenced to forty years of hard boredom. My big sister, Ann, would escape into town on her bicycle to play at her friend Goo's house. I didn't have any friends in town.

"You kids play quietly," my parents would order, as they headed for their bedroom. "Playing quietly" was an oxymoron in the lexicon of childhood. I also knew that it didn't matter whether it was Kay Kay, Gretchen or me who woke Mother and Daddy, we'd all pay the price of their bad moods the rest of the afternoon.

Although these family rides on the levee seemed harmless to all but Kay Kay, even our parents recognized the challenges and perils inherent in a car trip from Louisiana to Wisconsin. Sam's maps couldn't stop us from getting lost in the middle of nowhere or stranded somewhere with a flat tire. Speed limits along the way changed so often it was hard for Daddy to keep track of them. Suddenly there could be the high-pitched scream of a siren, a red light flashing behind us and a mean cop approaching to give Daddy a ticket he couldn't afford to pay. These highway police weren't friendly like Shaloo, Donaldsonville's Chief of Police. They might take my daddy to jail, and then what would we do?

Driving from Louisiana to Wisconsin was like trekking across Africa on a camel; it was a long, hot, dangerous trip. For two days my sisters and I rode crowded together in the backseat of an un-air-conditioned car. Since Daddy had a reputation for buying "lemons," there was always the threat a tire would blow or the engine overheat. We listened for clanks and clinks and sirens; we watched for smoke and flying rubber.

In spite of the discomfort, and the real or imagined dangers of such trips, I lived for them. There is no destination on any map of the world today that feels as far as that Wisconsin. There is no language that sounds as foreign as a Midwestern accent did. The world's most glorious landscapes cannot excite me more than the rolling hills and sparkling lakes of Wisconsin in 1958.

The waters of my state were invariably brown and there was water almost everywhere. Even Airline Highway, the main route into New Orleans, cut through swampland. Each time we sped through those marshes, I spied hundreds of turtles sunning themselves on half sunken logs that poked through the steamy waters at the edges of the highway. They looked like Oreo cookies lined up on a tray.

My best friend's family had a camp at nearby Lake Verette. When we cruised around the lake in her daddy's boat, I saw water moccasins in the branches of cypress trees. They looked as luxurious and entitled as mink stoles hanging on a coat rack at the Ritz. Camouflaged danger loomed everywhere. When I swam in Wisconsin, I never worried that something I couldn't see would bite me.

Everything above the Mason-Dixon seemed better than where I lived. The air was crisp and clean, devoid of the smothering heat and dust of the rural South. My grandparents' town had a library, a fourth of July parade, fireworks at night, ice-cream stands and beautiful parks with merry-go-rounds and swings that really worked. There were cozy attics and cool basements in the houses and hollyhocks and elm trees in the yards. Though Waukesha had many things Donaldsonville lacked, it was the one thing it did not have that impressed me most. Never once in any part of the whole town did I see a "Whites Only" sign.

No one I knew in Wisconsin used the word "Nigger," and no one made fun of me for saying "Negro." Until the summer of 1958, I thought "the North" was the most splendid place imaginable. It was worth the perils of the journey to finally arrive in such an enlightened, safe haven. But everything changed the summer we took Anne Christy with us to Wisconsin.

Anne Christy, or Chris as we called her (since we already had an "Ann" in our family,) was a young black woman who worked as our part-time maid for two years to earn money to go to college. She was 18 years old when I first met her, still young enough to share my interests—teen fashions, the mysteries of sex, sensational news and the future. She had one foot in the grown-up world and one in mine. My sisters and I thought Chris was incredibly cool, and we adored her. I could tell her any bad thing I'd ever done or thought. I knew she would never tell my parents. When I asked Chris stuff, she answered honestly and never made me feel stupid or patronized. For instance, she was the one who explained the whole deal with French kissing—how it wasn't as gross as it sounded.

"I know it's something I'm supposed to want to do someday," I told Chris, "but it seems disgusting to let a boy stick his tongue in your mouth!"

Chris was patient and sincere in her explanation. "When you really like the boy, French kissing is fun. You'll see."

"But what are you supposed to do with his tongue once he pokes it in there? I think I'd want to spit it out."

Chris laughed and told me it was hard to explain, but she knew I would like doing

French kissing someday.

"Your boyfriend doesn't 'poke' his tongue in your mouth. When you're kissing, your tongues just naturally find each other. It's like a caress inside your mouth."

The greatest fear I had by the end of fifth grade wasn't French Kissing but that I would never grow up. Janelle Laughlin and Linda Bessonet were already wearing bras, and my body showed no signs whatsoever of inching toward womanhood. From head to toe, I was still hopelessly a "little girl."

"I'm afraid I'll never get boobs," I confessed one day. With convincing certainty, Chris assured me I would be wearing a bra in a year or two at the most. Best of all, she gave me instructions on how to achieve a more-womanly size.

"Your boobs are gonna start growing all by themselves, but there are things you can do to make them bigger—bigger than your mama's," Chris said with a smile and a wink. One of her chores on the days she came to our house was to take the clothes out of the washing machine and hang them outside on the line. My mother's padded bras were probably the first she'd ever seen. No one in her family needed them.

"At night when you're in bed, rub your breasts. That stimulates the growth. If you do that every night, they're gonna get bigger and bigger."

I smiled imagining how surprised my classmates would be to see me walk in on the first day of sixth grade looking like Marilyn Monroe.

During the two years that Chris worked for us, she shortened those long River Road days waiting for Mother and Daddy to come home from work. A summer day in 1958 had twice as many hours as in later years. In the mornings, my sisters and I were the first kids in line at the town swimming pool. After lunch, I rode bikes with Myra Dugas down the River Road to the haunted house. When Myra was called home to help her mama buff the floors, I played dolls in the closet by myself or sat at the kitchen table talking with Anne Christy.

Chris told me lots of stories I've never forgotten. Most were about real life tragedies and murders— stories about children suffocating in old chiffarobes or getting chopped in half by speeding trains while they were looking for pennies on the tracks. She knew the details of several gruesome murders and freak accidents—like some man who fell into a bread machine and was baked into a dozen loaves of French bread. I could imagine his pinkie poking through the crust just as some hapless diner was about to take a bite.

Much as my mother tried to inoculate her children with Christopher Robin and Little Lulu, I was a Pit and the Pendulum kind of girl. I loved Grandpa Canright's stories about little girls getting scalped in the Wild West, just as I loved Freak Show Alley at the South Louisiana State Fair and Anne Christy's gruesome newspaper accounts of Louisiana tragedies.

Like every other kid in Donaldsonville, my greatest fear was of being trapped in a car that went off the end of the ferry. In our Mississippi River town, this fear was passed down from one generation to the next like family recipes or the crucifixes that hung on our parents' bedroom walls. My mother, however, was as immune to this particular fear as she was to all others—except the fear of financial ruin.

Mother's calm assurances did little to slow my racing heart every time the Oldsmobile's tires thumped across the steep wooden ramp leading onto the ferry. I felt the boat rock as Daddy turned the narrow corner in obedience to the arm signals of the ferryboat man. That man seemed unconcerned about the possibility of steering a car too close to the edge, just as long as he squeezed in the most cars possible on a single trip. Living in Donaldsonville, we couldn't go anywhere of interest without first crossing the Mississippi River on the Ollie K. Wilde or the George Prince.

Not only did Chris share my ferryboat fears, she increased them. The Christy family had known the black truck farmer who'd gone off the ferry the year before Chris started working for us. I couldn't hear enough about that terrible accident. However many times Chris told me the story, I would have to ask, "But, Chris, how did the truck go off the end of the ferry?"

This story was particularly tragic because it wasn't just the farmer who was killed; his little boy was with him, too. The father and son were sitting inside their vegetable truck when the ferry lurched and pitched them right into the river. That poor man and his son were swallowed up by the Mississippi River while a crowd of passengers leaned over the rail watching helplessly.

"No one knows for sure," Chris sighed. "It might have been Mr. Hawkins' brakes weren't working so good, or just as he reached that part where they put the chain across the opening, the boat rocked and the truck was thrown through the chain."

With horror, I imagined the scene— Mr. Hawkins and his little boy dressed in overalls, their surprise as they felt the front tires bump over the edge, the slowing down of time as the old pick up nose-dived into the Mississippi, their panicked faces at the windows just before the cab was sucked under—Creole tomatoes, peppers, corn and okra spilling into the water, bobbing gaily in the disaster's whirlpool, providing a temporary grave marker, the only one they would ever have. I could see the boy's small hands desperately fumbling for a way out of the truck, his dad blindly reaching for him through the dark, rushing waters.

"Chris, did they ever find them?"

"No, Jane, the Mississippi's too deep and the current's too fast. There's so much mud in that river, divers couldn't find the truck if they bumped into it."

That seemed particularly sad, the father and son floating inside the truck's cab, forever trapped in a watery grave. By now they'd probably turned to skeletons, skeletons in overalls."I won't ride in a car on the ferryboat," Chris said emphatically. "I get out and walk on the ferry and don't get back in that car 'til we pass the peanut man on the other side."

I wished my mother would let me get out of the car, but I would never have asked such a thing. She was always in a hurry to get wherever we were going. When we parked over the levee to wait for the ferry, she wouldn't even let us get out to buy a bag of roasted peanuts. Everybody else got them but not us. She feared the cars might start moving ahead before we returned. Being one car length behind constituted lateness in her book, and that was almost as big a sin as being overdrawn at the bank.

In addition to the foolishness of risking a slight delay, there was also the issue of foolishness itself. Mother thought this ferryboat phobia was irrational and just plain stupid. Having no fears herself, she could not understand those who did. I was too hungry for my mother's respect to risk her disdain. I learned to keep my worries to myself and waited for opportunities to discuss them with empathetic listeners. Chris was the best.

As fearful as I was about driving on and off the ferry, Chris was afraid of driving through the state of Mississippi... and I didn't blame her. Even before the three civil rights workers were murdered, we all knew it was a violent, hateful place, especially for Negroes.

I understood Chris' fear: Of all the states my family had to cross on our trips to Wisconsin, none was longer or more dreaded than Mississippi. Though it was our neighbor and shared similarities with South Louisiana, it also seemed vastly different; I felt it in my bones. Through the car window, I saw things I never saw in Louisiana—billboards screaming "Impeach Earl Warren!" and big signs in pastures announcing Ku Klux Klan meetings. Since the Klan hated Catholics almost as much as black people, it wasn't a popular club where I lived. In South Louisiana, people were more interested in parties than rallies and in celebrations than in lynchings. Our corner of the South had its own brand of racism, but it was softer, lazier, less angry and violent.

On those long drives through Mississippi, we saw mile after mile of cotton field with no tree in sight to provide a respite of shade from the sweltering heat. Dark figures stooped over dried brown plants in the blazing sun, picking little blobs of dirty white stuff. Most pickers, male and female, wore brightly colored bandanas on their heads. That splash of color seemed incongruous with the colorless life of cotton picking. Mississippi seemed a joyless place, hot and mean. The threat of violence was ever present—a latent force in the atmosphere, like heat lightning.

Despite having to cross Mississippi, the summer my parents asked Chris if she'd like to come with us to Wisconsin, she was beside herself with excitement. The only member of the Christy family who'd ever traveled far from home was her uncle who'd joined the service during the Korean War. Chris would be crossing more than a state line; she'd be going all the way up North. Most important of all, Anne Christy would cross the most significant line in a Southerner's psyche—the Mason Dixon!

We kids and Chris talked about it every day until the week arrived for our journey. Chris joked that she would duck below the window or hide on the car floor whenever we made a stop in Mississippi. "Or I can wrap my head in a kerchief like Aunt Jemima and pretend I'm your mammy." The jokes helped, but inside we all dreaded that part of the trip. After we got north of Mississippi, things would get better and better as we approached the North.

"Don't worry, Chris," I said, patting her hand, "once we cross the Mason Dixon Line, it'll be the same as if you were a white lady."

As much as I loved Chris's stories about disasters, she loved mine about the North. I enjoyed turning the tables, being the expert, having Chris hang on my every word. I reveled in the unconditional respect Chris gave me for being half Yankee. I was proud that my relatives never used the word "nigger" and that one of my great-grandfathers had fought on Lincoln's side of the Civil War. Perhaps I was too proud. Perhaps I was careless and exaggerated my accounts of the fabulous North…or maybe I just needed to believe them as much as Chris did.

For months before our trip, my sisters, Chris and I talked of nothing else besides

the North. Our excitement couldn't have been greater if we'd been setting out in a covered wagon for Shangri-la. I told Chris about driving through Tennessee and Kentucky— states famous for Elvis Presley and the Kentucky Derby—but Chris only wanted to hear about the North. I can picture her now, leaning across our kitchen table, chin resting on clasped dark hands, her full lips parted in a toothy smile that showed the small gaps between her front teeth. When I described the rolling hills and sparkling lakes that dotted the Wisconsin landscape, Chris shook her head, feigning disbelief. Our Louisiana minds could barely imagine natural water that wasn't muddy.

When I imitated those Midwestern accents with their sharp "R's" and crispy clear enunciations, Chris laughed and laughed, though she was ready to love Wisconsin people no matter how funny they talked. It was enough for her to know I'd never once seen a "Whites Only" or "Coloreds" sign in the North. It didn't seem to matter that there were no black people in Waukesha—the absence of the signs was more relevant.

In the summer of '58, instead of spending our vacation at Grandma and Grandpa's house in Waukesha, we were going to rent a cottage in Twin Lakes, the resort town where Uncle Maynard and Aunt Florence lived. I knew this vacation was going to be the best our family had ever had. Though I loved Grandma and Grandpa's house, a cottage by the lake sounded more exotic. I imagined walking out the door and jumping in the water. We'd swim in the lake all morning, play mermaids and water tag, dive off the floating raft, watch sailboats and motorboats pulling skiers. After lunch, Chris and I would walk downtown to Uncle Maynard's drug store. He would probably let us read his comic books and Seventeen for free. Chris and I might sit at a wooden booth, or perhaps on the tall stools that lined the soda fountain, and Uncle Maynard would give us free hot fudge sundaes and root beer floats.

I told Chris we would make a ton of friends in Twin Lakes since people in the North weren't prejudiced. I imagined slumber parties in our cottage with lots of cool, teenage girls from the North. When summer ended, Chris and I would have pen pals from Wisconsin. Although Chris indulged my fantasies, I knew they weren't the same as hers. It wasn't the lake or the free hot fudge sundaes that excited Chris about Twin Lakes; it was its proximity to Chicago.

I'd only been to Chicago once, but I never forgot what I saw there. Grandpa had taken my sisters and me to the Museum of Natural History so we could learn about dinosaurs and ancient Indian cultures. It was the first time in my life I'd ever been to a museum. There was a Tyrannosaurus Rex skeleton standing as tall as a house and dioramas depicting Eskimo families cast in blue light inside their igloos and a life-sized log cabin with a pioneer family gathered around the hearth.

As impressive as these sights were, I was more amazed by a scene I witnessed in the parking lot outside the museum. While Grandpa stood on the sidewalk asking directions, a very attractive Negro girl walked by holding hands with a white boy. They were smiling and behaving as if their relationship were the most normal thing in the world. If one of the dinosaurs had come to life and marched across the parking lot, it would not have fascinated me as much as that couple.

As I sat in the car watching them, I felt almost dizzy. I wanted to laugh and cry at the same time. It was as though the Tectonic plates of my reality had shifted, exposing something new and wonderful. In political arguments back home, Daddy said it would take generations before Negroes and Whites could live together as equals. That day in Chicago, I knew he was wrong.

"How were they dressed?" Chris asked when I told her about the black/white couple. I'd never seen Chris so interested and excited.

"Were people staring at them?" Chris wanted to know. "Did the colored girl have her hair straightened?" Imagining an interracial couple walking along a sidewalk in Chicago verified every good thing we'd ever thought or hoped about life north of the Mason Dixon. I was Chris's willing accomplice in promoting and expanding the vision of an enlightened North.

In early spring, when the new pattern books came out, Chris started preparing for her big trip to the North. It seemed like the whole Christy family was as excited as if Chris were heading to Atlantic City to be in the Miss America contest. Aunts and uncles gave her money. She bought patterns and material from Lemann's to make stylish new outfits like the ones she'd seen in Seventeen. Mrs. Christy helped her with the sewing and bought her a brand new pair of loafers. They were the style college kids at L.S.U. wore, but Chris would never have worn hers without socks.

Months became weeks, then days, and finally it was the eve of our departure for Wisconsin. Mother and Daddy planned to begin the trip long before dawn to knock off as many hours as possible before the hottest part of the day. They'd planned for Chris to sleep over at our house the night before we left. Late that afternoon, Daddy and I drove down Bayou LaFourche Road to pick her up. When we reached the Christy house, it looked like a family reunion. All her relatives were there to see her off—her mama and daddy, her aunties, brothers, sisters, cousins.

Daddy got out of the car and shook hands with Mr. Christy. While he put Chris's suitcase in the trunk, I stood by the car door watching the family. Chris's mama was smiling and crying at the same time. She leaned over and straightened Chris's collar. Then as Chris turned to go, Mrs. Christy suddenly reached for her. She wrapped her arms around Chris and kissed her over and over. I felt a twinge of envy. The only part of this scene I could imagine with my own mother was the collar part.

Once Chris was in the car, Daddy turned it around and headed back onto Bayou La Fourche Road. The Christy family stood on their gravel road waving to us until we went around the bend and were out of sight. When we pulled into the driveway at home, Ann, Kay Kay and Gretchen were waiting on the front steps for Chris. It felt like a slumber party, except Mother and Daddy said we had to get to sleep early.

Long after we were in our beds with the lights out, I heard them tip-toeing around the house, as if they thought we might actually be sleeping. Ann, Chris, and I whispered in the dark until we ran out of things to say. There was no door between the den where we slept and the kitchen. I lay listening to the hum of the refrigerator, punctuated by the rhythmic ticking of the clock. It was unbearably hot. Although I threw off the top sheet, my legs stuck to the bottom one. Droplets of sweat trickled from my temple down my neck. The hours crawled, marked only by the high-pitched whine of mosquitoes or the distant whistle of the City of New Orleans speeding through the sugarcane fields. That train would reach Chicago before we even got out of Mississippi. I wished our Oldsmobile could go as fast as the City of New Orleans. I wished we could get out of bed and get on the road. Would this night ever end?

A floorboard creaked.

"What's that?" I thought, a twinge of optimism rising in my restless heart. I sprang from my bed, tiptoed through the housed to the bathroom and bumped into Kay Kay along the way.

"Who's up?" called our mother from the bedroom. Kay Kay and I froze, expecting Mother to yell at us for waking her, but Ann called out from the den, "I am!" Suddenly, voices all over the house joined in, "Me, too!" "Me, too!"

"Hell, Candy," my father said, "we may as well get on the road."

"But Conrad, Gretchen's tennis shoes haven't had time to dry."

"What does she need shoes for in the car?"

We raced around the house gathering last minute books and paper dolls for the trip. In record time our entourage of seven cycled through our one bathroom, washing our faces and brushing our teeth. We dressed quickly, then headed out the front door into the pitch black night. The darkness was alive with insect voices—millions of them. Where were they? How could creatures so small have such loud voices? My peaceful reverie was interrupted by a very human, very familiar voice.

"Damn it! I forgot Gretchen's tennis shoes." Mother dashed back up the porch stairs, swinging the screen door so hard it sprang back with a bang. Daddy waited for her on the porch, then did one last check of the doors. While he locked the front door, Mother tied Gretchen's shoe laces to the car visor so the wind would dry her "tennies" before we stopped for breakfast.

Ann, Kay Kay, Gretchen, and I were in such high spirits we didn't even fight over who got to sit next to Chris. In the dark interior, I watched Daddy circle the car, kicking each tire to make sure it was safe before he climbed into the driver's seat and closed the door. He made the Sign of the Cross, said a short prayer, then turned the key to start the engine. Oyster shells crunched beneath the tires as he backed the car out of the driveway onto the River Road, heading north. A chorus of frogs and insects provided us a melancholy farewell.

When we finally stopped for breakfast we were famished and excited to be going to a restaurant for the first time since our last trip two years before. Gretchen's shoes had blown away somewhere along the highway, so Daddy carried her into the diner. The restaurant let Gretchen come in barefooted, but they wouldn't let Chris in with her neatly polished loafers and white ankle socks. She had to go around to the back of the restaurant and eat in the kitchen with the Negro help.

"It's not fair," I whined.

"No, it's not," my mother replied, "but Chris knew it would be like this before she decided to come."

"Is Chris going to get to sleep with us tonight at the motel?"

"Yes, we should be in southern Illinois by then," Daddy explained, "in the land of Lincoln!" A long, sweltering day stretched between breakfast and that distant motel in the Land of Lincoln.

Although we were traveling in a big car this summer, by noon it felt as cramped and hot as our old Chevy two-door. Every time Daddy stopped for gas, we shuffled places in the back seat, negotiating whose turn it was to sit next to Chris and which of us got to ride in the little shelf behind the seats. Chris never seemed to mind our fighting over her. No matter how whiney we got, she just smiled and teased us out of our bad moods.

At every filling station stop, Mother sent us in to get a drink from the water fountain and go to the bathroom. Chris stayed close to the car patiently waiting for us to bring a paper cup back for her. She never had to "go," and it didn't seem to bother her to miss the excitement of going inside a filling station, or maybe she just enjoyed these times alone with my mother.

By early afternoon we were still in Mississippi, dragging through yet another dusty town. Daddy slowed the car so he and Mother could read the sign post at the center of this sad and forlorn community. There must have been forty little signs of different colors and numbers nailed to a single telephone post. Mother's brow furrowed as she glanced back and forth between the maps on her lap and the helter-skelter directions provided by the Mississippi Department of Transportation. A barefoot black girl crossed the street, straining to get a better look at Chris as she passed our car. A yellow dog lay sleeping at the foot of the post, carefully wedged into the asymmetical shadow cast by the signs.

"Damn it, Conrad, I think we're lost!" my mother wailed, flinging the map across the car seat.

Kay Kay's eyes widened in the backseat. She reached for Chris's arm, but Chris looked just as scared.

"Now, Candy, don't worry. We'll just stop at that Esso up ahead and ask directions." Then Daddy glanced at our quiet, serious faces in the backseat and asked, "You kids wanna get some soda pops?"

Just like we never went to restaurants, we never got to have soda pop. Mother said cold drinks were expensive and would rot our teeth, but in that moment she was more worried about finding our way. After we pulled into the Esso, Daddy reached in his pocket and gave us each a nickel. He asked Chris what she wanted and nodded to Ann. With nickels in our sweaty fists, my sisters and I raced to the horizontal metal box standing just outside the station under the red awning. Ann lifted the lid. Inside there were cokes and 7-ups, strawberry sodas, orange pops and root beer. We could identify each kind of drink by its cap.

My throat felt cracked. I tasted dust and gasoline in my mouth and couldn't wait to wash it away. After agonizing over my selection, I put in my nickel, threaded an Orange Crush to the end of the line and pulled it out of the cooler. The cold glass bottle felt wonderful in my hand. I held it up to my face, ran it along my cheeks and nose, lifted the hair at the back of my neck and let the icy sweat of the bottle cool my sticky neck. Only then did I pop off the top and begin drinking. That orange drink was cold, and in that moment, more delicious than watermelon.

"Girls, get back in the car!" Mother's voice called from across the parking lot. Everyone else had finished their drinks. I quickly guzzled the last of my Orange Crush, put my glass bottle in the empties tray and ran back to the car.

"Did you see, Jane finished her drink!" Gretchen announced in her sweet voice, sounding rather proud of me.

Daddy smiled and held the door open. We scrambled in without our usual bickering for position. We weren't lost anymore; we had cold soda pop in our bellies and we were going to sleep in a motel that night. Could life be any better than this? Even Mother looked happy.

As we bounced down the road, my head began to feel heavy, as if it were being squeezed in a vise. The parched scenery whizzed past my window with an orange tint, causing flips in my stomach. I squeezed my eyes shut. My body felt hot and cold at the same time. Beneath closed eyelids, the world turned a horrible, sickening orange.

"Stop the car!" I shrieked, trembling. Daddy slammed on the brakes and pulled over to the side. Chris reached for the door handle and helped me navigate past Kay Kay to get outside. As soon as I was out, a strange force overtook my body. Something was happening to me over which I had no control. The color orange engulfed me like poison gas. I retched, and an orange, hot stream shot from my mouth to the dust covered weeds at the edge of the road. From the car, orange words surrounded me in a chorus of disapproval: "Disgusting!" "She made such a pig of herself." "Yuck!" "Damn it, we'll never get to Wisconsin!"

I vomited three more times that day by the side of the road. No one wanted to sit next to me, so I leaned against the car door feeling sorrier for myself than if I'd been an orphan. We would never get to Wisconsin, and it was all my fault. From across the car, Chris reached over and stroked my cheek.

On previous trips to Wisconsin, my sisters and I started begging Daddy to stop at a motel long before sunset but not on this trip. There was an unspoken understanding that we would wait to look for a motel until we'd left the segregated South. I didn't care if it was midnight, just as long as Chris could stay with us.

Spending the night in a motel was a highlight of our Wisconsin trips. With the voice of experience, I'd told Chris how cool it was to stay at a motel. It was like being a Rockefeller at the Ritz. In those days, every motel seemed fancy to us, whether or not it had a T.V. or swimming pool. Most had showers and air-conditioning, "modern" conveniences by our rural Louisiana standards.

Those vacations took place in a bygone era, long before the big chains dominated America's highway landscape. There was no standardization in motel color, size, design, featured amenities or name. Instead of Holiday Inn, Marriott or Ramada, we passed motels with names like "South of the Border," "Cozy Corner," "Sleepy Time" or with family names like Hitchcock's "Bates Motel."

I peered out the window longingly at each motel sign we passed. It seemed like we'd been driving forever. I finally asked the question in everyone's mind, "When will we be out of the South, Daddy?"

Mother and Daddy exchanged looks. We were all weary, and the sun was beginning to set. Mother reached for the map, bent her head down to study its maze-like features, then slid her index finger down the middle. She looked up and smiled. "If your Daddy steps on the gas and we don't get lost again, we should reach the Illinois state line in about an hour."

Cheers erupted in the backseat. Silence and sulks were replaced by animated discussion of the big event, choosing a motel for the night.

"Mama, can we stay at one with a T.V.?" Ann asked.

"Please pick one with a swimming pool."

"Ooh, I hope it has a restaurant with hamburgers and French fries."

"Do you think it'll have one of those showers like they have at the town pool?"

It was almost dark when Daddy's cheerful voice announced, "You're in the Land of Lincoln now, girls!" The air rushing past the window felt cool and refreshing, the way the North was supposed to feel. There was a crescent moon hanging like a Christmas tree ornament low in the sky. A sprinkling of stars sparkled across the navy-blue dome of early evening. What a beautiful night! Chris tilted her head to stare out the car window up at the sky. Suddenly, she reached over and gave me a hug. She looked happier than I'd ever seen her. I snuggled closer to her and asked, "So Chris, what do you think of the North?" She laughed and said, "It sure is cold up here!" but I knew it wasn't the temperature that was giving her shivers.

Mother started scanning road signs, anxious to find a motel. Gretchen was falling asleep, and we hadn't even had supper yet. Finally we saw a sign for Dale's Shamrock Inn, 5 miles away. Those five miles seemed the longest miles of the day. Like hawks, my sisters and I scanned the road with hungry eyes.

"Look, there's Dale's!" Kay Kay shouted from the back seat. Daddy put on his blinker and slowed the car for a turn. My hands were on the car handle before Daddy switched off the engine. Ann, Kay Kay and I scrambled out like Mexican jumping beans. I knew Chris was just as excited, but she lingered to help my sleepy little sister climb out of the car. We wanted to go with Mother and Daddy to the motel office, but they told us to stay behind with Chris and Gretchen.

"Make these kids run around the parking lot," Mother told Chris, "otherwise, we'll never get them to sleep tonight." Chris reached for Gretchen's hand and then turned to us with a pretend, stern look on her face, "You heard your mother—get on your marks!" As soon as we started running, Chris scooped Gretchen up to her hip and raced past us from the car to the sidewalk and back again. Gretchen was delighted to finally win a race with her elder sisters, even if it was Chris's feet that had done the running. Soon we were all laughing and panting and hugging each other.

"I've never slept in a motel before," Chris sighed, leaning against the car, looking up at Dale's neon sign.

My sisters and I interrupted each other, each wanting to be the one to tell Chris the most exciting detail of motels.

"They have carpets on the floor and big mirrors in the bathroom."

"And they're decorated really fancy, like bedrooms you see in the movies."

"And Chris, we can all get in bed together and watch T.V.!"

Chris smiled and shifted Gretchen to her other hip. Then she reached over and stroked my bangs. At that moment I loved Chris more than anyone in the world.

Daddy stuck his head out the door of the motel office and motioned us to come in. As he held the door, we entered the small office single file. The motel man was smiling...until he saw Chris. Then, he stiffened and turned to my father.

"Whoa, now wait a minute, mister!" He lowered his voice and said, "you didn't tell me you had a nigger with you."

"Nigger?" had Dale said the N-word? He didn't have a southern accent; he wasn't chewing tobacco; he looked nice, like a normal Yankee man. I wondered if my father had made some mistake, if we'd taken a wrong turn somewhere and landed back in the South. My sisters and I edged closer to Chris, as if to protect her from that word hanging in the air like a loaded gun. I reached for her hand, but she held herself rigid and didn't respond to my touch. She stood staring straight ahead, an icy expression on her face, her eyes glassy like when you have fever or are about to cry. In just one instant, one word had separated us. I could feel Chris moving away as surely as a train leaving the station.

Dale coughed nervously and shrugged his shoulders as if to relinquish blame. My parents exchanged worried looks; I could see Daddy's jaw jutting out the way it did when he was mad, and Mother seemed to slink into the background. My smart, articulate, fearless mother was suddenly mute. She could handle hurricanes and ferryboats and murderers in the dark. Why wasn't she handling this?! I wanted to shake them both. What was happening?! These were my parents, but suddenly I hated them.

Something was wrong! Something was terribly wrong. I felt sick again—sick and dizzy and shaky. I wanted to cry, and I wanted to hit someone. And then, I wanted to run away and hide somewhere. But where was there to go?

We had arrived.

We were in the North.

***

There was no drama, no shouting or cursing, and no turning back. It was late. My mother came outside and stood next to Chris in the parking lot. She spoke quietly to her. Chris's head was bowed. She nodded in understanding of whatever Mother told her. Meanwhile, my father stayed in the office with Dale while he called around to locate a respectable black family who would take Chris in for the night, a minister or schoolteacher. I can't remember, only that it seemed long—that wait out in the parking lot. The air felt cooler up here in the Land of Lincoln, but when I looked up at the sky, it wasn't beautiful like the sky above the River Road. I could only see two or three stars.

Finally, a pair of headlights appeared, and a truck pulled into Dale's. A black man stepped out. He and Daddy talked. When my father pulled out his wallet, the man shook his head. Then Mother and Chris walked toward the truck. The passenger door opened, and a black woman stepped out. She spoke with Mother and Chris for a few minutes. I wanted to hear everything, but my sisters and I knew to stay where we were. The black lady stepped to the side and Chris climbed in first, then the lady. My father closed the door for them and spoke to Chris through the window. After the truck's taillights disappeared down the road, we followed Mother and Daddy to our rooms. I don't remember a single thing about that motel except our arrival.

The next morning, Chris returned after breakfast, and we continued our journey to Twin Lakes. It felt like a different trip now, as if we'd detoured, or taken a wrong turn and were heading toward a land we'd never known. My sisters and I were quiet in the car. We had survived an ambush, like a pioneer family in a cowboy movie. The hostiles had taken Chris, but we got her back. I felt enormous love for Chris but also a sudden shyness. Chris seemed shy, too.

And then Mother turned to face Chris in the back seat. "You didn't miss anything," she said, "the Shamrock Inn can't even make coffee. It tasted like dishwater." Chris laughed. It was a simple thing, but it changed the feeling inside the car.

My mother had different ways that sometimes embarrassed me in our town. She wasn't friendly and lovey-dovey like other mothers, but in moments like this one, I wouldn't have traded my mother for June Cleaver. As a child, I didn't have words for the qualities that made her exceptional, but now I can say that one was her intuitive understanding of human dignity.

The worst part of our trip was over. We had made it past Mississippi and a mean motel man in southern Illinois. We hadn't gone far enough north last night, but now we were sailing along on much better roads, already spotting signs for Chicago. With hearts lightened, excitement about this special summer returned.

Rich people from Chicago spent vacations at lake resorts, not families like ours. Without our uncle's connections, it would have been impossible, but as town pharmacist, Uncle Maynard knew all the businesspeople in Twin Lakes and probably got us a pretty good rate. Everyone in Twin Lakes knew and liked the Canrights. Uncle Maynard was considered a fun guy. He could tell jokes better than Johnny Carson.

I could imagine my uncle and aunt hanging out with the "Rat Pack." They were the glamorous couple who danced at the clubs, speed-boated across the lakes, played golf, and drank cocktails every evening. I'd overheard Mother tell Connie that Aunt Florence had given my uncle silk sheets for their anniversary. Connie raised her eyebrows, and they both laughed. This little marital detail just added to my sense that everything was better and more modern in Wisconsin, even marriage.

And so it came as quite a shock to arrive at this resort—not someone's camp on Bayou Lafourche—and be told we could not stay there. "I'm sorry, Mr. Goette," the owner told my father, "there must have been some mistake. This is a respectable place, a family place. We don't allow coloreds."

Uncle Maynard was still at the drugstore at 4:00 p.m., but he rushed right over as soon as Mother called him. "What are we supposed to do now?" Mother asked, while Daddy glared at Maynard. My uncle reached for a cigarette in the front pocket of his white coat. "I'm sorry, Conrad," he said, "I'll fix this." He took a deep draw on his cigarette and headed up the lawn.

Despite his history and status in Twin Lakes, it took my uncle what seemed like an eternity of back and forth muted exchanges to convince his "friend" to allow "the Goettes" to stay. When deliberations concluded, the two men headed down the hill while we waited for the verdict. I wondered if we would have to get back in the car and abort this disastrous vacation without having a single swim in a Wisconsin lake or even one ice-cream cone.

Mother's shoulders stiffened; Daddy had his angry face. I watched as the owner marched toward us, a step ahead of my uncle as if to make it clear he was the man in charge. With no sign of apology in his face or warmth in his voice, he delivered his ultimatum.

"Since you're Maynard's family and you've come so far ..." but his condition was that Chris not ever be seen at the resort. She wasn't allowed to swim in the lake or walk on the grounds, and if she was ever spotted outside the cabin, our family would have to leave immediately.

All week my sisters and I took turns hanging out with Chris in the cottage. Whenever we went to Uncle Maynard's drugstore, we brought back a stack of outdated magazines for Chris. She read them cover to cover and anything else she could find, even my sister's horse books. If we got ice-cream in town or at our uncle's soda fountain, my parents would return with something much nicer than a cone for Chris—a banana split or big root beer float. We spent those long cottage days playing cards and Scrabble, talking about movies we had seen, or just looking out an opened window at a sparkling lake that seemed so near, and yet so far away.

Jeannette Jefferson Brings Her Spice

Genie and I sat at the kitchen table with our algebra books opened while Jeannette poured oil and flour into the big cast iron on the stove. I was thirteen years old at the time, didn't much like math, and lacked the mental discipline my homework required. My mind drifted to more interesting subjects. On that particular day, the subject was reincarnation. I don't remember what Genie or I said we wanted to be in our next lives, but I'll never forget what Jeannette said: "I don't care what I come back as, as long as it ain't black."

I glanced toward the stove where Jeannette stood in her gravy-stained apron, one hand crooked above her big belly, the other stirring the smoking roux, her stemless glasses balanced on the end of her nose. I studied her face expecting to find humor, but her gaze was serious, focused only on the roux. In that moment it had seemed she was speaking to the pot rather than to Genie and me. The sadness of her expression was as startling as it was unusual. Suddenly the steam rising from the pot seemed like tears. I had caught Jeannette in an unguarded moment. Its riddle seemed far more important than any equation in my book.

Jeannette Jefferson became our cook the year I started eighth grade. My family couldn't have afforded a cook even before my sister Ann went to boarding school. We were Donaldsonville middle-class. You either sent your kids to Donaldsonville High, which was free, or you sent them to Ascension Catholic, which was cheap. Only the daughters of wealthy families went to Grand Coteau. It was the equivalent of sending your daughter to the Sorbonne or your son, to Princeton.

Middle-class white families all had maids, or at least, an ironing lady, but only the rich had cooks. So how did the Goettes end up having the best cook in Donaldsonville? No one will ever be sure.

Mother first met Jeannette Jefferson at Connie Netter's house a month or so after our family moved to Donaldsonville. Mother had stopped by for afternoon coffee. Jeannette was in the Netters' kitchen when Connie introduced her to my mother. A newcomer to

Donaldsonville was rare, so I expect Jeannette was curious about the Goettes and especially excited to meet a woman who grew up in the state next to Abraham Lincoln's. She'd heard the gossip around town about Dolphie's cousin (by marriage) who'd long been a Brother but quit the order to marry a young reporter from the North.

I suspect my mother may have been equally interested to meet Jeannette. Though Mother wasn't working anymore, Jeannette's family was more than newsworthy. Had she not been black and female, Jeannette's daughter would have made the headlines when she was awarded a scholarship to Xavier University in New Orleans. In the early 1950's, college attendance was rare for a white man, rarer for a woman, and inconceivable for a black person.

Babbette's scholarship covered tuition, books, room and board, but not everything, like the clothes she would need in New Orleans. Dolphie and Aunt Emma—his progressive New Orleans aunt with a career but no husband, "Thank god!" she would say—found the scholarship, helped Babbette with the application process, and took her to New Orleans to meet the head of the music department. Though Babbette had performed many times for the hoity-toity, whites-only, women's music club in Donaldsonville, Dolphie had to twist the president's hand to get her to write Babbette's letter of recommendation.

Mother was eager to help. Though it had only been a few months since Gretchen's birth, Mother convinced herself that she'd never again fit into her regular clothes. She boxed up outfits she'd worn to work at the *Town Talk* and other less professional, but nice clothes she'd purchased between babies. Without a hint of the clothes being charity, because they weren't in her eyes, Mother offered the box to Jeannette. "If there's anything in here that Babbette would want to have, she'd be doing me a favor to take them."

All the years we lived in Donaldsonville, my mother was the most fashionable dresser in town, with a reputation for quality as well as style. When Jeannette got home from the Netters' that night and opened the box with Babbette, they were astonished. These clothes could have just been bought at Maison Blanche or Godchaux's!

This small kindness and show of respect seemed to have earned Jeannette's lifelong admiration for this woman from the North who spoke beautiful English without a trace of a southern accent. Candy Goette also turned out to be an integrationist—the only one in Donaldsonville, Louisiana in 1951.

Nine years later when Mother was working two jobs—buyer for the women's department at Lemann's, and editor of The Donaldsonville Chief—a convergence of circumstances prepared the way for Jeannette's entry into our lives. It began with a pain in Jeannette's back that spread to her legs. When it got so bad she could barely walk, Dolphie Netter insisted she go to Charity Hospital in New Orleans. It was the only reputable hospital in Louisiana that treated Black people. At Charity x-rays revealed severe damage to a couple of disks in Jeannette's spine. Without surgery, she would surely become crippled for life. But the surgery had risks. There was the possibility that Jeannette could become paralyzed or even die if something went wrong.

"Go 'head," Jeannette told the surgeon, "I got faith." The doctor thought she was talking about him, but she never trusted a white man she didn't know. Jeannette's faith was placed in "my boy, Jude," as she called the patron saint of hopeless cases. If St. Jude helped her to walk again, she'd thank him by performing a good deed every day for the rest of her life.

On the day that Jeannette Jefferson walked up to our front door to announce she would

begin cooking for our family, my mother was perplexed and embarrassed. "Jeannette, we'd love to have you, but we can't afford a cook. If we could, I assure you, there's no one we'd rather have, but…"

Jeannette interrupted her mid-stream. "Ma'm Goette, I already been paid. You see me walkin' don't you?" Though we never understood how we earned the honor of becoming Jeannette's good deed, my family did its best to try to deserve it. Meanwhile, my parents paid Jeannette what we could afford. "Bingo money," my father called it when he handed her the envelope before driving her home on Saturday afternoons.

Jeannette Jefferson was a legendary cook in Donaldsonville. She'd cooked dinner

for Clark Gable when he was up the River Road at Christine Hayward's grandma's plantation shooting the movie "A Band of Angels." Everybody in town knew Gable wanted to take Jeannette back to Hollywood to cook for the stars, but she wouldn't go.

"Jeannette, why didn't you?!" I asked in frustration every time she told the story. I

couldn't stop thinking of this missed opportunity, the life she could have had in Hollywood. I imagined movie stars in bathing suits sitting around Clark Gable's swimming pool—Audrey Hepburn, Cary Grant, Rock Hudson. In my fantasy version of the life she might have had, the glass door slides open and Jeannette steps onto the patio wearing a fancy starched uniform. Her hair is nicely coiffed like she gets it done for the "Les Dames" balls at the True Friends Hall. In my Hollywood fantasy Jeannette wears rhinestone-studded glasses with two stems.

Jeannette didn't see it that way. "Why I wan' be flumagattin' with all them movie stars when I got my own family right here in Donaldsonville?" she asked. I stopped arguing. Clark Gable's loss was my gain.

But it was a lot more than just family that kept her in our town. Jeannette was somebody in Donaldsonville, known and respected as a mover and shaker throughout the black community, as well as being the go-to person for any politician who hoped to get the black vote. 'Net knew everything that was going on in town and its surrounding areas. She had a voracious appetite for news anyway she could get it—print periodicals, across the fence gossip, social clubs, church organizations, meetings with town politicians, and cooking inside the homes of prominent white families. She was a magnet for news and an intelligent consumer sophisticated enough to know how to read between a newspaper's lines. No one could "bullshit" Jeannette Jefferson.

The Goettes were the only non-prominent, non-wealthy white family for whom she cooked. Later on, the other liberal, non-wealthy family in town, the Wiggins, were also graced with Jeannette's presence in their home. The irony is that while Daddy and the Goette daughters adored Jeannette's cooking, my mother did not. The culinary basics of Candy Goette's palate remained essentially, Midwestern. Mother would far rather have a ribeye steak and a baked potato with plenty of butter than a dish of Crawfish Bisque any day. Go figure!

Though Jeannette claimed her debt to St. Jude motivated her desire to cook for our family free of charge, her daughter Babbette says it was because my mother was a journalist. "Mama really admired her," and that was true. My father loved Jeannette for her cooking and her humor, but I don't think he saw her other, deeper qualities like Mother did. At first, Mother was simply grateful for not having to cook when she came home from work, but over time these two women developed a bond that nobody would ever be able to explain, probably not even the two of them.

It was spring 1960 when Jeannette started coming to our house every day after school to prepare our dinner. We lived in an old house with rats in the walls, yet we had the best cook in South Louisiana. Imagine being a kid coming home from school knowing you were going to have a dinner fit for movie stars. One day, you're eating your mother's meatloaf and frozen peas, and the next day, crawfish étouffée and gumbo z'herbes.

Net's crawfish bisque remains the most extraordinary dish I've ever tasted in my life. Rabbit sauce piquant, seafood gumbo, turtle soup, stuffed mirlitons, even her chicken dishes were better than anything I've ever eaten in the finest restaurants in New Orleans or any other city in the world. During the Jeannette years, a dinner invitation to the Goette house was rarely declined. It isn't true what people say about not knowing what you have 'til it's gone. My family knew from the first day Jeannette knocked on our door that we had won the lottery.

South Louisiana people know good cooking and value food more highly than any other basic need. We'll put up with air pollution and nasty water, but don't serve us a boring dinner. No other place in the world can match the way we cook, and Jeannette Jefferson was the best of our best.

After dinner when Daddy drove Jeannette home and we cleared the table, Mother would grumble about the messy kitchen. Splashes of roux formed dark patches of brown across the white stovetop and the floor around it was dusted in flour. Mother tolerated Jeannette's messy cooking, but what irritated her most was the act Jeannette would put on when we had "special" guests, like one of Ann's Grand Coteau friends. At such times, 'Net's sharp, irreverent humor was replaced with a stereotypical, self-deprecating, "happy negro" façade that others, including Daddy, seemed to enjoy.

Mother hated it. She liked the "real" Jeannette, the one well-versed in current events who cared about what was happening in the world as much as we did, the Jeannette who could imitate the speech and mannerisms of Ross Barnette and George Wallace, as well as various characters in our town. This was funny; the "mammy" act was not. Though we never spoke about it, I recognized the act black people put on for white people, the happy mask they wore like a shield. It made me wince to see Jeannette do that.

For the next five years until I went to college, I participated in my family's after-school routine of picking up Jeannette at her house on McGinnis Street before we headed down the River Road. After dinner one of us would drive her back into town to her little shotgun house that stood back-to-back with her daughter Tut's. My family came to really know Jeannette's tribe. The children and grandchildren who comprised her extended family moved seamlessly between the two houses, as if there were really only one house with a small yard and clothesline in the center.

The only two members of Jeannette's family I rarely saw were her eldest children, Babbette and Bro'man (pronounced,"Bro-main"). By the time I started eighth grade, Babbette had finished college and already established a successful career in the world of professional music. She sang with acclaimed groups that performed in some of the country's top concert halls. With Babbette's voice and training, she landed some of the most sought-after soprano roles, like Carmen and Bess. Had Babbette been white, her accomplishments would have been front page news in the Donaldsonville Chief, if not the Times Picayune. All the hoity-toity music club ladies of Donaldsonville would have beaten a path to

Jeannette's door and fawned over Babbette whenever she came to visit. My family had little exposure to classical music, didn't even have a record player, but we knew it was a big deal that Babbette Joseph from Donaldsonville, Louisiana had performed at Carnegie Hall.

She and Bro'main seemed polar opposites. I don't know if Bro'main ever finished school. By the time he appeared on my radar screen, he seemed a lost soul and a misfit in that family of hustling, bustling females. In addition to Tut and Babbette, three younger girls by a different father lived in the family houses. I would almost forget Bro'main existed until I heard 'Net or Tut tell a funny story about him tripping over the garbage can or challenging a passerby to a fistfight. I never saw him that the whites of his eyes were not red. Bro'main spent most of his days sitting with his dog under the Japanese Plum tree between the two houses, drinking whiskey.

I enjoyed our daily excursions to pick up Jeannette, even though the brief time between school and her house was the only time I got to spend in the front seat of the family car. Once we pulled up alongside the ditch bordering her sidewalk, I'd hop out, help her across the ditch and hold the car door open until she'd settled into the front seat. Unless it was raining or cold, she stuck her arm out the window, holding her wooden cane close to the side of the car.

Most afternoons before we headed for the River Road, Jeannette instructed Daddy to run her by Acosta's so she could tell the butcher exactly how she wanted our chickens cut (she liked bossing white men), or on Fridays, over to Bacala's to pick up oysters or shrimp that had come in that morning, fresh off boats in the Gulf of Mexico. As we wound through the quiet streets of Donaldsonville, Jeannette waved her cane whenever she spotted some acquaintance walking down the sidewalk. "Hey chile, how you doin'?"

She liked to call attention at such moments, as though it would impress her friends to see she was sitting in the front seat with "Mr. Goette," and his daughters were in the back. Jeannette Jefferson was both highly political and a shameless snob. Though we were the white family and she was black, Jeannette had more prejudices than anyone I knew. She was especially hard on white people who had once been poor.

She could not abide the nouveau riche. "They be thinkin' they so high falutin' with they new cars and fancy homes…" at which point Jeannette would stick her nose in the air and imitate her concept of a person putting on airs. If she were in the kitchen, she might put one hand on her hip and with the other, stick out her pinkie and pretend to sip from a fancy teacup. Then she'd raise her chin, frown and strut around the kitchen, holding the edge of her apron to the side in mock prissiness. With her big belly riding high under the gravy splattered apron, and her glasses perched like a pince nez, the contrast of her appearance and the fraudulent social sophisticate she impersonated cracked us up.

Jeannette was the most brilliant mimic I've ever known. Lord help the man or woman who gave any hint of being "uppity." Many an afternoon such people were mercilessly skewered in the Goette kitchen, royally roasted by Jeannette's sharp wit.

My favorite Jeannette impersonation was of Monsignor Gubler, head of Ascension Catholic church in Donaldsonville—the *white* Catholic church. A visitor to Donaldsonville would have to ask around to find Saint Catherine's, the *black* Catholic Church on Lessard Street. It was a sweet little church made of white clapboard with two wide steps leading up to the front doors. There was a cross on top of the roof but no steeple.

Though Jeannette had attended Ascension very rarely, she had memorized every detail of Monsignor Gubler's conduct during Mass. Blacks were only allowed in the "big" church on the rare occasion Father Calimary was too sick to perform mass at St. Catherine's, or when Bishop Tracy came from Baton Rouge to bestow his blessings on our small, Catholic town. On these special occasions, Father Calimary and his black parishioners were included in a high mass at Ascension. This seemed the one integrationist gesture of which the Catholic Church of Louisiana was capable before Lyndon Johnson passed the Civil Rights Act.

Given the size of Donaldsonville, Jeannette had many other opportunities to observe our esteemed church leader, whom she called "Monster Gobbler." Each time she assumed his personality,

Jeannette transformed her whole demeanor. She pursed her lips, fluttered her eyes, folded her hands piously across her belly and began to speak in an unctuous tone, giving modest responses to imaginary compliments. "Oh, you're far too kind, Jeanne Marie. I'm just a humble parish priest, hardly qualified to become a bishop, much less the Archbishop of New Orleans!" She strutted and preened like a peacock.

Her impersonation of Monsignor Gubler in the pulpit was brilliant—the boring drone of empty words, punctuated periodically by Monsignor's ministrations to nasal and throat purgings. With the microphone set on "high," he would pause in the middle of a sermon, pull out his handkerchief, take a deep breath, and emit an unearthly prolonged, guttural sound that gathered force, boomed through the speakers, echoed across the vaulted ceilings and relayed the progress report to every recessed corner, nook and cranny of Ascension Catholic.

We parishioners sat breathless in our pews, suspended in the long moment, dreading the final hack that would propel the gold glop mined from deep within Monsignor's chest, through his puffy, wet lips and into the big, lace-trimmed hankie Miss Jeanne Marie ironed for him on Saturday. That unearthly sound terrified babies, disgusted teenagers and frequently caused Gaye Blanchard to faint. I don't know how a woman standing at a stove with a spatula in her hand could evoke all that, but Jeannette did.

After Monsignor Gubler, Mississippians, and the nouveau riche, Italians came next on Jeannette's roster of prejudices. If pressed, she would admit she wasn't against all Italians—especially after my sister Gretchen married a professor from Torino, Italy—but she wouldn't hide her bitterness toward some Italians.

This prejudice was rooted in Jeannette's loyalty to the grandmother who had raised her and her siblings after their mother died. Her grandma worked several jobs to feed and clothe her grandchildren. In Donaldsonville for a long time, the only people poorer than Blacks were the Italian families who came over from Sicily in the early 1900's.

One day when 'Net's grandmother walked across Crescent Park, she spied a small cluster of scruffy white children rummaging for food in the garbage bins behind Lemann's. She took them home and fed the lot. From that day on, those little Italian faces remained as welcomed at her kitchen table as the black faces of her grandchildren.

In later years after Prohibition passed, those Italian "kids" made a killing on the bootlegging business. Jeannette said that once they got some money, they got amnesia, too, and became the biggest racists in town. She never forgave them.

Her low esteem for Italians was matched in *high* esteem for Jews. The first white family she ever came to love was the Eli Bloomenstiels, a prominent Jewish family whose name appears on a marker at the entrance to Crescent Park on Mississippi Street. Jeannette was a child herself when she became a nursemaid for the Bloomenstiel children. That family broadened Jeannette's horizons; they took her on trips away from Donaldsonville, treated her with respect, and never talked down to her. The Bloomenstiel home was filled with beautiful things: artwork, furniture, rugs, fine china, a grand piano and ... shelves and shelves of books.

Jeannette didn't know when she might have discovered her culinary talents if the Bloomenstiels hadn't drafted her into the kitchen the day their cook went AWOL. 'Net was fifteen years old and had never prepared a dinner in her life. But she'd watched her grandmother, and she remembered a thing or two. It didn't take long for the Bloomenstiels to realize Jeannette's talents were better suited to the kitchen than the nursery. There are a lot of things a person can learn from hanging around a kitchen.

I learned a lot of Donaldsonville history and gossip from sitting at the kitchen table listening to Jeannette those afternoons on the River Road. Though it took me twice as long to get my homework done, I studied at the kitchen table before dinner because I loved being around her. It wasn't just because she was funny or gave me sneak previews of each night's dinner, or that I felt the need to keep her company.

Even though I sat on the sidelines, head bent over some textbook, the nearness of Jeannette gave me a sense of well-being. I loved her voice, the soft plumpness of her body, her skin—silky and dark as her gravy. She never acted nervous or impatient like my mother. If a pot boiled over on the stove, the hiss and splatter did not alarm her any more than the sound of rain on a roof. It was as if she'd never learned my mother's mantra, "God damn it—it's ruined!" For Jeannette, nothing was ever ruined. You simply cleaned up the mess and went on. As she pulled the heavy iron pot to a back burner, a cloud of steam enveloped her like a halo.

When Kay Kay got home from school, as soon as she changed out of her Catholic school uniform, she would head to the kitchen to ask, "'Net, what happened today?" She and Jeannette shared an addiction to two soap operas, *As the World Turns* and *General Hospital*. While I memorized the causes of World War II, Kay Kay and Jeannette discussed the causes of Luke and Laura's breakup. Jeannette was not indifferent to history, but the Treaty of Versailles and Chamberlain's appeasements could not compete with Laura's discovery of Luke's affair with the secret daughter she'd conceived after being raped by the same greedy tycoon who'd pushed Luke's father off a cliff.

It seemed easier to follow the twists and turns of history than to follow the plot lines of that soap opera. History unfolded more slowly than the pace at which people fell in and out of love on "the stories."

"Ain't no reason Luke be messin' around with that young girl, but Laura can't be hidin' the truth from Luke. He got a right to know. Ain't no good ever come from a lie!"

Jeannette's moral code was strict and unyielding, especially when it came to human relationships. Because my own mother rarely devoted attention to such affairs, I enjoyed hearing 'Net's perspective. She seemed knowledgeable about the secrets of the human heart and confident in her interpretation and judgments of the things men and women did.

I found it puzzling, though, that Jeannette held such different standards of behavior for blacks and whites. She seemed stricter and more prudish with my sisters and me than with her own family. Jeannette would never have let me read Lolita as Mother had, and she would have lectured me about how to behave on dates, which Mother never did. She particularly didn't like it when my sisters and I went out with boys she thought beneath us.

One afternoon Jeannette looked out the kitchen window and spied Kay Kay kissing her boyfriend, Ralph, in the back yard. After Ralph roared away on his motorcycle, Kay Kay ambled into the kitchen smiling. Her smile faded as it met Jeannette's glare from across the room. Net told Kay Kay to sit down, and then she let her have it.

"You got a reputation to uphold in this town. Don't you be causin' people talk about a Goette girl actin' like some kinda low life! You better be behavin' yourself when you with that boy. I'm a hear about if you don't."

Kay Kay's backyard kissing didn't seem to bother our mother, so why did it upset Jeannette? Clearly, her own children had been fathered by different men. How could she have illegitimate children and lecture us on proper behavior with boyfriends? I once asked her why she'd never married, and she looked at me like I'd gone crazy.

"What I be wantin' with a man in my house? You think I ain't got enough troubles?"

I wondered why Jeannette thought men were so much "trouble." I knew it wasn't the same as for whites who feared black men for no apparent reason.

In Donaldsonville, black women ruled their households; the men were mostly invisible. Take Jeannette's family; there was Bro'main who stayed in the backyard with his dog, and there was Tut's husband, Eddy, who worked at the post office. When Eddy wasn't at work, Tut and Jeannette worried him to death with chores or had him running them all over town.

In the years I was in and out of Tut and Jeannette's houses, I never heard Eddy speak a word. You could hear the women from around the corner, but Eddy and Bro'main melted into the woodwork. So, why would a husband have been so much trouble for Jeannette?

During quieter afternoons in our River Road kitchen, I often found Jeannette sitting at the table engrossed in the newspaper. While she waited for water to boil or the oven to preheat, she rummaged through *The Morning Advocate* and *The Times Picayune* or read our latest issue of *Time Magazine*. During my high school years, everyone at our house was a news junkie, including

Jeannette. If you didn't keep up with the news, how could you talk about politics?

Every day seemed to hold a new and exciting development. Political events unfolded faster than a spool of thread in the wind. The hope for change—a hated word in the South—dominated the air we breathed and the headlines we read. In our home we had different heroes than most of our friends— Fannie Lou Hammer, Julian Bond, Martin Luther King, Andrew Young, Medgar Evers, James Meredith, John Lewis, James Farmer. 'Net was as informed on current events as my parents and their friends.

Everyone in town knew the Goettes were integrationists, which was almost as bad as being a Communist. After Genie and I became friends in the seventh grade, one day when I'd gone to her house after school, Mrs. Folse asked me whether my parents were for segregation or integration. I sloughed off her question, pretending to be confused about what those terms meant. I knew Mrs. Folse was fishing, and her smile told me she knew I was evading. In that moment I felt part fool and part Judas.

When I was in eighth grade, Mother gave me a disturbing book to read. I've forgotten its title but not the sad irony that drove the plot. It dealt with the cruelty of color codes and how they existed even within the black community. Light-skinned blacks had greater status than their darker-skinned sisters and brothers among whites but were not accepted as "family" in either community.

The story's main character, a black woman so light-skinned she could have passed for white, ends her life as a lonely outcast. After I closed the book, it stayed with me a long time. It left me with a nagging question--how could you be safe in the world if prejudice was part of the human condition? If it truly is a timeless, human tendency to fear and loathe those who are different, what about me?

My mother's teachings were rarely direct. She relied on the books she gave us to teach whatever lessons she might have intended. She simply handed me a book—*To Kill a Mockingbird*, *Black Like Me*, *The Ugly American*, *Cry the Beloved Country*—and assumed its message would be understood and absorbed. If not, there was nothing she could tell me that would make a difference. She was wrong about that. I never forgot Mother's off-the-cuff reply one morning when I said Jeannette was the best cook in the world.

"If she hadn't been born black in the South, Jeannette wouldn't have had to be anybody's cook. She could have done anything; she could have been anything she wanted to be," she said. "That's the real tragedy of racism."

For a long time after, I reflected on her startling reply to what I had thought a compliment to Jeannette.

That's how my mother did things—never consciously gave me moral instruction, never told me why she put a particular book in my hands, never lectured me about values. In fact, she never used that term. But she made me think. And she made me question. Everybody loved Jeannette the cook, and they loved her jovial personality; they loved the black Jeannette, including my father. But my mother saw another Jeannette, and 'Net loved her for it.

We only hear about the exceptional cases of people who rise above their circumstances, as if they were the only ones with potential to do wonderful things in the world. Jeannette, like every human being, had only one chance to live. My mother's impromptu remark somehow made something click for me, and I understood why Jeannette wanted to be reborn anything, "as long as it ain't black."

Jeannette Jefferson on River Road, 1966

Jane Goette

Ann Turns into a Teenager

Most children have to fight their way out of the nest, battle their parents for independence, struggle to escape the loving clutches of Mom and Dad. This was not the case with the Goette girls. Daddy didn't seem to have an opinion on the subject, but Mother let us know early on there was something wrong with young people who didn't want to leave home. They were either crazy, lazy, or complete losers.

The humiliation of Mother's disdain would have been enough to send us packing after high school, but my mother upped the ante. More than once I'd heard her tell Connie, "If the little birds don't leave the nest when it's time, the mother bird has to kick them out."

Ann was the first of Mother and Daddy's children to leave home, but she had never spent much time playing on the River Road anyway. She'd always had friends in town. Perhaps if she'd had a Dugas girl her own age she might have enjoyed playing with us, although my big sister was the only "Goette girl" whoever expressed a wish that she'd been an only child. Her happiest childhood memory was the brief period she had Daddy all to herself, September 1951, when Mother, Kay Kay, and I returned to Bunkie for Gretchen's birth.

While we were away, Ann lived like a queen. Daddy deposited her at Donaldsonville Elementary each morning before heading to his office at the high school. Ann hung out with the teachers before the other children arrived and the bell rang to start school. Those elementary teachers spoiled little Ann, assuming she must be missing her mother and sisters terribly.

After school, Daddy took Ann to the high school where she received the same treatment from the few female teachers on that faculty. Life had never been so good: teachers vying for the privilege of buying "poor little Ann" a coke from the vending machine in the teacher's lounge. Instead of eating meat, potatoes, and brussel sprouts at home, Ann dined on hamburgers and French fries at the First and Last Chance. I imagine my confident big sister twirling on the bar stool sipping a cherry coke through a straw while at the same time Kay Kay and I were drinking milk in Bunkie.

After so many years wearing a black robe, when Daddy left the Brothers to marry Mother, he was helpless picking out clothes and relieved to have Mother do it for him. While we were in Bunkie, he let Ann dress herself for school each morning, even when she chose to wear a pair of Mother's earrings. Daddy was happy to have us back, but Ann wished we'd stayed in Bunkie forever.

I have no memory of that special bond that must have existed between Daddy and Ann, but I remember vividly the period during which they fought all the time. By today's standards, Ann's adolescent "rebellion" seems rather quaint. The kid just wanted to wear lipstick, peroxide her hair, and flirt with teenage boys. She was ready for some smooching, perhaps, but mostly it was *Gone with the Wind* drama my sister sought. I'm quite certain she was years away from wanting to "go all the way," the term we used for intercourse.

Like all Donaldsonville teenagers I knew at that time, Ann smoked cigarettes—not pot. Our town hadn't even heard about "Reefer Madness." With her lifelong aversion to needles, Ann would never have been a candidate for today's hallmarks of rebellion—body piercings and tattoos. She wanted red lips and blonde hair like Sandra Dee. She wanted to ride in cars with boys and pretend to be Natalie Wood in *Rebel Without a Cause.* Unfortunately, our father didn't know how good he had it. He was too old and out of touch with adolescence to understand why his little girl would want to be a blonde or wear lipstick or flirt with boys. His childhood had occurred in horse and buggy times, and he'd spent his adolescence in the equivalent of a monastery. To use one of Daddy's favorite expressions, he "didn't know da da from ya ya" about being a teenager, much less the female version.

I don't remember Ann being "sweet," but Daddy did. The idealized image of his first born grew in proportion to the outrageousness of her teenage incarnation—the sassiness, the yawn she would feign when Daddy talked to her, her rolled eyes and withering disdain. I suppose Daddy must have been tortured by memories of a fair-haired little Ann, a girl I never knew. Love, longing, and loathing were tearing him apart. He was also making Ann's life miserable. They were locked on opposing sides of a battle with time, a violent tug-of-war— Daddy pulling Ann toward the safety of the past, while Ann strained toward the music he couldn't hear, the call of the future.

Where Ann Goette's name appeared on girls' bathroom wall

"Candy, can't you do something about Ann?" Daddy would plead as Ann slammed a door and disappeared to sulk somewhere.

"Conrad, don't make such a big deal. When I was a teenager I wanted to be 'cool,' too. Ann's just trying things out; she's still the same Ann underneath it all. You're taking this far too seriously."

I believed my mother was probably right, though Ann was not just nasty to Daddy after she turned into a teenager—and that's how I thought of it—she was cranky and condescending. Like the time Kay Kay tried to tell her a little story about something that had happened at school and Ann responded, "You're about as funny as a truckload of dead babies." After that, I kept my stories to myself, but I loved those times when Ann was in a good mood. One afternoon, she put down her book, smiled at something I said, and called me a little "fruit." I took it as a compliment. Brimming with pride, I walked into the kitchen and told my mother, "Ann called me a little fruit." I thought it was an endearment, as if she'd referred to me as a little peach, but my mother's expression informed me I was on the wrong track.

The fights between Ann and my father continued and intensified when she started high school at Ascension Catholic. Daddy had spent his adult career in high schools, but he wasn't prepared for Ann's behavior. Wearing earrings to first grade was one thing, but wearing lipstick to high school was another. As Ann's freshman year progressed, lipstick became the least of Daddy's worries.

Sometime after Christmas, to cure the post-holiday doldrums, Ann and her friends decided to form a gang. They had seen *Rebel Without a Cause* at the Grand and its title inspired the name they chose for the gang, "The Rebels." Since none of them had driver's licenses yet and couldn't go drag-racing, it was difficult for them to find meaningful gang activities in Donaldsonville. How exactly does one start "a rumble"? Mostly, Ann's gang just wrote their logo on the covers of books and on bathroom walls. Nancy Griffin's mother embroidered "The Rebels" on the back of one of Nancy's jackets. Mother would never have done that for Ann; she didn't even know how to sew.

Aside from the trouble the graffiti caused the school janitor, Ann's "gang" was as harmless as Alfalfa and Spanky's. It wasn't drag racing or switchblade fights that kept Ann in trouble; it was her complete indifference to school. Disapproving notes from her teachers multiplied as the months passed by, and each new report card was worse than the last.

"Ann, don't you want to go to college?" I asked once, my voice full of worry.

"College is for squares," Ann replied, giving me an Elvis Presley curl of the lip as she glanced in the mirror to see how she looked.

By the end of Ann's academically alarming first year of high school, Daddy was convinced Ann was going to the dogs, and Mother was convinced he would kill her if something didn't change soon. "Conrad has lost all perspective," I heard her tell Miss Connie. "If he doesn't loosen up with Ann, I'm afraid she's going to really give him something to worry about."

A short time later, when Kay Kay returned from the picture show one Saturday, she ran through the house shouting the exciting discovery she'd made at the Grand—"Ann's famous! Ann's famous! I saw her name on the bathroom wall!"

"What did it say about Ann?" Gretchen asked, as wide-eyed as if her sister's name had appeared in lights on Broadway, rather than in purple crayon above the mirror of the girls' bathroom. Daddy grimaced and Mother smiled when Kay Kay replied—"Shit on Ann Goette!"

This was Daddy's "last straw." Mother's came a month later with Ann's end-of-year report card. As lackadaisical a student as mother had been, her grades were never as bad as Ann's. My parents must have stayed up late that night in May (which means past 9:00 p.m.) worrying and searching for a way to save their daughter from herself. The next morning, their decision was made. Ann would be going to Grand Coteau in the fall.

"Grand Coteau?!" Ann screamed, in horror and disbelief.

"Grand Coteau?" I whispered, the very name inspiring awe.

Main building, Academy of the Sacred Heart, Grand Coteau

Campus scene at Academy of the Sacred Heart

Grand Coteau: Ann's Finishing School

It's impossible to understand the significance of their decision without understanding the place in south Louisiana Catholic society at that time of Academy of the Sacred Heart, a boarding school. Run by Mothers of the Sacred Heart not only was it socially prestigious (less important to my family) but this school had an excellent academic reputation. For Daddy, its location was an additional plus. Grand Coteau was in the middle of the woods near Opelousas—no boys, no cars, no lipstick—*Rebel Without a Cause* replaced by uniformed convent girls scurrying down polished oak hallways, stopping to curtsy to Blessed Mother as they rounded the bend to their classes.

Rich Catholic families from Mexico, Puerto Rico and British Guyana, as well as Louisiana, sent their daughters to Grand Coteau, and after Fidel Castro's Revolution, gorgeous girls from elite Cuban families flocked to the school. The only *Donaldsonville* girls who went to boarding school were from the town's elite, not from families like ours.

My parents were way out of their economic league, but they would have done anything to save Ann—from what, I was not really sure. Now I understand how worried Daddy had been that his daughter was turning bad, that she might follow the path of the morally loose, as evidenced by her interest in boys, cars, lipstick, and "gangs." While Daddy worried about Ann's soul, Mother worried about her mind. Ann was still a good reader, but she only read fiction. All the other subjects—math, science, history—were as irrelevant to Ann as the square root of the hypotenuse of a fig tree.

It was easier for me to understand Daddy's concern than Mother's. Ann seemed so much like the teenage version of my mother. I had eavesdropped on many of her conversations with Miss Connie in the kitchen while they sat sipping their Community Dark Roast. Mother had been as bored by math and science as Ann. She laughed telling Connie how she'd slept through chemistry class junior year and had passed only because a humane and very

Jane Goette

understanding teacher had taken pity on her—"Canni, chemistry's just not your thing. There would be no point in failing you." My sisters and I grew up knowing that math and science were simply not cool. Our mother had no use for them.

Given Ann's similarity, I wondered why her academic indifference so alarmed my mother. I guess she was afraid Ann would end up like her— stuck with four children in a little town where nothing much ever happened. The Great Depression had cast a long shadow over my mother's life. She didn't want us to ever experience the economic insecurity that plagued her early years. She didn't want us to be stuck in poverty, as her mother had been, or stuck in Donaldsonville, like her.

My mother's home circumstances precluded a college education, but because she got a job with a newspaper right out of high school, she knew it was possible for a girl to have a career without going to college. The issue of "security" played a prominent role in both my parents' thinking about college ... but for very different reasons. In this area, my father was the progressive and my mother old fashioned. My mother's opinions about her daughters' futures seemed to belong in the pages of *Pride and Prejudice*, certainly not in the mid-twentieth century.

The main reason my strong, independent, working mother wanted us to go to college was so we'd find smart, progressive men to marry. In her view, the key to an interesting life was finding a husband who would provide it. An interesting life meant getting out of racist, parochial, Louisiana; seeing other parts of the country and the world; being part of an intellectual community rather than one like Donaldsonville where ties were based on blood rather than ideas. Her assumption that we had to get married to go places now seems as absurd and outdated as it was incongruous with her own reality. It wasn't Daddy who took her to Dallas and New York, but her job. It wasn't Daddy who commanded the greatest respect in a room full of educated people discussing politics or literature, but my mother.

Daddy, on the other hand, thought of college education as insurance, the antidote to hardship. One of the reasons my father could never save any money was as soon as he had a little extra cash, a life insurance salesman would come by and Daddy would buy another policy. It was as if buying life insurance could inoculate his family against disaster. Daddy was not about to put his faith in the men we might marry. Whether they were "smart and progressive" or dumb as mules, he knew a woman couldn't count on a man. Men could go crazy and leave a wife for some floozy or gamble away all the family's money, or just up and die leaving a wife and kids stranded. The best insurance against that kind of misfortune was a college education, and he meant for his girls to have it.

Aside from the security issues, my parents both believed in the enlightenment potential of a good education. Learning was a far more relevant yardstick by which they measured a person's worth than the amount of money they possessed, so a college education was the one luxury they deeply admired.

Even though Mother's formal schooling had ended with high school, she was an intellectual by just about anyone's standards. When Ann was a baby, Daddy worked full time during the day and took night classes at LSU to earn a master's degree in history. Mother, who had never set foot in a college classroom in her life, wrote my father's master's thesis. She was a voracious reader and a knowledgeable, talented writer her entire adult life.

My parents truly believed that most of the world's ills sprang from ignorance. The most treasured items in our home were always its books and magazines. Mother and Daddy were united in their desire to see Ann go on to college, even if their reasons were somewhat different. Although they disagreed about the seriousness of Ann's social behavior, they were equally alarmed by her grades. In view of all this, I guess it was not surprising my parents would send Ann to a boarding school we couldn't afford.

While my parents worried about finances, my sisters and I were excited that our big sister was going to Grand Coteau, a prestigious school with girls from foreign countries as well as other parts of Louisiana. We were happy to be the little mice cheering her on as she headed toward a more glamorous life. She would come home and tell us all about it. I was hungry for every detail. I felt nothing but excited until the day Ann actually left.

All summer long the family focus had been getting Ann ready for boarding school—buying the uniforms, checking the list of supplies she needed, wondering about her roommates, imagining the interesting people she would meet. Not until I saw the suitcases heading to the front door did it suddenly hit me—my sister was leaving home, and she would never live with us again. The first bird was flying away; the nest would be irrevocably altered. The word "forever" had a forlorn sound.

I sat on the front steps watching the car back onto the River Road and head north carrying my sister toward her future. It would be my future, too. This home, this nest, was going to empty. It would be my turn next. I wasn't ready. I wasn't even ready to sleep alone for the first time in my life, as I did that night. Ann and I had fought for years, staking opposing claims to territory on this thin, lumpy mattress. Now that I had it all to myself, it felt too big, and the distance from the den to the other side of the house seemed a continent away.

In the days and weeks and months that followed, while I lay awake worrying about every sound in the night, my parents worried about how they would pay for Grand Coteau. Pink overdraft slips from the bank appeared more regularly in the little glass window of P.O. Box 203. Daddy tried to hide them from Mother, but when two or more were ignored, even Dolphie's friendship didn't stop a phone call from the First National. Each time this happened, Mother fell apart—flashbacks to her Depression childhood in Pewaukee, eviction notices, gray potatoes for dinner. We were going to "The Poor House"!

"Don't worry, Candy," Daddy would say more from optimism than knowledge, "it'll all work out." On the rare occasions that Mother cried, Daddy would leave the house and return later hoping her sadness had run its course. Kay Kay, Gretchen, and I worried about our parents getting a divorce far more than we did about going to the Poor House. When the atmosphere of our home sizzled with tension, tears, and conflict, my sisters and I shuffled through the house like nervous little ghosts. We kept our heads low, eavesdropped a lot, and worried. No one had to tell us not to ask for "things." Besides, there was nothing we wanted more than peace at home.

On the rare weekends that Ann came home, often accompanied by a Grand Coteau friend, the atmosphere lightened. In the mornings, Daddy served Ann and her friend Bloody Mary's in bed. Mother served coffee and pie in the living room in the afternoon when Connie came over to see Ann and meet each new friend she brought home. Ann seemed one of them, now—the grown-ups in the living room.

Jeannette pulled out all the stops for those dinners, insisting we sit in the dining room before she made a grand entrance carrying our Thanksgiving platter loaded with dark-brown, glistening, pieces of roasted chicken, each piece cut just as she had directed of her favorite butcher, Mr. Acosta. For special occasions and to impress Goette guests, Jeannette also took pride in presenting the dishes with artistic flair. Parsley springs, chopped scallions, and sautéed mushrooms were her garnishes. Around the chicken, Jeannette placed individual molds of rice she had formed by pressing rice into coffee cups to create a more elegant presentation. There were more mushrooms in the gravy and more laughter at the table on those nights. Everything was better on the weekends Ann came home, except for one.

By the spring of 1963, the days of paying Grand Coteau tuition were drawing to a close. In a few months, the first Goette daughter would be graduating from high school. When my parents received a letter from Ann that she was coming home the following weekend, in anticipation of that visit, Daddy ordered a sack of crawfish and picked them up early Friday afternoon. Jeannette spent the rest of the day making crawfish bisque, the most labor-intensive, heavenly dish in all the world, and nobody made it better than Jeannette Jefferson. Mother had baked a chocolate cream pie topped with whipped cream and shaved, dark chocolate swirls. Each time I opened the refrigerator that afternoon, I sneaked another peek at the pie. I'd been thinking about it all day.

***

The reason for Ann's visit home that weekend was not for the food and family but to tell her parents that in the fall she wanted to go to a small, private Sacred Heart College right outside of Chicago.

In the early 1960's, at least in my community, those who went beyond high school to college were the exceptions, and of those, most were boys. Ann had never expressed any interest in going to college, and despite doing well in English and Art at Grand Coteau, the rest of her grades would not have qualified her for college.

It was during the before-dinner socializing that spring visit that Ann sprang her news. My parents were caught off-guard, stunned, and speechless. Before they could recover, my sister began her lobbying campaign. "Father Coyle says Barat is the perfect college for me. The head person at Barat is a good friend of Mother Mohoneke's. Mother-M has already written to her; she's sure she can get me in despite my grades."

Mother and Daddy listened, not surprised that their charismatic daughter had become a star at Grand Coteau but impressed that the school's most powerful leaders were aligned and lobbying for her to get into Barat. Mother Mohoneke had been a great influence on Ann and thought well enough of her talent to enter Ann's poem in a contest, which she won. Father Coyle, the Rector at Grand Coteau, had a special place in his heart for my sister. His stature and status at Grand Coteau meant a lot.

"But Ann," my mother said, "Barat tuition and board will cost much more than Grand Coteau; I just don't know how we could manage this, and…"

"I'll apply for a scholarship! Mother Mohoneke will write a letter about that, too, and I can get letters from other teachers. They really love me; they really want me to go!" My parents exchanged worried glances. "Mother Mohoneke thinks I can get reduced tuition, some kind of work-study. They really want me!"

"Sweetheart," Daddy began, cocking his head and looking at Ann with a half-smile and sympathy in his eyes, "I know how much you want this. Your mother and I are so proud of you, but…" Ann began to cry, and Daddy couldn't finish his sentence.

"Ann, there's more to it than just the tuition," Mother said, "Lake Forest is outside Chicago. That's a long way from home;

train fares are expensive. You would need new uniforms and a whole new wardrobe for that climate, and..."

"I thought you'd be so happy," Ann said in a choked voice as she turned and ran to the bathroom to cry.

I don't remember the details, but it came to pass that my sister started her freshman year at Barat College in the fall of 1963 as I began my junior year at Donaldsonville High School.

Students at Grand Coteau

Jane Goette

1963, A Tragic Year

Our family's financial problems continued, but Gretchen, Kay Kay and I were used to that. The Civil Rights movement dominated the news; support for its cause grew daily and increased momentum. Change was in the air. College kids participated in freedom rides and sit-ins at "whites only" lunch counters. Young people were joining the Peace Corps and Berkeley's free speech movement was in gestation.

It seemed a time of great promise, the best time in the world to be young. A clock that had stood still for a hundred years was beginning to tick, its dusty hands, moving forward at last. Everything was going to change, and I couldn't wait to be part of it.

Life in Donaldsonville seemed no life at all. Every exciting thing in the world was taking place far from my home. I wanted "out" in the most excruciating way. Would the world wait for me? Would the Civil Rights movement end before I was old enough to join it? I was restless, tired of waiting for my life to start.

Perhaps my restlessness was the reason my financially strapped parents bought me a train ticket from New Orleans to Chicago that November, 1963. I'm not sure whose idea it was for me to visit Ann at Barat over Thanksgiving break—perhaps I'd nagged my parents; perhaps Ann had really wanted me to come—whatever the reason, I was ecstatic.

My best friend was going with me. Genie and I could think of nothing else all fall. We felt excited just to be leaving Donaldsonville, but we were going to travel alone on a train all the way from New Orleans to one of the country's most famous cities. Carl Sandburg had written a poem about "Chicago," a poem we read in our junior English textbook. Genie and I were heading to the glamorous North, to one of the biggest, most exciting cities in the country to stay in a college dormitory with my cool big sister.

Since it was late November, we might even get to see snow. The mature part of us thought about handsome, smart boys with Beatle haircuts, northern accents and snow in their hair; the little girls in us longed to roll in the snow, build snowmen and have snowball fights.

The morning of November 22, I stood on the porch with my mother watching for Rose Folse's blue and white Buick station wagon to pass the Jambois house and pull into our driveway. Mother had to go to work, so Genie's mother was taking us to the train. Daddy, Kay Kay, and Gretchen had already left for a school day Genie and I got to miss. It felt intimate, being alone with my mother, the suitcase between us on the porch. She had helped me choose exactly what to take. This attention from her was new and wonderful.

This was the first trip of my life where it seemed to matter what was in my suitcase. I wanted to look cool, not like a kid and certainly not like a hick. Genie and I wanted to be stylish, like the girls in Seventeen Magazine; we wanted those Yankees to think we were college girls. My sister had also hinted that she might be able to find dates for us. What stories we'd have to tell when we returned from "up North"! I knew this would be a time I would never forget. I shivered with pride and joy and gratitude standing on the porch with my mother that November morning, waiting.

I suppose all of us who were six years old or older at that time remember today where we were when we heard the news from Dallas on November 22, 1963. I was on a train with my friend Genie speeding through the dead cotton fields of Mississippi. The night before, I'd lain awake for hours, too excited to sleep, my head filled with images and stories of what I thought awaited me in Chicago. Even now, I remember those imaginary images and vignettes because they were the best part of the trip. Where do memories go that never happened? I have so many.

I leaned my head against the cool, foggy train window, closed my eyes and pictured the station in Chicago, steam rising from the tracks, and through the mist, Ann standing on her toes in the crowd, waving. Mississippi was such a long state. Would we ever reach Chicago? The hum of the train lulled me to sleep—the rhythmic chug of metal wheels on the tracks comingled with the muffled swirl of voices in the aisle, gently rocking me to sleep.

Snow swirled around me as if I were inside a glass paperweight village, a boy with curly hair and a red muffler around his neck, coming toward me, smiling. I was smiling, too, waiting for him to reach …

Suddenly, I was awake, my heart racing wildly. Before I knew, before I actually heard the words, something struck me, rattled my sleeping brain. Like electricity, it screamed through my bones, and I knew something terrible had happened. I heard male voices in the aisle, two conductors, their Mississippi drawl, slow-as-molasses. From the amorphous pool of thick, slow sound, words coalesced:

"Well, I'm just glad they shot the sonfabitch in Texas insteada Miss'ssippi."

The other conductor laughed, "Now ain't that the damned truth! You know the Feds'd be all over this state if they'd a kilt him here."

I sat bolt upright. "Is he dead? Is he dead?" I blurted, startling the two conductors. They exchanged looks, as if I were a crazy person, then one of them said, "Yeah, they come on the radio a few minutes ago saying that hospital in Dallas just declared Kennedy dead."

I glared at him with hate-filled eyes. The conductors looked uncomfortable and moved down the aisle to continue their conversation. Moments later, I heard them laughing. These two grown-up men were actually laughing! Our President's assassination seemed no more significant to them than if a stranger's dog had been hit by a car.

Oh, my God, Kennedy was dead! They shot our beautiful, smart, young president. We would never have another like him. At the same moment I learned the news, back in Donaldsonville, my father had just switched off the intercom after announcing the news to the whole school. Later his secretary told me, "Your daddy switched off the microphone, went into his office, and closed the door." Miss Pardo worried about Daddy. The long mourning had begun.

I can't remember a time in my life when I needed to be with my family more than on November 22, 1963. Instead, I was trapped on a hostile train traveling through the "gret stet of Miss'ssippi," toward some imaginary happiness that would never materialize. Would anything wonderful ever happen in this hateful, cruel world?

I was heartsick and scared. Though Genie was sitting beside me, I was alone in my grief. All the snow in all the world wasn't enough to cover the blackness that engulfed me. There had been a death in the family; I needed to be home.

enette. I hated

being away from home around happy people. I resented my
teachers and friends for not caring as much as I did. It was as if we
lived on two entirely different planets.

Pouring salt on our collective wound, Daddy bought every new
book that was published on Kennedy—his family, his
administration, his thousand days, his assassination. The hundreds
of photographs in all the books and magazines in our home—Jack
and Jackie standing next to Charles DeGaulle at some glittering
Paris affair, little John John playing under his father's desk, the
Kennedy clan scattered across the lawn at Hyannis Port, a football
sailing through the air—all these happy, hopeful images of our lost
Camelot.

After the Kennedy assassination, it seemed nothing could lift
my spirits, not even Jeannette's jambalaya or Mother's homemade
fudge—nothing, that is, until the Beatles came to America.

John, Paul, George, and Ringo arrived just in time to rescue my
junior year in high school and propel me out into the irrepressibly
hopeful world of teenagers—boys, cars, smooching, rock music,
sweaty dancing. I was mildly aware of this British phenomenon,
"The Beatles," but when I saw footage of girls screaming, crying,
and pulling their teased hair, the whole scene seemed ridiculous
and immature. These mobbed concerts were retrograde, more like
the Elvis Presley era than my own. My heart was singing a dirge
while those boys shook their mop heads belting out silly words like,
"Yeah, yeah, yeah." How could I respond to something so light-
hearted and simplistic as, "with a love like that, you know you
should be glad!"

"Glad?" This word had no place in my vocabulary; it was a
foreign emotion. For weeks, the newspapers were full of stories

- 257 -

about The Beatles and their upcoming appearance on the Ed Sullivan Show. These boys didn't look like any I'd ever seen before, with their strange, longish haircuts and collarless suits. They were really cute, but there was something else. It was obvious John, Paul, George, and Ringo were having fun. They seemed smart and edgy—not afraid to look the camera smack in the eye. It was as though they knew something we didn't know yet, something fun and wonderful and they were going to let us in on it. They were speaking to us, kids like me. This was going to be our time, and it was going to be the best!

That February of 1964, everybody talked about the Beatles and asked, "You gonna watch Ed Sullivan?!" Cynical and dejected as I may have been, I wasn't about to miss the show. That Sunday night, Kay Kay, Gretchen, and I crowded together on the couch waiting to see what the hullabaloo was all about. Mother and Daddy peeked through the doorway of the kitchen. Ed Sullivan came out on stage amidst anticipatory roars from the teens in the audience. They were waiting for the "Fab Four"; I was waiting for a miracle. That night, we all got what we came for.

Ed waved his hand, and the Beatles appeared. *One, two, three,* their guitars strummed, heads bobbed, and "I felt hap-py inside," really happy for the first time in months. Maybe that's why America fell head over heels instantly; we needed to love those boys; we needed to twist and shout and scream "yeah, yeah, yeah!"

I loved the Beatles the moment I saw them. Suddenly, I wanted to go ridin' up and down Railroad Avenue with my friends, listen to the radio, look for cute boys who might or might not wave at us. I wanted to smoke cigarettes, drive fast, make out behind the Chance, turn the radio up loud, dissect the lyrics of every song, and sit up all night talking with Genie, Janelle, Kat, and Mary Lou.

My weekends were no longer spent poring over Time/Life books about the Kennedys. I started traveling down muddy country roads, through sugarcane fields and down the bayous to dance at

Cajun honky-tonks. Some of the little clubs on these Louisiana back roads played music that would later make Motown seem tame. The most notorious were the Gear Room and the Bon Chance. I couldn't wait to go. From the outside, Bon Chance appeared to be a large wooden shack surrounded by Cypress trees. It reminded me of the Rainbow Inn at Pierre Part where Daddy took us to eat crawfish bisque once a year.

One Friday night in early spring, Genie picked me up in her mama's car to go riding up and down the Avenue with a carful of friends. We knew a few of the boys in our class had started going to the Bon Chance. Back at school on Monday, they told us big stories. We didn't have any. We felt left behind, little goldfish swimming back and forth in the same old bowl. Meanwhile, the boys had found a channel to the sea.

One Friday night after a couple of loops down the Avenue and behind the Chance, Genie said, "Y'all wanna go find the Bon Chance?" I loved the thrill and adventure of traveling those unknown roads. From Sid Marchand, Genie had a vague idea of where this little Cajun club might be. We would find it even if we got lost in the process. With each mile, houses grew sparser along Bayou Lafourche Road; the darkness grew deeper. Trees draped in Spanish Moss leaned toward the car as if reaching for us.

When Genie turned onto another, less familiar road, I feared we were lost forever deep in Cajun country. The car's headlights transformed trees to inky shadows, alive and quietly threatening. I was about to suggest we head back as we rounded a curve to see a line of cars turning into an oyster shell parking lot lit by multi-colored lights, and behind them, a flashy 4-leaf clover sign above the entrance to "Bon Chance."

With pacing pulses, we parked, already feeling the bass in our chests. Music, laughing, the wail of a woman's voice streamed through the cracks of the backwoods nightclub. The warm night air carried the scent of oysters, beer, aftershave lotion, perfume, and sex. Though I'd been to Ralph Falsetto's Club in Donaldsonville, this place felt dangerous in the best sense of that word. My friends and I crunched through the gravel in our pointy-toed pumps and headed to the weathered steps of Le Bon Chance.

Jane Goette

The world that existed on the other side of that door was as unfamiliar as Dorothy's OZ or Lucy's wardrobe. A fog of smoke hovered above a long, bar where men, *only* men, leaned as comfortably as I would at a kitchen table, as if they were at home. Beer glasses, shot glasses, ashtrays brimming with cigarettes, and sea of elbows and shoulders crowded the bartop. Heads turned as we approached the far end where an archway led to a dance floor surrounded by tables. We searched for an empty one.

I don't remember many details from those Bon Chance evenings except waiting for the fast songs. I didn't like the entrapment of slow dancing, a stranger's arms wrapping around my body so close I could barely breathe, imprisoned in a cloud of after-shave, sweat and breath soured by alcohol. Sometimes a complete stranger would press his pelvis so close to mine I'd feel the hard knot inside his jeans, like a dirty little secret he whispered in my ear when no one else was listening. When the song ended, I'd pull away, relieved to feel the slight tug of my clean hair as it became unglued from his cheek. I resented the sense of entitlement some men assumed the moment they entered a bar. The deck seemed stacked in their favor. They chose the partners, they did the leading, and if a man's hands strayed from your back to your butt, if his fingers slid under your arm to the soft outer part of your breast—well, you were lucky to be on the dance floor rather than standing alone feeling unwanted. I longed to be wanted but not like that, not as a thing to press against in the dark.

It wasn't slow songs with strangers that drew me to a honkytonk like the Bon Chance. I learned to light a cigarette just as a slow song began to buy time 'til it ended. I waited for rock songs so the *real* dancing could begin. I loved being an equal partner—I shake my hips, you shake yours—no one really leading. You could feel the energy when the band banged out a Beatles or Stones song. We crowded onto the dance floor, wagged our heads, bent our knees, stuck out our butts, snapped our fingers and let it rip. These were the moments that sent an explosive sense of power and joy coursing through my body.

White kids called it the "Nigger Twist." I called it "fast dancin'." I was having fun, feeling alive, looking forward to things.

I was a month shy of sixteen when JFK died, but I'd felt like my life was over. Silly as it seems, the Beatles brought me back to life. They made me want to be in love and dance and scream and celebrate. They made me believe I was beginning the happiest days of my life.

Jane in plaid on right with high school friends:
Gene, Mary Lou, Judy, and Kat in curlers.

Jane Goette

The Happiest Days of Your Life

I don't know how the rumor got started, but word had it that high school years were the happiest of your life. The older people who perpetuated this myth did so with gusto and authority. "They'll be the happiest days of your life!" they'd say, nodding their heads and smiling brightly. When I was younger I believed what older people told me. I was hungry for some kind of compass on life, and they seemed so certain about things. They were far more experienced with life than I, and besides, what reason could they possibly have for lying?

Whenever I pressed for more details about the high school years and why exactly they were so happy, the responses were more vague than authoritative: "Well, you're so carefree. You don't have kids or housework, no job, no bills."

True, I'd think, but we do have school all day long and homework and tests and grown-ups bossing us around. Whenever I thought I had them cornered with the logic of my argument, they'd come back with the zinger, "But, Honey...you get to start dating!"

I didn't have very many dates in high school. By dating age, I had acquired a reputation for being a "nice" girl, the kind who doesn't like to hurt anyone's feelings. Consequently, the only boys interested in me seemed to be the ones who couldn't get dates with anyone else. I became a magnet for rejects. The boys tended to be chubby, nerdy or unbearably obnoxious. When they called, I'd gesture frantically to my mother to get me off the hook—tell them I'm not home, had a terrible accident, was too busy doing homework—I had no pride, any excuse would do; it didn't have to be creative. My mother seemed to derive sadistic pleasure from handing me the receiver. Why couldn't she have been like those mothers on '50's TV shows, the kind who were always on the kid's side, who'd sit on the daughter's bed listening to her problems and standing up for her in times of trouble.

My first official date was with a nice Italian boy who loved his mama. Let's call him Benny Lonadonna, though that wasn't his real name. When Benny called to ask me to go to a dance, it sounded like the real thing—at last, my first date! I didn't know Benny very well since he went to Catholic High and I, DHS, but from a distance he seemed sort of cute and rather non-threatening. Proudly, I strolled into the kitchen to tell my family there was a boy on the phone asking me for a date.

"Who is it?" my mother asked.

"Benny Lonadonna."

"Isn't he that boy who walks down the street holding his mother's hand?"

My mother looked more amused than impressed by this sudden turn in my social fortunes. Okay, he wasn't Troy Donohue, but why did my mother have to tell me he held his mother's hand?

"Where is he taking you?" she asked.

"To a dance in Plaquemine," a little town up the road from ours.

"I'll bet his mother's going with you," my mother said with an irritating smile.

The night of my big date, at the appointed hour a car pulled into our driveway and honked the horn. This threw me into a panic, for I knew it was considered the height of bad manners for a guy to sit in a car honking for his date to come out. What was I to do? Pretend I hadn't heard the horn and force Benny to do the right thing? I ran into the kitchen where my parents were enjoying their after-dinner coffee and cigarettes.

"Oh, God, he's tooting!" I cried, at which point my parents burst out laughing.

They took wicked pleasure in repeating that line for years after. Had my death preceded theirs I'm sure they'd have had those words inscribed on my tombstone: "My God, he's tooting!"

Benny finally came to the door obviously puzzled that I had not heard the car horn. There stood a boy with black hair styled in a Frank Sinatra sort of coif, wearing a blue blazer, khaki pants and penny loafers. At least he *looked* like a boy going on a date. His parents were in the front seat of the car, and after Benny and I climbed into the back, his mother turned around and snapped our picture with her Kodak Brownie.

"Jane, how ya'momma and daddy doin'?" Mr. Lonadonna asked.

"They're just fine, Mr. Lonadonna."

During the ride to Plaquemine, Mr. Lonadonna never said another word; he was chauffeur and I was straight man for the comedy team of Lonadonna and Lonadonna. The whole way to Plaquemine I was entertained by their act. Benny's mother would feed him a line to which Benny would respond with some joke. While I can't remember a thing Benny said, I do remember his mother responding with robust laughter to almost every line he uttered.

"Benny could be on TV. Don't you think, Jane?"

"Yes, Mrs. Lonadonna."

By the time we reached Plaquemine, the muscles in my face were so sore from fake smiling I had to go into the ladies' room and frown into the mirror for several minutes to ease the ache. When I emerged, I found Mrs. Lonadonna happily engaged in conversation with other nice Italian ladies. At the center of their circle stood my date, Benny, smiling proudly and turning around so all the ladies could see his neat duds. Mrs. Lonadonna was laughing and smacking Lonny on the back; the other ladies seemed to mirror my own face with its hearty fake smile. As I approached, Mrs. Lonadonna reached for my hand and pulled me into the circle.

"This is Jane Goette, Benny's little girlfriend. Y'all know her mama and daddy-- her mama works for *The Donaldsonville Chief* and her daddy, Mr. Goette, he's the principal of D.H.S.?"

The ladies all shook their heads and studied me in light of this fascinating information. I felt transformed. I was no longer a teenage girl but some sort of trophy for Benny. Was he collecting them? Who would be next—the daughter of the butcher? The baker? The candlestick maker? Was this why boys asked girls on dates, to build a collection they could show off like charms on a bracelet? And what kind of charm did I make? Would I be a little gold one with a typewriter or perhaps, a little silver schoolhouse? What did any of this have to do with me? I'm not my parents!

The band began to play *In the Still of the Night*. Mrs. Lonadonna pushed Benny and me toward the dance floor. "You kids go dance," she said, as she winked at her friends. We did dance—twice that night, thank God. At least I'd have something to report from my evening that might sound a little like a normal date. This was the first of many that required embellishment in order to avoid humiliation at home. Dates were supposed to be fun. I hated them.

I cannot recall high school dating without an immediate association with two dreadful smells—Juicy Fruit gum and Old Spice after-shave. Market studies from the sixties would surely show the primary consumers of these products were adolescent boys. *All* adolescents worried about breath. You never knew when the big moment might come, the one which would turn high school into "the happiest days of your life," that enchanted evening when "you may see a stranger, across a crowded room." I prepared by brushing my teeth six times a day, twenty minutes each time just to make sure I hadn't skipped a spot. Thank God flossing hadn't been invented yet; I might have had to drop out of school to stay home and take care of my teeth. Since my twenties, dentists have been fussing at me for brushing my teeth too hard and wearing down the enamel. "Enough already!" I want to say, "it all happened before I was twenty."

Another adolescent phobia was body odor. Deodorant could only do so much. How long was it expected to protect a teenager, twisting the night away at the St. Joseph's Hall on an August night in Donaldsonville, Louisiana?

Part of my ritual for a night out was to suffocate my body with after-bath talcum powder. I put so much on the bottoms of my feet it frequently turned to a sticky paste by the time my evening was over. A few girls wore a popular perfume called *Evening in Paris*; you could buy it at the dime store, and it came in a pretty blue bottle shaped like the Eiffel Tower. But aftershave use among boys was universal. Almost every boy I ever went out with wore *Old Spice* and too much of it. Toward the end of high school, the coolest boys (I'd hear from my friends who dated them) had moved on to stuff like *Jade East*.

The hot spot for us teenagers was The Chance—I had no idea where black teenagers hung out. The Chance was located at the dead end of Railroad Avenue across from the train depot. This restaurant and bar was named The First and Last Chance, because it was your first or last chance to get a drink upon arriving or departing our town by train. It had a drive-through, big parking lot out back, with oyster shells for gravel; it was always a little fishy back there in more ways than one. A wooden fence bordered the Chance, fronted by a few sickly banana trees (banana weeds, we called them).

Teenagers parked in the banana weeds when they wanted to make out on their dates. The guy would make a complete loop through the lot first, just to make sure all his friends had seen him, then he'd double back and park at the back by the banana weeds, turn out his lights and honk his horn. A few minutes later, a tired looking black woman with swollen feet (lowest employee on the totem pole) would come out to take the order. It didn't matter how old you were; if you were there, you could drink alcohol. Sloe Gin Fizz was my drink of choice, while most of my dates drank Jax Beer, Dixie or bourbon and coke. I saw kids as young as twelve years old sitting in cars "back 'da Chance" drinking mixed drinks and smoking cigarettes.

Whenever your date pulled into the Chance, you knew what he had on his mind.

My dates, the ones who were challenged in the "cool" department, would cruise up and down the avenue, trying to work up the nerve. Each time we approached the end of Railroad Avenue, I revved up the conversation, throwing out some topic designed to break his concentration, destroy whatever game plan he'd devised for easing that car into the Chance parking lot with me at his side. My avoidance strategies backfired on me one time.

I had accepted a date with another Catholic High boy (because I didn't know how to turn him down) and this date made me nostalgic for my evening with the Lonadonnas. Steve was so inarticulate, he made Benny seem like Shakespeare or Johnny Carson, at least. I couldn't get a conversation going no matter how hard I tried. I knew better than to ask about what books he'd read or what he thought about integration, but this boy didn't even respond to my hottest topics, cool stuff like UFO's and "What do you think is in that secret letter from the Pope?" I even stooped so low as to ask him how he thought the L.S.U. Tigers would do this year. The sum total of the words Steve spoke that night were: "Yeah," "No,"

"Hunh?" "Hey, man, where y'at!" "Good" "Ya wanna beeah?" (He was too cheap to even offer me a Sloe Gin Fizz!)

We drove up and down Railroad Avenue about fifty times. I'd see him eyeing the Chance driveway each time we got to that end of Railroad Avenue, but he was at least smart enough to know he didn't have a prayer of parking with me. Each time we got to the other end of the avenue and looped around the corner of Lessard St., I desperately studied the big clock on the First National Bank, hoping it was almost time for me to be able to go home. Steve seemed happy enough, honking his horn each time he passed one of his friends and shouting out the window, "Hey man, where y'at!" He never looked at me or made the slightest attempt to respond to my frantic efforts at conversation. I could have been one of those big "Patty Play Pal" dolls and he'd have been happier, just as long as I wasn't the "Chatty Cathy" model I had come to resemble on this date.

Steve also seemed conscious of the time and aware that my get-away was imminent. He was certainly as eager for our date to be over as I was, but what cool deeds would he have to brag about? He reached for another Dixie (the six-pack was now down to three), honked at a passing friend and motioned the guy to pull up next to his car.

"Hey, man, ya wanna go draggin' on the White Castle highway?"

"Yeah, Man...cool!"

Holy shit, what could I do now?! If only he'd made one more loop up the avenue, I could have asked to go home. It would have been on the early side but not alarmingly so. Now I was trapped. His car headed past the Dairy Queen, around the bend, passed Jay's Drive-In, reached the intersection and hung a right. I wanted to shout, "NO!!!" but I didn't know how. Would he think I was square? Why should I care what this dumb jerk thought about me? Why couldn't I stop this?

Steve was a loser--a half-drunk, stupid, not very cute, adolescent boy who'd only been driving one year. If he didn't even have the decency to ask me if I wanted to go drag racing, why didn't I have the nerve to tell him "over my dead body!" I could picture my dead body, too, trapped in the twisted steel of a wrecked car, dead on the White Castle highway at sixteen. What a tragedy it would be. I hadn't had the happiest days of my life yet, not by a long shot, and now I never would. As we passed the Smoke Bend Church, I silently prayed: "Please, God, don't let me die! If you get me out of this one, I'll go to mass every first Friday for the next year; I'll put half my allowance in the collection each Sunday and if you really want me to, I'll …I'll become a nun!" (At least I wouldn't have to go on dates anymore.)

The White Castle was a two-lane, ten-mile highway between two small towns where most grown-ups went to bed by 9:00 if there was nothing good on T.V. The police were in their beds, too, or would be until someone called to tell them they'd better get out to the White Castle highway. Why couldn't they come now, before I died?!

The cars idled side by side for a few minutes while Steve and the other guy hung their heads out the window. Except for "hey man, where y'at?" and a fake laugh or two, they didn't have much to say to each other. They clunked beer cans, took last slugs, crushed the cans, and tossed them out the window. Steve revved his engine, and then we were off! My head jerked back. I clutched the arm of the door, shut my eyes, listened to the roar of engines and waited to die.

I could picture Sheriff Shaloo knocking on my parents' front door to break the bad news. My mother would be irritated that someone had the nerve to disturb her this late at night. Though roused from a sound sleep, her feet would hit the floor quickly and she'd make her way to the front door at a rapid clip, her footsteps echoing her irritation. Her curlers would bounce, dislodging a bobby pin or two. There would be a frown on her face as she pulled the door open, ready to confront…a daughter who'd forgotten we never locked our door? How surprised she would be to see the sad-faced sheriff standing in the shadows of our front porch. My father would notice the twirling red reflected on the bedroom wall from the police car's flashing lights. From the bedroom, he'd call out, "Candy, who is it?"

I was practically in tears anticipating the weeping and wailing my parents would emit upon Shaloo's report of my demise. My visions were interrupted. Suddenly, the drag race was over; the cars were side by side again and the boys were whooping and laughing, thoroughly satisfied with themselves and the cool adventure they'd just had. This was no drag race! They hadn't established rules; there wasn't even a finish line. They were just two teenagers driving fast for a few minutes on the White Castle highway, but... I had survived.

"I have to go home now," I said, startling Steve, who seemed to have forgotten I was there. He smiled all the way into town and out the other end, heading down the River Road to my house. I was smiling, too. The River Road was dark until we rounded the curve, and I could see the light shining on the front porch of my house, shining just for me. It was as beautiful to me as a lighthouse to a sailor on a stormy night.

Those dating years held countless anxieties, not the least of which was worrying about what my father might say to my date. My sister Kay Kay's first date was with a nice Italian boy, Kenny Matassa, and Daddy told Kay Kay not to worry.

"I'm just gonna ask the boy if it's true Italians eat spaghetti for breakfast." This was our father's idea of a joke, typical of his sense of humor. Our angst over the small talk he might choose to make with our dates just spurred him on.

One time Boozie Dugas asked me for a date. His family had lived downstairs from us briefly when we first moved to Donaldsonville. Boozie and I were three years old when we had been neighbors and had had little contact between then and high school. My early recollections of Boozie were two things—that he was the first child I'd ever seen wearing eyeglasses (his had little cowboy guns up at the top between the lenses and the stem; they were real cute) and he once hit Kay Kay on the head with a brick. Before I could begin to worry about what we might possibly have to talk about on our date, I had to worry about what my father would say to him.

"Daddy, promise me you won't say anything embarrassing," I pleaded.

"Jane, I'm just gonna set the boy at ease, remind him we're old neighbors from way back. 'Why, Boozie,' I'll say, 'I remember when you were runnin' around with shit in your diapers, boy!'"

I did have one wonderful time back 'da Chance with a Cajun boy named Leon LeSeur. His first name was pronounced "Lay-on," the "n" so soft you couldn't hear it. That boy was every bit as beautiful as his name. Leon had blond hair and blue eyes, which were unusual for a French boy. He was short and cute in a Paul Simon sort of way. Leon lived down the bayou in a smaller town than ours called Paincourtville (short bread town), though it didn't even have a bakery.

Leon and I had seen each other at a basketball game and exchanged eyes "across a crowded room." I asked around to find out his name and story. He apparently asked about me, too, and the next weekend I saw his car drive by my house while I was sitting on the front porch. I rushed to the phone to call my friends, and we spent the rest of the afternoon talking about that two-second event. After ten hours on the phone, intense data analysis and numerous consultations with various authorities, I cracked the case, concluding that Leon LeSeur must like me.

Our house was not on the main drag, being a little outside of town. The River Road was at the foot of the levee and followed the Mississippi River all the way to New Orleans. A person would have to have some reason for driving on it, especially a teenaged person who couldn't possibly be heading for New Orleans without his parents. Could it have been mere coincidence that one week after having eye contact with me across a high school gymnasium, he had gotten lost and wandered down the River Road by accident? Certainly not, your Honor! Leon LeSeur rode past my house seven times because...he liked me! Of course, he never stopped the car and didn't wave or anything, but still, I got a thrill each time I saw that car go by.

Every weekend Leon would drive to our town, then out the River Road past my house and back again. I began to wonder if we'd ever move on to the next step of the passionate love affair I was anticipating. Leon had more sex appeal than James Dean but about as much nerve as Barney Fife. Finally, his boyfriends and my girlfriends took the situation into their hands and arranged a meeting at the Chance. Lame excuses were devised to have us all shuffling between cars and before we could chicken out, Leon and I found ourselves side by side and alone in a car back 'da Chance. My usual verbal dexterity abandoned me. We sat there smiling at each other like idiots.

At last I was in the banana weeds with someone I wanted to kiss. I felt like Sandra Dee or Gidget, a teenage princess with bouffant hair and a perky personality. With some effort I could approximate the hair, but "perky" was not a word anyone would ever have used to describe me. I'd read too much Edgar Allan Poe and found English novels like Wuthering Heights more engrossing than any sports event. I had destroyed my personality long before I met Leon.

If only I could have another chance, turn the clock back—it would be different this time. I would go to football games and learn to really care about the team. I'd memorize all the words to Soldier Boy and sing it with pathos in my voice. I'd learn to twirl a baton and practice cheers in the backyard. I'd break the habit of speaking good grammar, and even if my mother grounded me, I'd never again say "To whom do you wish to speak?" when someone called our house and asked, "Who 'dis?" Why couldn't my mother have been a housewife and Girl Scout leader like Linda Bessonet's? Why'd she have to work for a newspaper, of all things? With other parents, I might have had a chance, might have been a contender!

I still smile remembering that night at the Chance. I don't recall a thing we said to each other, if anything. Looking at Leon just made me smile. I wanted to touch that boy's face, hold his hand, kiss him. He had shy eyes and the most endearing smile. I couldn't help smiling back. Without premeditation, slick moves, or reliance upon what we'd seen in the movies, our heads leaned forward, and we kissed.

We kept kissing until it was time to go home. The kisses were as natural and easy as the smiles. His lips were soft; his kisses, tender. The boy was sensual, a natural, not like other boys I'd kissed, who pressed so hard against my lips it hurt. Until Leon, the boys I'd kissed always seemed in such a hurry to get to the next step (probably so they could brag to their friends) they bungled the present moment. I hated when a boy tried to poke his tongue in my mouth before I'd even felt his lips.

There was something appealingly vulnerable about Leon, although I never got to know him well enough to find out who he was besides a fantastic kisser. It turned out he had a girlfriend back in Paincourtville, and after that night at the Chance, it was she I'd see cruising past my house on weekends.

My junior year in high school I had a terrific crush on a dark-haired, handsome boy who lived across the river and went to Catholic High in our town. I would see him at the Grand Theater on weekends, or at basketball games and other high school functions. I never saw him behaving like a jerk, like most of the boys at my school, and I knew the word "nigger" had never crossed his lips. As I studied him from afar, he grew in perfection. He was certainly a smart boy and kind, too. Perhaps he was a closet integrationist, just waiting to find a soul mate with whom he could share his frustrations at growing up in a racist community like ours. Perhaps he, too, had dreamed of running away to become a freedom rider when he was in middle school, had felt as sick as I had when Chaney, Schwerner and Goodman disappeared the previous summer in Mississippi.

All that spring, I dreamed about Ron Dupree. When I got home from school, I'd dump my books on the living room desk and head for the levee. I took long walks up there, staring out across the river, knowing my true love lived on the other side. I was so ready for love; it's all I thought about.

"Call him!" Genie said, one weekend I spent at her house. "It's your prom; you can do the asking. What have you got to lose?"

"Genie, I've never talked to him in my life— he'll think I'm crazy, or even worse, he won't even know who I am!"

"Of course, he knows who you are! Y'all are the only Goettes in Ascension Parish; everyone knows your mama and daddy."

"If he'd wanted to ask me out, he would have by now."

"How do you know he's not feeling the same way you are? He's probably just shy. He looks like the quiet type to me."

Al was a blank slate. Because I knew absolutely nothing about him, it was easy to imagine anything I wanted. In novels and the movies Genie and I loved, it was often true that two lovers quietly pined for each other long before something happened to bring them together. In fact, the greater their initial reluctance, the greater their love turned out to be.

"C'mon, Jane--no guts, no glory!"

When I returned from Genie's, I casually mentioned to my sister Kay Kay that I was thinking about asking Ron Dupree to my prom.

"Are you crazy?!! He doesn't even know who you are! You'll make a fool of yourself; I'll never be able to show my head in public again if you do this!"

"Genie thinks I should. He doesn't have a girlfriend or anything, so why wouldn't he want to go to my prom?"

"Jane, you're not in the same league. Ron Dupree is somebody; he's popular. You can't just ask him out!"

"Oh, yeah, just watch me," I said, faking the nerve I lacked in real life.

"You'll be sorrrrry," she sang in an irritatingly confident voice.

After several more pep talks from Genie, I finally worked up the nerve to call Ron Dupree. He said "yes," and sounded nice on the phone. I couldn't wait to tell Kay Kay and gloat about my triumph. "Maybe I'm not a nobody, after all," I thought, closing my eyes and seeing myself walk into green sugarcane fields with my new love. Suddenly, Ron was Warren Beatty, and I, Natalie Wood in *Splendor in the Grass*, the sexiest depiction of teen romance I'd ever seen. I was so happy. At last my true life was about to begin. I would have my "hour of splendor in the grass, glory in the flower."

The following week, my mother helped me pick out a cute pattern for a prom dress. I would look my best that night, wash my hair in beer the night before to give it extra body and brush it two hundred strokes. I would have to sneak a bottle of Jax because my father thought it a sin to pour a good beer over your hair. Of all the things his teenage daughters did in that time period, this act was the single most disturbing one to my father.

I realized my date with Ron was going to be my big chance to change my life. I thought of all the topics I would bring up for discussion so that we could get past the superficialities and on to deeper stuff. I was sure that Ron was the kind of guy who wouldn't care that I still wore a triple-A bra; he'd be far more interested in my brains than my breasts. I had funny stories to tell him, too, about Donaldsonville characters and my sisters. We would talk about everything once we had a chance to fall in love.

Ron and I wouldn't do the usual things teenage couples did, like driving up and down Railroad Avenue and parking in the banana weeds. We would take walks on the levee and in the sugar fields, hold hands and ride the ferryboat back and forth across the river. We would both be interested in exotic places like China and India, Africa and the Mayan ruins in Mexico. Ron and I would go to all those places after we finished college. On summer nights, we'd find a private spot behind the levee and go for moonlight swims.

For weeks after I'd invited Ron, I waited for his call to inquire about the color of my dress so he would know what kind of corsage to bring me on prom night. This was common practice. As prom night drew closer and closer, I grew sick with worry. Mrs. Torres had already made my prom gown, an ankle-length green and white dotted-swiss dress with spaghetti straps. Mother had advised me to suggest to Ron that he bring a daisy corsage; it would look great on my dress. I liked the idea also because Ron would see I wasn't the kind of girl who tried to get a date to spend all his money. Daisies were a lot cheaper than the usual orchids. He'd see, …if only he'd call.

Three days before the prom, the phone rang. It was Ron. It was a short, awkward conversation. He had called simply to ask what kind of flowers I wanted. With a mixture of disappointment and relief I hung up the phone.

Unbeknownst to me, Ron had fallen in love with a girl from Paincourtville shortly after he'd accepted my prom invitation. I imagine he only went through with our date because his mother made him. From the moment we left my house, I sensed impending doom. His aloofness was more than simple shyness. All night his eyes avoided mine and searched the crowded room for someone else. The conversations, funny stories and creative questions I'd stored up for this boy settled in my stomach, heavy as river clay. Kay Kay had been right all along. I was nobody.

The night of my junior prom I was the first girl home. Later, my friends would tell me that Ron had returned to the Club after dropping me off, that he'd spent the rest of the night making out on the dance floor with a pretty girl from Paincourtville.

The morning after prom, my daisy corsage sat wilting on the kitchen counter. The beautiful dress Mrs. Torres and Mother had designed for me lay in a crumpled pile on my bedroom floor. My prom date had never even noticed my pretty dotted-swiss dress or my shiny, 200-stroked brown hair, my new shoes or my modest request for daisies.

One evening, a month or so later, I was moping around the living room when my mother suddenly put down her book. I assumed she was going to tell me I was "as irritating as a cat hanging on a screen door," her usual response to bored kids.

"You know, Jane, for some people high school years are the happiest days of their lives, but then it's all over. The glories of high school quickly fade in the world beyond graduation. You shouldn't begrudge them that. It may be all they'll have. I know it's hard for you to believe right now, but your best days are ahead of you."

Waiting to Start my Life

I had waited for that magic place called "college" for a long time, and I placed it in the North. Mother left the North as a young woman and got stuck in the South for the rest of her life. I was stuck in the South determined to end up in the North. I'd had enough southern education.

Like the black people in my hometown, my sisters and I grew up thinking of the North as the promised land—a place devoid of racism, bigotry and violence. We imagined Yankees to be smarter and more progressive; lovers of poetry, plays, and concerts; people who spoke correct English, and, well—just plain better than us southerners in all respects except storytelling and food.

In fifth grade it hadn't been enough to read about the explorers; I wanted to be one. My world was small then. Scooting under Miz Abadie's barbed-wire fence, crossing her field, and the next and the next, undaunted by irrigation ditches that ran between cow pastures and canefields. I wasn't reckless, I watched for water moccasins. Excitement outpaced fear each time I led my small band of explorers into the long green tunnels of sugarcane. Who knew what we might find on the other side?

By teen years, my band of fellow explorers had all fallen away, and I'd outgrown pretend play much as I had my town, much as I had size four shoes. The sense of being an outsider increased. I felt restless and sad. I wanted to learn new things, things beyond what my family could teach. I was hungry to find people my own age who cared about embarrassing stuff like justice and beauty, not the boxed-up kind imprisoned inside books, but the real thing. Much as I loved to read, even more, I wanted to *live*.

Until my senior year of high school I had assumed that when my turn came, I, too would go to school in the North, but my choice would be very different than Ann's. When Genie and I had visited Barat in November 1963, it had seemed quaint and lovely, set in a storybook town, but small and Catholic had never been what I wanted. For me, that magic place called "college" was the University of Wisconsin.

I had only seen the Madison campus once. Years before I reached college age, we had taken a side trip to see the university on our way to Twin Lakes. We all thought it beautiful. Bascom Hill seemed as high as a mountain to my Louisiana eyes, and as we drove up the steep road that skirted the hill, below us flickers of sunlight sparkled across the pristine waters of Lake Mendota. At the top of the hill, a sprinkle of students sat scattered across the grass, some with books in their hands, others bent over notebooks, writing. Most of the girls wore shorts and sandals, like my Aunt Marilyn.

The most dominant image at the top of the hill directly in front of Bascom Hall was the commanding statue of Abraham Lincoln seated in an imposing chair, much like the one at the Lincoln Memorial in Washington but smaller and less austere. Instead of cold marble, the setting for this monument was a lovely, grassy hill with a sparkling lake he could almost see.

I don't remember ever seeing a Lincoln statue anywhere in Louisiana, nor any other place I'd been in the South. Memorials to Confederate generals were abundant throughout the South. Robert E. Lee stood high on a pedestal at the very center of the historic circle that separated downtown and uptown New Orleans.

The lasting impression formed by this brief visit was of Abe Lincoln sitting atop this big, beautiful hill looking out at students sprinkled across the grass, as if this were his reward for saving the Union, to spend eternity looking out at American children as hungry to learn as he had been. If Abraham Lincoln had founded a university instead of saving a democracy, Wisconsin would have been the one. I fell in love with it the first time I saw Bascom Hill.

As I matured and heard stories about the free-thinking ways at Madison, my longing to go to UW grew. Uncle Glen told me about an informal debate that had taken place in the Rathskeller at the Madison student union. The debate was about nudity. Where I grew up, there was no debate, naked bodies were not to be seen, and if you thought about them too much, you probably better get to confession soon. Our local picture show followed the Catholic Church's ratings with the same attention I now give to the *New Yorker* or *Times* reviews.

"The body is beautiful," one student says, "why should it be covered up?"

"So, we should all run around naked?" another shouts in response.

Other students, male and female gather around the two, joining the debate. The nudity proponent counters, "Is that any more ridiculous than women wearing bras and girdles to hide their curves? Or men wearing neckties or bowties, those silly, uncomfortable things we all hate? Nudity frees us to be our truer selves."

I anticipated the side my Uncle Glen would support. He was an artist, an atheist, and a non-conformist in every category, so I was surprised by the end of his story:

A beautiful girl somewhere in the crowd suddenly rises from her chair and calls out to the avowed nudist, "Then stand on the table and take off your clothes!" The whole Rathskeller erupted into laughter.

If Uncle Glen's intention had been to shock me, it failed because the topic of the debate thrilled me less than the fact that students in Madison did that sort of thing, that they could have an intelligent debate while socializing over a couple of beers, argue in good spirit, and still be friends at the end. These boys were competing over ideas like Louisiana boys did sports and drinking. A girl had joined them, in fact, beat them at their game, and the others had applauded, rather than blackballing her.

The Rathskeller must be a marvelous place, and to have it inside the university's student union seemed unbelievable. Uncle Glen described it in such detail—its murals, fireplace, atmosphere, and voices—I could put myself inside the picture. I imagined the Rathskeller smelling of history, like Grandpa's attic, rather than cigarettes, warm beer, and vomit. Until the summer of 1964, I had assumed that if I got good grades, earned and saved money, this dream was not out of reach.

So many assumptions we make in life, in relationships, and especially in families, are wrong. Kay Kay, Gretchen, and I had been happy Ann would go to private boarding school at Grand Coteau. It wasn't for the social status but that Ann would meet smarter kids, have better teachers, and experience classes that didn't exist in Donaldsonville, like art and creative writing. Not until our own children were born did we younger sisters question the inequities in our family. Ann was the first born. Her education was Mother and Daddy's first investment in their children's futures.

My parents were never good with money.

After Ann graduated from Grand Coteau, she went to Barat College of the Sacred Heart in Lake Forest, Illinois. I don't remember the details surrounding that decision; I was at the age of being more interested in hanging out with my friends than around the house eavesdropping on my parents' conversations.

By spring of 1963, the year Ann graduated from Grand Coteau and I finished tenth grade, I'd lost my Catholic faith and wasn't even sure I believed in God anymore. Ann's Grand Coteau stories about racing past the statue of Mother Mater (Jesus' mother) and running back because she'd forgotten to genuflect seemed more stupid than charming. I loved my sister but didn't really know her.

Ann had never seemed to live in our world, even before she left for boarding school in tenth grade. I have a host of memories of playing with Kay Kay and Gretchen, none of Ann. We slept in the same pull-out bed every night, rode in the same car, ate meals around the same table, shared a family bathroom. It's not that I don't have memories of Ann, but that none of them are intimate.

She was the star of the family more than a participant in it. She wasn't the kind of sister you'd hang out with on the back steps shooting the breeze. You listened to her stories; she never asked about yours. I knew very little about my sister's internal life. I had inklings of the life she wanted to live, the people she wanted to be around, but nothing about what she wanted to do in the world. I loved and admired Ann but didn't really know her as I did Kay Kay and Gretchen.

As much as I'd always wanted to go to college, Barat would never have been my choice. It seemed the college equivalent of Grand Coteau in every respect: private, elite, expensive, Catholic, and all-girls. I was happy if it made Ann happy to go there.

It hadn't occurred to me that my sister's Barat experience would doom my Wisconsin dream, not until May, 1964. I was sitting in my chemistry class in the middle of an exam when I heard my name on the intercom: "Jane Goette, report to the office." The intercom seemed so loud when the only sound in the room had been pencils moving across paper. All heads popped up to look at me. Jane Goette wouldn't be in trouble. Had someone died? An accident? I looked at Mr. Falcon. He must have assumed this, too, for he never excused you from class, much less an exam, but he nodded and opened the door, patting me on the shoulder as I passed.

I bolted down the stairs, lifting my heels to lessen the sound, and shot down the hall to the office. When I opened the door, Daddy motioned to me from across the counter to come around to his office. Grim-faced, he closed the door behind me. The hum of the air-conditioner ensured our privacy. It was cold in his office, and I was scared. If Daddy had detected my shivering, he would have taken off his suit jacket and given it to me. He was that kind of man. I studied his face, dreading whatever he was about to tell me: something had happened to Ann; a car had hit my mother as she crossed the street to Connie's. Oh God, Mother was dead! Nothing could be worse than that.

The Bursar's office at Barat had just called my father. He still had not paid Ann's spring tuition, and now that the semester was about to end, the account had to be settled or Ann would not be permitted to take final exams. Ann would earn no credits for her entire 2nd semester. As with overdraft notices from Dolphie's bank, Daddy hid bad news from Mother. I don't know why he didn't have the money this time any more than I understand the others. Daddy kept secrets. Not out of malice but something else. Perhaps a stubborn refusal to disappoint or a failure of courage to say no. It doesn't matter to me, he is my father and a good man. That May day in 1964 he was in trouble, and though my sister didn't know it, Ann was in trouble, too.

We got in the car and drove to the Savings and Loan. Daddy stayed in the car while I went inside, withdrew my savings account and returned to the car, placing the envelope on the seat between us. I think it was enough to cover all of Ann's spring tuition. Neither of us looked at each other or spoke on the ride back to the high school. What was there to say that we didn't both understand? It was a secret I knew to keep, just as I knew how painful it was for my father to have to do this.

Spring slid into summer. Nothing much happened that hadn't happened before: Crawfish shells grew harder; mornings still began with the nutty scent of Community Dark Roast wafting in from the kitchen. In the afternoons, I would head to the Netters to babysit Patty. I'd spend the night with friends and they, with me. My sisters' friends, too, would come and go through the doors of our River Road house—all familiar and welcomed. On weekend nights, I might go dancing at Big Ralph's on Saturday nights with Chuck Savoie, my boyfriend at the time.

Summer mornings after breakfast, I headed to the town pool for daily practice with Mr. Boutte, who treated his fledging swim team the same as his seasoned footballers. It wasn't Mr. Boutte's boot camp ways or daily commands, "Hit the water, Goette!" that made me do it. The first time he'd yelled, "Goette, ten laps, and don't stop!" I'd thought it would kill me. I don't know why, but I pushed myself to do more laps than Mr. Boutte demanded. It was not to please; I was too angry for that. "Hit the water!" Mr. Boutte had said, neither of us knowing how much I needed to "hit" something. I swam in defiance, a quiet but fierce rebellion against something I couldn't name. If Mr. Boutte said, "Ten laps!" I swam fifteen, then twenty; every day, more. I became a machine, and it felt good. In a few weeks, Mr. Boutte and I had both stopped counting. I was a long-distance swimmer.

Ann did not come home when spring semester at Barat ended. She had already started a job at a swanky resort hotel on the shores of Lake Michigan, just outside Chicago. It would have been a dream job anyway, certainly more exciting than another summer in Twin Lakes, but once Ann learned that the Royal Shakespeare company from England would be staying at the Hotel Moran, she was desperate to work there. The company was preparing a production of Hamlet for the Chicago stage.

As far as the rest of my family, this is what I remember about the summer of 1964: We did not have a vacation; my parents spent a lot of time poring over their bank statements; Kay Kay's friends dumped her; Mother said a trip to visit Ann would cheer her up;

Jeannette seemed down in the dumps; we all missed Kennedy. While the rest of her family was in a slump, Ann was falling in serious love for the first time in her life.

Ian McCulloch was playing Laertes that summer he and Ann met at the Hotel Moran. He was ten years older than my sister; handsome, smart, professionally accomplished, and committed to a life in the arts. He was as enamored of Ann's youthful "American-ness" as she, of his artsy "British-ness." He and his friends in the company invited Ann to their rehearsals. She sat in on their conversations during and after rehearsal, as if she'd been one of them. She was happy and glowing, confident, charismatic, and those Brits loved "Annie's" stories. She and Ian spent all their free time together. It was love; it was the real thing. Just like our father, Ann never worried about practical stuff; she assumed things would work out, and they usually did. Ian epitomized the life Ann wanted. Ian and Annie were the star-crossed lovers whose story would have a happy ending. Ian would want her at his side from now on. He would ask Ann to go to London with him; she was sure of it.

At about the same time that Ian flew home to London to resume his life without Ann, my parents received news that was as stunning and devastating to them as Ian's abandonment was to Ann.

A letter arrived from Barat informing them that Ann had failed to pass her second semester and would not be allowed to return to Barat in the fall. The letter lay on the kitchen table like a grenade my parents didn't want to touch, not even when it was time for us to set the table. No one had much appetite for dinner that night, anyway.

"What's she going to do now?" Mother and Daddy asked each other, neither of them having an answer. A pall fell over our household.

With Ian and Barat gone, at summer's end Ann packed her bags and headed home on the train from Chicago to New Orleans. Her heart was broken. For the first time in our lives, Ann's homecoming did not feel celebratory. When Daddy and Ann came through the door, my sisters and I didn't know what to say to make Ann feel better. Neither did our parents, but they knew what they would tell their other three daughters.

As I started my senior year at DHS, my parents adopted a brand-new perspective about higher education. When I talked about University of Wisconsin, they told me, "It doesn't matter where you go to college. If you really want a good education, you can get it at LSU as easily as at a college in the North."

I don't think I argued or even resented my parents' new line of reasoning. Everything had changed; the future didn't seem as hopeful as it once had. Kennedy was dead; my sister had flunked out of college; my parents were already struggling and had three more daughters to launch.

Third girl from left: Jane swam through her disappointment, increasing her endurance with each practice.

Failed Flower at LSU

The summer I graduated from Donaldsonville High, Genie and I started classes together at Louisiana State University. I took an English course taught by an unknown, untenured, acne-scarred, amazingly smart professor whose class I have never forgotten. "Maybe my parents were right," I thought. And they might have been had I graduated at a different time or in a different place. Between 1965 and 1969, what happened outside the lecture halls was even more important to my young mind than what I could learn from my classes.

In the fall of 1965, I moved into Power Hall, a much newer and larger girls' dorm that had not been available in the summer. Genie and I had both wanted to meet new people and had decided not to room together come fall. I hadn't expected to be the only girl on my floor who did not pledge a sorority. I'd never heard of "ice-water parties," the kind LSU sororities hosted to check out the freshmen girls, separate the wheat from the chaff, and make final decisions about who got in and who didn't. Power Hall was an anxious beehive as girls buzzed in and out, all their hopes and dreams for college riding on which sororities would accept them. I didn't know one from the other.

My first semester of college I was surrounded by girls who talked endlessly about frat parties and who got "pinned" by so-and-so from such-and-such fraternity. They tended to dress alike, talk alike, and love the same things. LSU boys were like that, too. I felt lonely and miserable. The Dean of Women had hoped I would flower, but I felt myself wilting fast.

I didn't want to talk about stupid things. These LSU conversations were not nearly as stimulating as the ones we had in my own home on the River Road. College was supposed to be the place where I would learn more than I could learn at home. The whole experience was supposed to be more enlightening. There were serious issues like Civil Rights and the War in Vietnam, and serious young people who cared about them.

Lyndon Johnson had defeated Barry Goldwater in the 1964 presidential election. Goldwater was the trigger-happy one, so why was Johnson escalating the war in Vietnam? The political discussions in the Goette living room on Friday nights shifted from Civil Rights to Vietnam. The discussions my parents had with their friends, Jean and J.P. Wiggin and Harry Stille, were far more interesting than any conversation I heard among my peers at LSU.

Mother and J.P. were the first in their gang to argue against the war, and Daddy, the last. He defended Johnson's decision to send more troops, still believing the anti-communist domino theory. He had studied history, loved history, but didn't recognize the changes stirring the pot in this historical moment—the issues, forces, voices relevant to the 1960's, unleashed and already writing new history while my father talked about the Romans and the Hapsburgs or quoted Lincoln and Thomas Aquinas. Mother would roll her eyes. "Conrad, climb off that soapbox and join the 20th century."

Mother had loaned me her copy of *The Ugly American* during my senior year of high school. After reading it, I knew Daddy was as wrong about the war as he had been in saying it would take 100 years for the South to accept integration, when all it took was the Civil Rights Bill. I had graduated the last year of segregation.in the public schools of Donaldsonville. Though Gretchen was only four years younger, the attitudes of her peers were far more accepting of integration than mine had been.

It seemed the greatest concern now was this war. At Aunt Marilyn's I had read the issue of *Ramparts Magazine* with an unforgettable spread of black and white pictures taken in Viet Nam: A young girl and boy, running down a dirt road, their arms flung out away from their bodies; faces, contorted with fear and pain. Little children in Vietnam, running for their lives, running to escape the napalm we had dropped on them. Through tatters of burned off clothing, you could see burn marks on their flesh.

Once I'd read about Napalm I couldn't stop thinking about the war. Students in Madison held a sit-in at the administration building to protest the university's investment in Dow Chemical stock. "Not with our tuition money!" they said, while my peers at LSU talked about the Tigers, got drunk, and pinned in whatever order those things happened.

Soon after that protest, Wisconsin was dubbed Berkeley of the Midwest.

I longed to be there and felt I would shrivel up and die if I had to spend another three years at LSU surrounded by frat boys who would sow their wild oats, keep score as to how many girls they had "deflowered," but save that engagement ring for a virgin. Meanwhile, the girls had strict curfews, tried not to get pregnant (by praying?), talked about boys, and hoped to become one of those lucky "flowers of southern womanhood" whose finger would be graced with a diamond by the time she graduated.

In the spring of my freshman year, I went home one weekend to celebrate my sister Ann's engagement to Tony Distler, a professor in the Theatre Department at Tulane University in New Orleans. Our family and friends were quite excited about it. Tony was from Pennsylvania, liberal and sophisticated, ten years older than Ann— a real grown-up with an established career. He had an actor's sonorous voice that lacked even a trace of a southern accent, and he could quote Shakespeare effortlessly. When Ann told stories about their romance, people in the room got starry-eyed. My parents seemed proud of Ann and relieved that she was marrying Tony. Father Coyle, Ann's mentor from Grand Coteau, told her, "If anyone gives you a hard time about not having a college degree, you just tell them: "I married my degree, and it's a Ph.D.!"

Friday night Ann and Tony arrived from New Orleans shortly after my ride from Baton Rouge dropped me off at home. My memory of the weekend is that I felt as excited as the rest of my family. I really liked Tony and saw that Ann was in love and happy. Nothing happened to change my good feelings, absolutely nothing. I can't explain what happened later. After dinner that Saturday night in April 1966, friends arrived as they did most Friday and Saturday nights. The house was noisy and full of life. I loved and enjoyed all those people in the living room, but I didn't want their lives. I felt happy that Ann was in love and getting married, but I didn't want that either, not yet.

I peeled away from the party to attend to schoolwork. I had to finish a paper before I returned to LSU the next day. I didn't mind missing out on the party; I had heard all the stories already, so I pulled out my books and notes, sat at the typewriter, and continued the paper I had started on a subject I no longer remember, on a topic I neither hated nor loved. It had to be done, and so I was doing it.

With no warning and for no reason I understood, my fingers froze on the keys. An overwhelming wave of sadness came over me. It was quite sudden, as if a stranger had sneaked up behind and squeezed me so hard I could barely breathe. My fingers froze on the keyboard. Tears blurred my vision, spilling down my cheeks. There was no sound to my crying, only tears.

Someone walked past me on the way to refresh a drink. I don't remember who. "What's wrong?!" Speechless, I did not reject the kind hand that led me onto the back porch, repeating that question over and over. I had no words to explain a profound loneliness. I have only this image from that night on the back porch in Donaldsonville: the quiet sky suspended above the sugar cane fields, stretching toward infinity; the beautiful, limitless black sky that held millions of stars, alive and twinkling; all that mystery, possibility, beauty. I wanted that.

The next morning I saw the worried looks my parents exchanged at the breakfast table. I couldn't eat, and so I drank a cup of coffee and smoked a cigarette. That Sunday afternoon before I returned to LSU, I sat by the living room window waiting for my ride back to Baton Rouge, hoping it would arrive soon. Daddy pulled up a chair beside me, cupped my chin in his hand and looked into my eyes. It was the way he looked at me when I was a little girl. I expected him to smile and say what he always said at such moments, "Jane, you're a tree full of owls." This time his face appeared more sad than amused, his voice, quiet and tired.

"Jane, you know that if we had the money we'd send you to Wisconsin." I nodded. I understood my parents' finances better than he did. I wasn't angry with anyone. It just felt like I'd forgotten how to breathe. My chest hurt. I didn't know about burkas yet or Harry Potter's invisibility cloak, but that's what I needed. I couldn't wait for my ride to pull into the driveway and rescue me from this fishbowl moment. The relative anonymity of LSU would be a relief. I could lie on my dorm bed with the covers over my head.

Kappa Alpha fraternity's celebration of the Confederacy 1998

Jane Goette

Love Letter

A week later a letter from my mother arrived in my LSU mailbox. I took it up to my room to read in private. I expected to be scolded for embarrassing my family and knew I deserved it. But that's not the letter she wrote me. Mother said I should go ahead and apply to Wisconsin. If I got accepted, if I could get a decent summer job, and if Wisconsin would give me a semester-by-semester student loan, it just might work out. All this was written in Mother's practical voice, but I could read between the lines and knew my parents would have to tighten the family belt to help me, and I knew my little sisters wanted them to do it. Like a prisoner who receives a letter from the governor pardoning her, I felt the chains fall away and a rush of joy and hope, of gratitude. I would have a chance at life, but there was another message that meant even more. I had received a love letter from my family.

A few weeks later I went home for Kathleen Lemann's wedding. Afterwards, Camille and Bubba held a lavish reception for Kathleen and Jess at Palo Alto, the Lemann's plantation home. Mother knew Dolphie would be there, and though he wasn't much of a drinker, he couldn't resist free champagne. Mother had advised me to wait until Dolphie had drunk a few glasses, then I should ask him for a job at the Gonzales National Bank. Dolphie was now its vice-president. As Mother and I stood together sipping our champagne in the front hall, Daddy nudged me towards Dolphie. "This is a good time, Topper," Daddy said with a smile and a wink.

I spent the summer working the drive-in window at Dolphie's bank. He picked me up each morning and we drove together across the Sunshine Bridge to the east bank of the Mississippi, on to Gonzales. I hadn't ridden alone in a car with Dolphie since he picked me up after school one September day in eighth grade to go to New Orleans to see his newborn baby girl, Patty. I'd been Patty's babysitter ever since and spent almost as much time in Connie and Dolphie's house as I did my own.

Now I was trading my part-time job in Dolphie's home for a full-time job at his bank. I would miss my Patty, but I was a girl with a mission.

Bank-telling was not exactly my forte, but it was my ticket to Wisconsin. On Friday afternoons when the workers at the chemical plants got their checks, they headed straight to the drive-in window at the Gonzales First National to cash them. One Friday, Dolphie suddenly appeared at my side. He was smiling at me, like he was about to tell me what a good job I was doing. He leaned over and in a Ralph Cramden voice whispered, "Don't worry about hurrying, Sweetheart, you've only got 'em backed up to the Sunshine Bridge." Dolphie always made me laugh. I loved him more than ever that summer at Gonzales First National—that bittersweet summer, the last I would ever live with my family on the old River Road.

Now that a door out had finally opened, another door opened, too—the door in. I began to see all that was lovably special about Louisiana, which included Dolphie Netter and a host of Donaldsonville people I'd known all my life. I loved the afternoon thunderstorms and Mrs. Abadie's cows in the pasture behind our house. I loved the panoramic view I had each day when we crossed the Sunshine Bridge: the long levee on each side of the wide Mississippi River, green arms holding back the brown water as it rushed down the continent toward home, at last entering the vast expanse where it could lose its river self and finally become one with something large and accepting—the Gulf of Mexico.

On the west side of the river where I lived, green sugarcane fields stretched as far as the eye could see. How many times had I stood on our River Road porch watching rain race across the green fields towards me, faster than a river, even the Mighty Mississip'. I would miss it all: Louisiana humor, Cajun accents, mornings in our family kitchen; Mother and Daddy drinking Community Dark Roast, smoking cigarettes, reading *The Morning Advocate*, sharing sections and comments while I listened and learned.

During my last month and new days of noticing, I watched Kay Kay across the table as she consumed her breakfast: a stuffed crab left-over from last night's dinner, a bowl of cream of mushroom soup followed by a bowl of Cheerios and two slices of cinnamon toast. As she ate, she swung her legs under the table. My younger sister who cried for the Little Drummer Boy, but skewered her sisters, humiliating them with every opportunity, completely unconscious of her power to hurt others. She was wickedly funny, smart, and as courageous in some situations as she was cowardly in others: not hesitating a second before leaping onto the back of our big sister's would-be rapist, pounding him with her fists while she screamed, "Let my sister go!" But in her own life, this sister would not venture far from family.

At 7:00 a.m. that summer of 1966, my baby sister Gretchen would already be on the phone making plans with her friends. I felt a flood of admiration as I watched, remembering our little baby "Butchie," realizing she'd grown competent and confident in the world, become a take-charge girl, and the chief organizer in her crowd of friends. Gretchen made things happen that had been unimaginable during my high school days like quietly boycotting the official, still-segregated prom, to organize an alternative "prom" that included the black students in her class. Gretchen wasn't waiting for her life to begin, as I had; instead, she made life happen, even in Donaldsonville.

Perhaps the trait I admired most in her was her intellectual tenacity and courage. She tried things that were hard and asked questions when she didn't understand something or didn't recognize one of those names we're supposed to know. Her honest, inquisitive mind always overshadowed her ego, as a little girl, a young woman, a teacher and mother, and now.

Though my sister Ann had left home years before, I still missed her. She was so full of life and fun, always in the thick of things— the undisputed star of our family, as cool as she was charismatic. Ann was expecting her first baby that November of 1966. She would be giving birth in New Orleans, while I was hundreds of miles away in Madison. I would miss being there to welcome my first nephew (as it turned out) into the world.

I would miss so many things—Daddy, boiling crawfish in the back yard, mixing whiskey sours; Mother, baking a German Chocolate cake or one of her pies; friends dropping by our house;

Ann's dramatic stories created out of whatever she did—a visit to the doctor, streetcar ride, trip to the grocery; Kay Kay, leaning over Jeannette's pot, noting every ingredient she threw into the black cast iron. That image remains strong, the two of them standing side by side at the stove.

We all loved Jeannette, but she and Kay Kay had a special bond forged by their mutual interest in cooking and soap operas. If Kay Kay missed an episode of *Guiding Light* or *As the World Turns*, 'Net would fill her in, pausing to sample the dish she was cooking, never tasting directly from the spoon, always pouring or plopping a sample into the palm of her hand before handing the spoon to Kay Kay, studying her face for its inevitable approval. "Doesn't that burn your hand?" I once asked Jeannette as she lifted a steaming ladle and poured a sample directly into her palm. "No, I been doing this so long, I don't feel the heat."

It was a decade or two before I made the connection between racism and Jeannette's small peculiarities—never using the toilet when we were home and never sipping from the same spoon as us. These were learned survival behaviors, ingrained habits she would never break in a white family's house, even in ours. It took distance and time for me to look back and see all that I'd learned as a quiet observer within my family, my town, my Louisiana. All those growing-up years had instilled me with a deep, complicated love for the River Road, a love hidden beneath layers of longing.

In the summer of 1966, while I worked at Dolphie's bank and counted the days until my departure for Wisconsin, I began to see the things I would miss from my life on the River Road: the food, fun, and fights we had around our dinner table; the people who flowed in and out of "the Goette house"; the abundance of colorful Donaldsonville characters whose exploits, words, and accents were reenacted at our kitchen table.

I would miss my high school friends with whom I'd shared every crush on every boy, cigarettes and secrets, anxieties about my hair, figure, and future. We listened to music together, dissecting the lyrics of Peter, Paul, and Mary, Bob Dylan and Joan Baez. When we were old enough to get into honky-tonk dance clubs, we traveled together along dark, bayou roads to reach destinations like the Bon

Chance to hear live bands and dance fast and slow on shadowy dance floors with strangers who didn't know or care who our parents were. My family. I would miss them most of all.

May 27, 1955

Dear Neeley,

You have been so much in my thoughts all week that I have finally been driven to my desk to unburden myself of these thoughts on paper. No one could ever accuse me of not being talkative but never have I had the gift of expressing verbally any deep thoughts or feelings that I possess. Maybe a psychiatrist would discover that this is a result of having a mother whose lack of emotional display made her seem cold and who was embarrassed by any demonstration of affection. Whatever the cause, the fact remains that I can best express myself on paper.

As this 1955 letter to Neely shows, my mother had a wise and loving heart but could not express her deeper thoughts and feelings verbally, only in writing. Her letters ranged from amusing to life-changing.

Jane Goette

Madison at Last, Fall 1966

At summer's end, I packed up my Samsonite, Olivetti typewriter, and every warm piece of clothing I owned, which did not yet include scarves, mittens, boots or even a heavy coat. I took my first stand-by flight—in fact, the *first* airplane of my life—to Milwaukee, Wisconsin. Aunt Marilyn met me at the airport, and a few days later, drove me to Madison in her Volkswagen bug. Billy and Karl fought in the back seat the whole trip.

Marilyn had to pull the car off the highway a couple of times to stop them. Thirty minutes later, another ruckus erupted. This one crossed the essential boundary between front and back seats. In the process of trying to kick his brother, Bill's foot came flying between the two front seats, hitting the stick shift and causing the car to lurch into another gear. Marilyn screamed, hands clutching the wheel so tightly her knuckles turned white, reminding me very much of Grandpa Canright. After my aunt regained control of the car, she pulled over for the last time, ordering her sons to "Get the hell out of the car!" If Billy and Karl couldn't behave any better she would leave them on the highway. "You can hitch-hike home or walk back to West Allis!"

By the time we reached Cole Hall, the designated dorm for freshmen girls and new transfers, Aunt Marilyn was ready for the loony bin. She had inherited the Canright driving gene, which rendered her a complete wreck behind the wheel of a car—not aggressive like Mother and Grandpa, but easily rattled.

Marilyn and Glen were almost as excited as I that I'd been accepted to Wisconsin, "the Berkley of the Midwest." When we set out for Madison, I had assumed my aunt would help me move into the dorm, and maybe we'd get a hot fudge sundae afterwards and talk, but it wasn't like that. Marilyn was so anxious by the time we reached the campus, all she could think about was getting back to Milwaukee. When we reached Cole Hall, she left the motor running, opened the trunk, handed me my suitcase and typewriter, hopped back in, and drove off. I stood on the sidewalk watching as her turquoise bug sailed back down the hill, two blonde heads poking out the back window, their hands waving goodbye.

So here I was. After years of longing, I had finally arrived at the great University of Wisconsin. This was not the arrival I had imagined, this girl standing alone on a sidewalk holding a suitcase in one hand and a typewriter in the other, feeling lost and forlorn. Terror and excitement raced through me in equal measure as I stood outside Cole Hall waiting for my life to begin—and soon, it did.

With no help from anyone, I figured out my classes, managed to sign up for them, located buildings, and navigated this enormous, hilly campus all before the other students arrived. First, I went to Student Financial Aid and got a job working 30 hours a week at the University Photo Lab. Being a morning person, I scheduled all my classes before noon so I could work in the afternoons. I felt proud that I'd managed all this alone, but also, lonely. There was no one to talk to until the weekend before classes began and other kids started to arrive.

By their accents, hair styles, and dress, I could tell the girls in my dorm were a diverse group, and it wouldn't be hard to make friends. Rose Sullivan from Boston became my first and best friend at UW. Though Rose had grown up in the Northeast, and I, in the Deep South, we had more in common with each other than with others in our dorm. As a fallen-away Catholic from Donaldsonville with no exposure to religion other than Catholic and Southern Baptist, I was curious and wanted to learn about other faiths, not shop for a new one. And Rose, having grown up Catholic in an Irish neighborhood of Boston, felt the same. Winthrop was predominantly Irish Catholic and almost as provincial as Donaldsonville.

Rose and I were awed by the sophistication of the New York girls at Cole, especially Rose's roommate, Libby Davis. With blonde, textured hair, hazel eyes and olive skin, Libby would have been striking even if she hadn't worn large, African, dangle earrings. She parted her hair in the middle from forehead to the nape of her neck, French-braided each side, and then crisscrossed the braids at the back to form a wide, braided bun.

For parties and special occasions Libby pulled her braids to the front, to the crown of her head, tucking the braids' edges into her tight, wavy hair. Sometimes she might stick a flower or some other ornament into her braided crown. Never had I imagined that a hairstyle I associated with Louisiana widows and spinsters could appear so stunning and chic. The first time I saw a picture of Frida Kahlo, I thought of Libby. What had seemed a hairstyle that expressed subservient acceptance of cultural dictates for women, even when joyless and drab, was reimagined and transformed by Libby Davis and Frida Kahlo into expressions of triumphal, female beauty.

Libby had grown up in "the city," which I soon understood to mean New York, rather than New Orleans as it had back home. While I attended DHS with a World History teacher who referred to Hitler's regime as the Third "Reach," Libby had been educated at a progressive NYC high school. I arrived at UW as a sophomore and Libby, a freshman, but she possessed a worldliness and knowledge base light years beyond mine. She came to Madison knowing everything about every topic that interested me, from sex and birth control to history and literature; she knew art, music, theater, psychology, and politics.

In the fall of 1966, I had presumed our shared positions against the war and interest in political activism would mean Libby and I were both integrationists. Libby quickly dispelled that assumption. She did not support integration and had little interest in the leaders of the Civil Rights movement in the South. While in Donaldsonville, people still thought of King, Farmer, Young, and Lewis as "Communists," Libby thought them hopelessly blind to political realities and behind the times. The "movement," as she called it, had left them behind. She didn't share or admire their Christianity because it was the faith taught to African slaves by their white oppressors hundreds of years before, a faith slave descendants still shared with the white, southern Baptists who burned down their churches.

What had Christian faith and non-violent tactics achieved for black people? It shocked me to learn that Libby Davis not only had no interest in Martin Luther King, but she didn't support integration any more than George Wallace or Ross Barnett. I had left a community where peers made fun of me for using "Negro" instead of the N-word; a few weeks later, I'm at a university where peers from New York roll their eyes if I say "Negro" instead of "Black."

When Libby asked Rose how much wall space she needed for her things, Rose responded, "None. I don't have anything to hang." In fact, Rose was thrilled to have Libby take charge of making their room look cool. I would have felt the same. Later, after Libby had decorated and gone out to buy books, Rose knocked on my door.

"Wanna see what Libby put on the walls?" I expected to find Monet and Picasso prints, and knowing Libby had attended live theater in New York and traveled to Europe, I wouldn't have been surprised to see posters of dancers, Broadway shows, or the Eiffel Tower. Instead, when Rose opened the door to their room, I had my introduction to Black Power or "the movement" as Libby called it. No visitor to that room could ignore the large black and white posters of two guys I barely recognized, Stokely Carmichael and H. Rap Brown.

The larger of the two black and white posters featured Stokely Carmichael leaning into a microphone, his face serious and posture defiant. He's handsome, his eyes shine with intelligence. In the slightly smaller poster at Stokely's right, H. Rap Brown stands with clenched fist raised high above his head. He's wearing a leather jacket, sunglasses, and a Che Guevara beret tilted to the right and perched atop his bushy Afro. Clearly, this Brown was different from the "Brown" who had challenged the Board of Education in Arkansas.

Rose and Libby got along well during the little time Libby spent at the dorm. Mostly, except when she attended classes, Libby hung out at her "brother's" apartment on Mifflin St. Dave had recently become Libby's brother when their parents—her mother, a psychiatrist, and his father, a professor, I think—got married the summer before. Dave's African heritage was apparent, but Libby could have "passed," as they say in the South. Rose and I were fascinated, especially when Libby started sleeping with her brother at his apartment.

I stopped cutting my hair, and on my first visit back to West Allis, Uncle Glen pierced my ears with a hypodermic needle. Marilyn assisted, holding ice cubes on either side of each ear lobe before Glen stuck the needle in. Sharing my thriftiness and knowing I didn't have much money, my aunt and uncle encouraged me to hitch-hike between Madison and Milwaukee. They would drop me off and pick me up at the West Allis exit. Glen went down to the basement after dinner and returned after Marilyn and I had finished the dishes and sat down to enjoy a slice of warm apple pie. "Here you go, Jane," he said, handing me an 18-inch square sign with a string attached to two sides, "here's your round-trip ticket." Uncle Glen had produced a neat, hand-painted sign for me to hold as I stood on the side of the road with my thumb out. One side read, "Student to Madison," and the flip side, "Student to Milwaukee."

Lincoln overlooking Bascom Hill

Jane's new Madison style

Smokin' on Mifflin

The next weekend, Libby invited Rose and me to a party at Dave's apartment on Mifflin, the "coolest" street in Madison. We couldn't believe our good fortune. The Friday of the party, I went back and forth between my room and Rose's, seeking her advice about which top looked better with which skirt. We were going to a party with a bunch of New Yorkers; I didn't want to look like a girl from down the bayou!

Rose dressed more casually than I, thinking you could never go wrong with a pair of jeans. (I didn't own any.) "Jane, this isn't a cocktail party on Fifth Avenue; we're trying to look cool." I knew exactly what "cool" looked like at LSU where every girl dressed the same, as if they'd all come off the assembly line at the Villager factory. So the litmus test I applied for the night was to dress as anti-LSU as I could.

The walk from Cole to Mifflin St. took about thirty minutes. It was dark. As we got deeper into the student-occupied neighborhoods, Rose and I strained our eyes for glimpses inside lighted apartment windows. Like Margaret Mead disciples researching an unfamiliar culture, we compared observations and took mental notes along the way. And we laughed a lot. Rose and I were not vested members of *any*thing, just two girls flying by the seat of our pants—a "Connecticut Yankee" and "Coon-ass Cajun" going to "King Arthur's Court."

We didn't have to look at the number on the house to know when we'd arrived at Dave's. A blue light hung from the ceiling of the porch illuminating a big PEACE sign tacked to the right of an opened front door through which Mo-Town blared. Rose and I looked at each other for encouragement, then braved an entrance. Inside, black lights pulsed through a halo of marijuana smoke, the aroma, comingling with incense. A haze of smoke swirled and swayed to the beat of Martha and the Vandellas.

"The beers are in the bathtub!" Libby shouted into Rose's ear, pointing to a room at the back that had to be the bathroom. Rose nodded. Getting the beers gave us a mission, forward momentum, and something to do other than stand awkwardly against the living room wall, gawking. We threaded a path through the crowd toward the bathroom. Neither of us liked beer, but so what? We returned to the living room just as "Stop, in the Name of Love!" started to blast from the stereo. A hand tapped my shoulder. I turned to see a boy in a black turtleneck and jeans, a mop of curls, ("Jew-fro," I was to learn) and a warm smile.

"Want to dance?"

Rose smiled encouragingly, extending a hand to take my beer. I danced with Danny through that song and the next, also a Supremes' hit; there were so many. I glanced around searching for Rose, then spotted her in the crowd of dancers. I relaxed and kept dancing. Danny and I exchanged smiles, made a few fruitless attempts to shout things to each other, then laughed and gave it up. Finally, there was a pause in the music, but before I could head back to the beer I didn't want, Danny reached for my hand and tilted his head in the direction of the porch. I spotted my purse on the floor and grabbed it on the way to the door.

Pulling out a cigarette had been a preemptive defense against unwanted kisses in high school, and smoking, a reliable way to fill awkward moments when I'd exhausted my short repertoire of small talk phrases. As soon as we stepped outside to the porch, I reached for a cigarette. Before I had time to light it, Danny had already pulled a lighter from his pocket, flicked, and extended its flame. I bent my head toward his hand, took two quick puffs to make sure it was lit, and lifted my head to see Danny closing the lighter and putting it back in his pocket. He didn't smoke.

I liked this New York boy. Later, when we were ready to leave, Danny walked Rose and me back to Cole Hall. His dorm was two buildings away from ours, so close in fact that we shared a dining hall. That was the bad part. Financial Aid had helped me get a shift at the cafeteria to lessen my dorm fee. I was just getting to know Danny and liked him. I prayed that he wasn't an early riser; I worked the first breakfast shift at the cafeteria. Whatever hope I held for seeming cool and attractive would turn to toast!

Cafeteria workers were required to wear a hairnet and a uniform. I had to buy my own hairnet, but the supervisor had provided me with a crisp, harvest gold uniform. It hung six inches below my knees. At home, we used safety pins to hold up hems, but I didn't have any here, so I turned the hem under—almost to my waist—slapped masking tape over it, and prayed it would hold. I scurried to work the morning after the Mifflin party, keeping my head down, just in case.

As I came to learn, Danny admired me for working my way through college. It gave me the status of being part of the proletariat. This hip, smart, New York "red diaper baby," soon became my boyfriend. His parents were almost as old as my father. They had been activists in the labor movement and members of the Communist party before its split over Stalin.

After word got around Cole that Rose and I had been at Dave's party, the New York girls on our floor started inviting us into their rooms to listen to the Stones, Bob Dylan, Donovan, and the Doors. They also introduced us to "grass," which I had known only through anti-marijuana propaganda with its references to "reefer madness." All the teenagers in Donaldsonville smoked cigarettes, but Rose had never smoked anything. "I don't smoke," she had told me the first time I offered her one of my Salems. Rose didn't care for the taste of a cigarette, but after we'd smoked our first joint, she concluded that pot tasted much better.

That first high at Cole Hall was the best marijuana experience I ever had. We couldn't stop laughing. Audrey and Frances took turns listening at the door for campus police coming to bust us. Each time one of them put her finger to her lips, tip-toed to the door, and leaned her ear to the crack, the rest of us would collapse onto the beds, grabbing pillows to put over our mouths, which only made us laugh harder. It was fun, and god, we were cool!

On weekends, between studying and going to parties, Rose and I stayed true to our mission of investigating different religions. We attended a variety of churches: Presbyterian, B'hai, Quaker, Unitarian (designed by Frank Lloyd Wright), and we educated ourselves politically, too, stopping to read every poster and flyer we saw on bulletin boards and every graffiti on every construction wall throughout UW's wide-spread, hilly campus. I searched for signs that would guide me to an anti-war meeting and found "The

Committee to End the War in Vietnam." I think it later morphed into SDS.

In the fall of 1966, I attended my first demonstration at Madison. Danny and I were among a group of about 25 people standing in front of Bascom Hall with signs protesting Dow Chemical's recruitment on campus. Whatever else that company may have manufactured, and I knew and loved at least one Louisiana family friend who worked for Dow, its production of the Napalm we dropped in the Vietnam War meant I didn't want Dow on my campus.

Although the Dow demonstration in Madison had been small in 1966, a year later when Dow returned to our campus for job recruitment, a much larger and better planned protest took place. The Vietnam War had escalated during that year, with a hundred-thousand more troops being sent, most of them draftees. College deferments had an expiration date; this war did not, and with its production of Napalm, Dow Chemical had become its symbol.

The Fall 1967 protest included a student sit-in at Commerce Hall where Dow had set up a recruitment station. I headed to the protest after my morning class, but the doors had already been locked. A fortress of helmeted Madison police stood guard around the entrances. I didn't understand what was happening but soon found myself choking inside a cloud of teargas. People started running. Rumor spread that cops were beating up students inside Commerce. I didn't know until hours later that the rumor was true.

The violent response by police to this peaceful demonstration ignited the now legendary antiwar movement in Madison. The University of Wisconsin became ground zero for the anti-war movement on college campuses.

All my years in Madison were exciting and exhilarating, but none quite as wondrous and joyful as the first year when nothing bad had happened yet. By Thanksgiving of 1966 I had been to a protest where no one got beat up or tear-gassed; I'd smoked my first joint, gone to parties on Mifflin St., and had a New York boyfriend, but I had not seen snow. Images from old-fashioned Christmas cards and the recent movie, "Dr. Zhivago" made me impatient each chilly day that came to Madison without a flake of snow yet. Rose and our New York friends groaned, "Just wait," they said, "you'll come to hate it," but I knew they were wrong. And they were.

Danny had promised me that when the first snow came, he would drop everything and find me. He wanted to be the first to take me on a snow date. With each snowless day, my craving for it grew, much to my worldly friends' amusement.

Late one afternoon between Thanksgiving and Christmas, Danny showed up at my door apple-cheeked and smiling, his bushy hair, suddenly white. It took me a nanosecond to realize, "Snow!" I rushed back to my room to put on my coat and brand new pair of boots. Like little kids, Danny and I ran down the street, laughing, holding out our tongues to catch snowflakes, scooping up handfuls to toss at each other. We walked all over campus and through beautiful Madison neighborhoods in the muffled quiet of that first snowy twilight in Madison. As it grew darker, we sometimes stopped beneath streetlights just to watch the snow tumble from the sky.

Lawns, sidewalks, and streets blended together like mounds of melting ice-cream, their borders, indistinguishable beneath a blanket of pure white not yet disturbed by a single footprint. I gave Danny's hand a tug. I didn't want to talk or walk or do anything but stand and watch. All the Christmas cards, calendars, and movies had not prepared me for the living, sparkling reality of snow, vaguely blue in the whispery hush of evening.

But it wasn't like that in February. My friends were right. By then I'd grown sick of navigating treacherous ice-packed sidewalks, discouraged by the sight of gray, pock-marked mounds of snow that refused to melt. When the calendar rounded the corner to February, my seasonal clock ticked toward spring; time for camellias, azaleas, Mardi Gras, and soon…crawfish boils in the backyard and clover on the levee.

Lake Mendota was still frozen solid. People walked across it. Some, dressed like Eskimos, sat on milk crates beside holes cut deep into the ice. They held short fishing poles in their mittened hands. Boats with razor sharp rudders whizzed across the ice, their white sails flapping like surrender flags in the bitter wind. My friends lured me out onto the frozen lake one Sunday afternoon, insisting it would be fun, but I couldn't wait to get back to the Rathskellar to warm my hands and feet before its friendly fire.

Spring break approached with no organic sign of the season for which this break had been named. My eyes longed for green, my ears, for familiar stories told in slow soft accents. I wanted *Donaldsonville* stories—told in that inimitable Donaldsonville accent which, like its gumbo, is a spicy blend of Cajun-Italian-Black—where punchlines are perfectly pitched to unleash laughter at the finish line. I wanted Buddy Lemann's voice in the living room, telling about Grover. Sweet, toothless, white-haired Grover with a body like Tarzan—former lifeguard and supposed pedophile, he taught all the little girls to swim, oblivious to the little boys who called out, "Watch me, Grover!" before bellyflopping into the pool, their small hands folded close to thin chests, as if they were praying. "Yeah, son, yeah," Grover would shout back, never taking his eyes off the little girl he rocked on his knee, up and down in the water. Buddy would shake his head and exclaim, "All the girls in Donaldsonville swim like Esther Williams. Damn boys can't make it across the pool!"

Spring Break Trip Home

I *had* to go home but didn't have the money for a Greyhound bus ticket. I convinced Danny, who'd never been south of New Jersey, to come with me—it would be an adventure—so we hitched a ride with some kids heading to Texas. Along the way, the snowy landscape gradually surrendered to green. Each mile nourished a hunger I hadn't realized, the way you forget how much you love food when you've been sick a day or two. After driving through the night, famished but excited to see green again, we finally stopped for breakfast at a diner in Mississippi. Two crew-cut guys walked past our table giving Danny dirty looks. "Why don't you get a haircut?!" they said as they headed to the cash register. Danny looked scared.

After we finished breakfast and continued our drive, that look intensified as we every 10 miles or so we passed an "Impeach Earl Warren" billboard. Nothing in his experience prepared Danny for the shock he experienced when we passed a large banner in the middle of a field, announcing an upcoming Ku Klux Klan rally.

"It's not like that in South Louisiana," I assured my New York boyfriend, "the KKK hates Catholics almost as much as Blacks and Jews." It was true. When we reached my River Road home, the welcome we received more than made up for each miserable, Mississippi mile. As we climbed the front porch steps, I heard strains of *Missa Luba* coming from our living room windows. I felt myself crying and laughing at the same time.

Six months before on the day I had gone to State Street to shop for an Indian scarf to tie back my hair, I had also bought the first record album of my life. The scarf hadn't been needed for any practical reason, only to project the image I sought for the new "Jane." I had saved money, rationed cigarettes and stopped buying pumpkin pie at the student union. French fries and pie were the two cheapest, most-filling foods I could afford at lunch.

I had only intended to purchase a scarf, but while inside that shop I lingered to listen to the music that played in the background—mesmerizing sounds came from the speakers: voices singing; drums beating; it seemed familiar and foreign; sacred and wild. I recognized the Latin lyrics; I had heard them every Sunday from the first mass I had attended to the last, but this music felt deep, warm, and personal, as if it had come from a place inside the body close to the heart.

"What is that?" I asked the girl at the cash register. "*Missa Luba,*" she said. When my face remained blank, she added, "you know, that African interpretation of the Catholic mass."

I left the shop, walked down the street to a record shop, and bought it. I didn't have a record player and doubted my New York, Jewish, dorm friends would care for it, but now I had a Christmas present to give my parents. Daddy would love this new version of the Mass; mother would love that it was African.

To climb the steps and hear *Missa Luba* pouring from the River Road windows of my home was an even better welcome than Daddy's whiskey sours. My family was excited to finally meet Danny. In her weekly letters to the Goettes on the River Road, Marilyn had included accounts of the two weekends Danny and I had spent in West Allis: staying up late talking politics, going folk-dancing at the Saratoga, and a later weekend in the dead of winter, we'd gone ice-skating on a small lake with their friends, the Konles.

The first time Danny and I visited, after Billy, Karl, and Hans went to bed, my aunt and uncle wanted to try pot, so we passed around a joint—Marilyn complaining that she didn't feel anything—but soon my aunt and uncle were taking turns imitating Grandma Canright, running back and forth to shut the kitchen door to the basement. Though Danny didn't understand the joke, watching my aunt and uncle chase each other was enough to see they were higher than kites and hysterically funny. (I don't think Marilyn included the pot part in the letters she sent to my parents.)

Before we met, Danny didn't know anyone who'd ever eaten a crawfish, nor had he ever had a cocktail. Now he was in a backyard in Louisiana watching my father pour a sack of "mud bugs" into boiling water along with a lot of Zatarain's, extra cayenne, and onions. He'd had a walk on the levee and heard accents he didn't know existed in English.

After dinner that first night, the Wiggins, Harry, and a few other friends arrived to talk politics, tell stories, and hang out in the Goette living room as they did most weekends. Mother served Pecan Bread Pudding with Bourbon Sauce and strong cups of Community Dark Roast. Daddy poured bottles of Jax into chilled beer mugs and made another batch of whiskey sours. J. P. Wiggin, who was becoming more obsessed with Vietnam each time I saw him, wanted to hear about student protest plans in Madison.

Though my parents' Friday night gang showed no signs of running out of steam, Mother noticed Danny struggling to suppress a yawn, and broke up the party. "These kids drove all night to get here; they need to go to bed." I can't remember whether it was Danny or one of my sisters who slept on the couch, but for the first time in a year I got to sleep in a bed with spring-scented, crisp sheets—a child again, lying with closed eyes on a bed of levee clover.

That whole visit my mother never said a word about my dangly earrings, long hair, and Indian print scarf. She treated me more like a grown-up than her daughter and seemed more interested in my experiences and political views than my earrings and hair. It was Danny's Jew-Fro that garnered family and friends' attention. Harry referred to him as "Little Orphan Annie."

When the Texas boys pulled into the driveway to take us back to Madison, part of me wanted to climb into that car, and part of me wanted to stay. If only we could put bookmarks in our lives and come back to the parts we love, or straddle the pages of two different lives before we decide which story will have the happy ending. When the crowded car backed out of that shell-paved driveway and turned north onto the River Road, I tried not to look back, but when we rounded the curve at the Persons' house, I turned for a last glimpse of home. Mother had already reached the top step of our front porch.

Hours later when our Texas driver stopped for gas, I took a short walk near the station. It was windy with a chill in the air. A sudden gust ruffled my hair. I pulled up my collar and instinctively felt for the Indian-print scarf I had worn every day since my hair grew long enough to tie back. It had come to symbolize the new "Jane" I was trying so hard to become. I reached for it as you reach for a hand when you're lost. It was gone. I watched as my Indian-print scarf sailed past me toward the median strip. It skipped across the wind like a child running away from home, pausing just a moment, like a hand waving goodbye.

***

Madison had undergone a transformation while I had been eating crawfish on the River Road. Our crew of sun-starved youth had left Wisconsin in winter and returned one week later to find a version of spring I had never experienced. All the sooty, pock-marked piles of snow had melted from street corners, lawns, and sidewalks. Mirage-like whispers of green shone through dried grass; tightly wrapped buds jutted from bare tree limbs. "Look!" I gasped, as I glimpsed little peeks of blue through the crowded streets that bordered Lake Mendota. I felt like Wendy surrounded by a carful of sleeping Lost Boys, all of whom lurched awake with small grunts and groans, emitting a cloud of bad breath in the back seat.

Lake Mendota looked even more beautiful than it had the first time I saw it from my parents' car window. As if by miracle, a wave of an invisible wand, that enormous expanse of gray ice had turned back into blue, sparkling water, but Lake Mendota no longer seemed foreign to my eyes. In fact, *nothing* in Madison felt unfamiliar anymore. This town, this university, had become mine.

Goodbye to Madison

I had set out for the University of Wisconsin like Puss N' Boots. I, too, had left my country home to seek a different kind of fortune in the wider world. Like Puss, I was willing to work hard to change my fate; Madison would be my London Town. When I left my family nest on the River Road in the fall of 1966, I had assumed that I would know what to do and where I was going by the time I graduated. After all, I would be 21 by then, not just a grown-up in my parents' eyes but in the eyes of the law.

Early 1968 was one of the most exciting, hopeful times of my life. Eugene McCarthy surprised his party as well as the nation by winning the Democratic primary in New Hampshire, March 12, 1968. Four days later, Robert F. Kennedy entered the presidential race, also as an anti-war candidate. Adding to that harbinger of springtime was the unseasonably warm weather that arrived like a special delivery package to our doorstep in Madison, Wisconsin on March 31, the night President Johnson had scheduled an address to the nation.

Tosh, Rose, a few other Doty St. friends, and I had planned an early dinner together sensing that something big was coming but not knowing if it would be good or bad, an escalation or de-escalation of the war. Either way, we wanted to be together for whatever was about to come. It's impossible for generations that followed ours to grasp what it was like to be young at a time when our nation was sending thousands of young men to distant jungles to fight a war most of them didn't understand and many also opposed.

By 1968 that war had become a ravenous monster, devouring more and more young bodies each day that the war dragged on. We didn't have control over our lives; we couldn't really plan a future. Friends, boyfriends, brothers might be snatched up any day with the appearance of a draft notice in their mailboxes. The shadow of Vietnam loomed over our lives like a thunder cloud. Who would the lightning strike next?

With a mixture of hope and dread, we crowded around our ten-inch black and white television screen and turned on CBS; we liked Walter Cronkite. The windows in the apartment were wide open, it was that warm the evening of March 31. Some of us lit cigarettes as we braced for whatever was coming. The mood in the room teetered between hope and anxiety; the tension was palpable. All squirming and small talk ceased the moment Johnson began his address with its familiar opening, "Ma fellow Amuricans…" delivered in a Texas drawl we had come to despise.

I can't remember now how many minutes passed into his speech before he uttered those immortal lines, "I will not seek, nor will I accept my party's nomination for president of the United State…" and then everyone froze, stunned and stupid, exchanging questioning looks, "Did he just say what I thought he said?!"

As if in answer to that unspoken question, a distant, raw and raucous roar burst through the windows. A joy too big for any apartment to contain spilled out onto the streets of Madison. It was a school night. There were papers to write, books to read, studying to do, but that night, the students of Madison played hooky and celebrated their hearts out.

We thought the nightmare of Vietnam was going to end soon. It seemed inevitable in that moment, as if President Johnson himself were acknowledging this mistaken war. We would be able to get on with our lives. Young people of my generation were challenging the entrenched, white establishment in all areas: government, business, education, religion, art…. We would live up to the principles *those* leaders had abandoned. They called us Commies and dirty hippies, but this rebellion wasn't *against* American values, it was against the betrayal of those values, and now the torch was passing to my generation. We had brought down a president. We would bring down the other barriers standing in the way of the better world we knew was possible.

Never before, and never after early spring of 1968, had I felt so alive and hopeful about the future—the world's and my own. I was in love with art, music, friends, teachers, the sparkling lakes of Madison, the murky Mississippi of home, short skirts, long hair, dance parties, late night conversations… and I was in love with Tosh Lee.

He had skin like toasted honey and eyes dark as ripe plums. One June night in Madison lying side by side in the single bed we shared, Tosh recited a Haiku poem. I'll remember the image the rest of my life; a man wakes the morning after a hard rain and wonders "how many rose petals fell in the night?" As a young boy in Formosa, he had wandered down to the beach one morning just to look at the sea. The water was strewn with bloated bodies.

A short time later, he was at the market with his mother when shouting began. People were pushed aside to clear a path for a band of soldiers waving their rifles. With the butts of their guns, they pushed along three men tied side by side, their hands bound behind their backs. Early the next day, Tosh had awakened in the predawn. He was a little boy who had to pee. His family lived a small distance from the train depot. As he stumbled sleepily toward the outhouse the wind was blowing. Something moved in the distance that arrested his attention. He stopped, peered through the predawn light, to see silhouetted against the backdrop of the train station, three heads hung from its rafters, bobbing in the wind.

Poetry and stories, his and mine. Candlelight baths and massages; the latter, a first for me. Full body, head, neck, back, but my favorite was Tosh's foot massage. Who knew that warm, knowing fingers could explore the bottoms of feet and send tingles to a scalp? I adored this new Morse Code; our fingers, feet, sending each other love messages.

Tosh was simple to please. "Lovey," he'd say as we lay naked in bed, "would you please walk on my back?" I feared I would break his bones. My feet soon learned the art of shifting body weight, balancing on opposite sides of his spine, my toes kneading the places most in need. He read my body's needs, needs I didn't even know I had, and I read his, the ones I could understand. I came to love this man with my whole self, head to toe.

And God, the man was fun! Tosh infused every party or made-up game with an infectious, uncensored playfulness. Once in a charades game Tosh had given us a clue that amounted to "Ding,

Jane and Tosh on River Road visit in 1968

dong, ding, dong." To us Americans the presumed response was "the wicked witch is dead."

"No," Tosh insisted, "it's cherry blossom time!" as though this were the most obvious answer in the world. Everyone burst out laughing. It was that spit-out-your wine kind of laughing you can't control. And Tosh laughed, too.

My friends and I were more recent political activists, but Tosh was older and had been seasoned by experiences foreign to us. Tosh was a boy when World War II ended. We hadn't been born yet. As soon as the war ended, Tosh's older, very ambitious brother left Formosa for Japan. With its economy wrecked, confidence broken, and reeling from its devastating defeat, Japan was a great place for a young man with big ideas and mountains of energy. Big Brother's small ventures turned into larger ones. He soon accumulated enough money to bring the rest of his family to Tokyo where Tosh spent his teen years and attended the University of Tokyo. His first protest marches had been against the Bomb.

Tosh's lifelong pacifism was deeply rooted. For different reasons, mine was too. Though I'd never been physically close to war like Tosh, Grandpa Canright's graphic, gruesome accounts of sights, sounds, and smells he experienced at the French Front had left their mark. I was a 19 year old, idealistic girl from the River Road when I fell in love with Tosh Lee, a 29 year old man of the world. Tosh already possessed the life skills I lacked and knew how to take care of himself and others. Like Jeannette, Tosh could rummage through a refrigerator, find a few half-eaten pork chops, some forgotten vegetables, and transform these forlorn ingredients into a feast that fed everyone seated around our Doty St. table.

We hadn't been a couple very long when I found out Tosh was cheating on me. "She doesn't mean anything to me," he cried, blocking the door as I pushed it against him. "I love YOU, only you!" This was probably true, but it didn't make sense in my universe. If a man cheated on his woman, it meant he didn't love her, or she was frigid, and he had to seek sex elsewhere. And yet, I knew Tosh loved me and sex between us was outrageously good. I wanted to break up with him, but my stubborn heart betrayed me.

Like Michael Corleone's futile attempts to step away from his dangerous family, love kept pushing me back in.

I should have left Tosh and let my heart take its licks, but the euphoria of early 1968 had given way to tragedy, one after another. My heart couldn't take it. The world was too scary to go it alone. I was supposed to be a grown-up by the time I graduated from college, but I wasn't. Everyone thought of me as a gutsy girl—my parents, Aunt Marilyn, sister Gretchen, my friends. I had learned my way around that enormous campus, managed its hills and outlying regions, hitch-hiked, found jobs and places to live, lived well with sparse resources, participated in protests where violence was possible and tear gas a certainty. I wasn't afraid to be alone in voicing an unpopular opinion or cause; I never had been and never would be.

But I *was* afraid of being alone. So, I married Tosh on New Year's Eve that year and spent spring semester living in Tokyo in the small one-room bedroom-study-bathroom Big Brother had built beside his parents' house—for us. I got a short term, part-time job with NHK, the Japanese equivalent of today's PBS and NPR. I did a couple of televised English conversation skits, which were stilted and silly, but then they gave me a weekly radio spot. The only instruction was that I write a weekly, short essay detailing some experience or impression I had as an American living in Japan. I loved writing those weekly essays, and since I read them into a microphone in a small room rather than before a live audience, I felt relaxed and confident, as if I were reading to a friend or a sister.

During the semester I spent in Tokyo with Tosh, I taught an English conversation class for Japanese employees of IBM. Though I was by far the youngest person in the classroom, they felt shy around me and uncertain of their English. My job was to engage them in discussion, which was easy for me because I was as curious about their lives as they were about mine. Whether it was the dynamism of my teaching or the novelty of having a young American woman teach them, these earnest, young, short-haired businessmen in out-of-style suits developed a trusting bond with their earnest, young, short-skirted American teacher.

On the day I flew home to New Orleans with Tosh's younger sister Kazuko, we left on an early morning flight. After entering the Tokyo airport with Tosh and his parents, I was surprised to find my students there, all dressed up in their business suits, waiting for me. They presented me with a bouquet of flowers and thanked me for being their teacher.

Going to Louisiana before flying to Madison would be a nice experience for Kazuko, but mostly I wanted to be home to see my youngest sister walk down the aisle of the DHS gymnasium, and my father hand his last child her high school diploma. After Gretchen's graduation, I returned to Madison to complete my course work and graduated in August. My baby sister began her undergraduate education just as I finished mine.

Two months later, I left Tosh. He had a cheatin' heart that just couldn't change. My views were very progressive in all areas, but not when it came to that. At twenty-one, I was the first Goette sister to graduate from college and the first to end a marriage. The brief pride I experienced at my educational accomplishment was completely overshadowed by the shame of failing at marriage. It isn't what my parents *said* about education and marriage that revealed which held greater currency in a daughter's life, it is what they *showed*.

My sister had failed at college but succeeded at choosing a husband. She had married up. After so many years of worrying about Ann, my parents wouldn't have to worry about her anymore. Instead, that concern would shift to their level-headed second daughter, the one who did her homework, never got into trouble, and had just graduated from a great university.

As the second daughter I was the observer in my family. I had witnessed the pain and anxiety my big sister had caused our parents. I was a solitary, silent listener those nights they had come into the kitchen to smoke and drink coffee after we kids were in bed. From the darkened den doorway, I heard their anxious, hushed voices. These parents who seemed to know everything in the daytime, seemed lost and worried sick. It was heartbreaking. I didn't want to ever cause them a moment's worry if I could help it. They had been through enough.

My parents would be so disappointed in me now, but even worse, it would cause them pain if they saw mine. I've never been good at hiding my feelings. I didn't go home again until the following spring after I'd moved to Boston and had a job at MIT. I don't remember exactly when or how I broke my shameful news to these parents I adored, but it wasn't in person. When I left Tosh, I went to Blacksburg, Virginia to sister Ann and her husband Tony's house.

It made sense to my parents that I would go to help my sister who was about to give birth to her second child. The two months I spent in Blacksburg gave me time to figure out what the hell I would do next. Meanwhile, I actually *did* help Ann, and she helped me, too. She kept my confidence and I kept hers. As I quickly observed, being married to a workaholic husband when you're young and stuck in a house by yourself with a little kid was no bed of roses.

My sister and I have never felt closer than we did during that time. We bonded through a newfound sense of sibling solidarity and the unspoken shared knowledge that neither of us was happy. Ann has always been good at hiding things, making others believe the reality she wishes to project, as if pretending hard enough can make something true.

 But in that unique moment of mutual need, all pretense vanished when we were alone. We laughed through our misery, whiling away long afternoons listening to the radio as we danced across the chilly rooms and waxed floors of the Big House with rags on our feet, buffing the shine like good little housewives. That drafty old 18th century house was only warm when guests came to the upstairs living room for cocktails or parties. At one of those parties, I told the husband of a friend of Ann's that I wanted to move to Boston but didn't have a job. He encouraged me to apply to MIT. His sister worked for the provost and could easily get me an appointment with the personnel office.

And so, like the Cat in Puss 'n Boots, I headed to the big city to make my fortune, which in my case simply meant saving face and securing a job that appeared more promising than working at Rossi's Five and Dime in Donaldsonville. When I finally visited River Road that spring of 1970, I did feel hopeful about my future, and so did my parents. Daddy was already preparing to retire from Ascension Parish Public Schools, and at last, my mother could leave Donaldsonville.

My parents moved to Baton Rouge and purchased their first and only home. A Brother of the Sacred Heart was superintendent of the Baton Rouge Catholic school system at that time. He was an old friend of my father's from his previous life as Brother Jerome. He offered Daddy a position as Director of Elementary Education, a job my father came to love.

My mother got a job at a newspaper across the river from Baton Rouge, *The Plaquemine Post*. The paper had a wonderful editor at that time, Gary Hebert, who saw in my mother a "real newspaper woman." She and Daddy were both experiencing a level of career satisfaction, challenge, freedom, and recognition absent from their lives in Donaldsonville. They reconnected with old friends, like Billie and Boyd Roane, Dolphie's Aunt Emma, Daddy's cousins, and my old friend Gene, now living in Baton Rouge, quickly became Candy and Conrad's Fifth Goette daughter. The Goette family had left the River Road, all of them, forever. Ready or not, I had to make my own life.

Goette sisters on Shadow Lake Road in Blacksburg, 1977

Goette sisters on Shadow Lake Road, 2017

Jane Goette

Honeycomb

Cigarette burns on windowsills.

Calcified bodies of bees.

Children's fingerprints on glass panes,

names smeared across autumn-steamed windows,

Ann Jane Mary-Kay Gretchen,

signatures as varied as our hair,

brown blonde curly straight short long.

Corncobs in the bedroom walls

where fat rats stashed food for winter.

After the cane fields burned and

the temperatures dropped

they scratched and nibbled

all through the night—

an inch of wall between us,

so close they could hear us breathe.

We snuggled under thin blankets,

listening on windy nights:

pecans pelted the sides of the house,

thuds and plunks on the roof,

gas heaters hissed and purred.

The bones of our old house

creaked and groaned

as we settled in for winter.

Every spring the bees returned,

hotly humming inside the dining room wall.

After school, a sprinkling of thumb-sized bodies

littered the floor where some squeezed in.

Barefoot and hungry

I hopscotched my way to the kitchen

conjuring biscuits and honey.

I imagine honeycombs inside those walls today,

dark gold and time thickened,

hard as amber these decades later.

Are our long-ago words trapped inside, too?

Can voices stick to honey?

Mother reading "The Listeners": Is anybody there?

asked the Traveler, knocking on the moonlit door..."

Seasons came and went on the River Road.

And one season, we did not return.

Did we leave part of our selves?

Where do words go?

And the harmony or dissonance

with which they are spoken?

Somewhere inside those walls

surely the hum and tick of our lives

reverberates still

beside quiet honeycomb, decayed corncob.

Are we still there? I wonder,

Traveler and Listener both,

as moonlight shines on the closed door

of our old River Road house.

Afterword
Reflections on Race

In coming to the conclusion of this memoir, which has been years in the making, I'd like to add a few words that might have interrupted the flow of the stories but need to be expressed.

The term used for people of African descent underwent a series of changes during my life, from "colored" in my childhood to "negro" in adolescence, then "black" during the late sixties, and more recently, "African American." Jeannette Jefferson's daughter Babbette told me she wouldn't use "African American" until white people start calling themselves Irish American, Italian American, German American, etc. Settling on the term "black" for use in this book was an attempt to bridge the gap between authenticity and respect.

***

It wasn't just Louisiana dogs like Patches and Nig in the world of my childhood who were racists. Though the white people I knew expressed it in more polite ways, it seemed that all the whites in my town shared an unspoken credo of inequality; blacks were less, and white people, more. More what? Intelligent, trust-worthy, deserving, knowledgeable, and just plain valuable.

I don't remember the elders in my town—not the priests at church, nor teachers at school; not even my own parents actually talking to us about the reality in which we lived, for it was a tale of two towns, two states, and as I came to realize, a tale of two nations. One for white people and the other for black. In the 1950's the most admired on this spectrum of black and white were the whitest people, fair-haired and fair-skinned, epitomized by movie star princess Grace Kelly. Who wouldn't want to marry *her*?

Though the grown-ups talked about the importance of work and how it built character, it seemed to me the people most admired were those who worked the least and had at least one maid, a yard man, and a cook; families in which the father had a lot of people working for him and the mother spent most of her time at social clubs playing cards, planning parties, and talking about culture, which I think meant symphonies, not bands; opera, not the kind of singing black people did, and theatre, not a picture show like the Grand or school plays like Mrs. Kahn's fifth grade operettas. The rich people had to go to New Orleans or even farther away for culture.

The hardest working people I saw were black men. What could be harder than working all day in the sugarcane fields in hot weather? Yet, "field hands" were the least admired of all people in my world. No child would want to become one when he grew up. Field hands were poor no matter how hard they worked, and they didn't get any respect. In fact, white people didn't even like to look at these men. They should stay in their place; live back in the quarters by the cane fields where we wouldn't see them, be grateful they were paid for their work, and not make trouble.

One incident that has stayed with me as if I heard it yesterday is Kay Kay's account of what happened one Saturday, probably in the sixties, when she was hanging around Lemann's waiting to get a ride home. A black man dressed in overalls entered the store through the side door nearest the shoe department. He stood there looking uncomfortable, like someone might yell at him and run him off at any moment. Miss Mina saw him, and though the store was nearly empty and she wasn't doing anything, she leaned against the checkout counter rubbing her back up and down its wooden edge to scratch an itch her hands couldn't reach. She usually did this when no one was around.

The black man held a little girl's hand, his daughter it seemed. The child was barefoot and visibly excited, leaning behind her father, then peeking out and surveying her surroundings like it was Disneyland or something. Finally, Miss Mina sauntered over.

"What do you want?" she asked him with a tight smile.

"I come to buy my chile a pair a shoes," he said, nodding down at his little girl and smiling at her.

Miss Mina turned and he followed her to the shoe department. This was a novel occurrence at Lemann's, so my bored sister tagged along behind them. "What size is she?" Miss Mina asked. "I don't know. She ain't never had no shoes before, but she fixin' to go to school." At this, the child bristled with pride, twisting the fabric of her daddy's pant leg and smiling up at Miss Mina. Instead of measuring the child's foot, the usual procedure, Miss Mina looked down at the girl's feet and headed to the storage room behind the curtain, returning moments later with two boxes of sneakers. Though Lemann's carried an assortment of brands, Miss Mina had brought Keds, the most expensive canvas shoes the store carried. She handed the man the boxes and a pair of socks and said, "Go ahead, try them on her," as she lifted the lids of a white pair and a red. The child looked at her daddy and pointed to the red. After he'd put the socks on her feet, he slipped the shoes on and tied them quickly. "Go 'head, now," the man said to her, "see you can walk in 'em." She took a couple of steps and then ran to the wall and back, laughing. The man reached down and pinched the toes. There was plenty of space.

"How much these run me?" the father asked reaching into his pocket. I don't recall what anything cost back then, but whatever sum Miss Mina cited, that man looked stunned, gut-punched, like a person who'd expected an A right up to the moment the teacher hands him an F. He stiffened and bent down to take the shoes off the girl's feet, then handed the box back to Miss Mina. "I'm sorry m'am, I can't be buyin no shoes like that." He was a black man and she was a white woman. He couldn't peruse the shelves comparing prices and touching the shoes or ask this woman to show him other ones. Miss Mina had all the power. They both knew it. It had been a mistake for him to come to this store.

In Donaldsonville, white children and black children knew the score. We understood the unspoken rules of our town. Once you were big, if you were black you couldn't have eye contact with a white person other than a child, and you sure better watch your mouth. Away from their parents, black and white children might play together and abide by a common sense of justice—no cheating, and you had to take turns. They could push and yell at each other when fairness had been breached. It was the grown-ups who taught children other ways.

Mixed races might play together back-a-town on an empty lot or in an alley between houses, but every kid-friendly *official* structure or sanctioned play area—a playground, school, swimming pool, skating rink, fair—separated the races. On the rural River Road where I lived, there weren't many children, period. The Dugas girls and the Person boys were the only ones we ever saw, though there had to be a lot of black families farther down the road and back near the fields.

There were many unspoken rules of the world in which I lived. I watched the masks slip on and off people's faces. The black mask, a façade of perpetual cheeriness; their easy, rolling laughter and thigh slaps, the constant humoring and deference that white people expected–or required—of black men and women. It seems obvious now that black people in our community knew us better than we knew ourselves, and we didn't know *them* at all.

Even in my own family I noticed that my father behaved differently when my mother was not around. He was a child of the South, accustomed to its ways and speech. Daddy seemed to possess an innate social ease and sense of belonging. He enjoyed the jokes and storytelling shared among white men in informal situations. The humor was often at the expense of black people, exaggerating their fear, ignorance, naivete, or gullibility. "You shoulda seen that 'nigga,' run!" the story might go, "like he had seen his mama's ghost!" and the men would all get a kick out of it. Daddy sometimes told his own stories and used the N-word when he was talking to an acquaintance at the post office or picking up a case of Jax Beer.

The most puzzling story though, was the one my yankee mother told about her presumably non-racist high school friends back in Waukesha. My mother was the first of her school chums to marry and have a baby. When she went home to Waukesha to visit between Ann's birth and mine, her friends had asked how she managed to do things outside the house. "Who takes care of Ann?" they wanted to know. Mother told them about Ellie, a black woman, who babysat Ann from time to time. They looked shocked. "Canni, you let a black woman touch your baby?!"

Mother was as surprised by her friends' reactions as they were by her comfort with up-close association with black people. I'm not sure there were any black people in Waukesha, but if there had been, there was no law prohibiting them from going to the same schools as my mother had. Wisconsin didn't have segregation laws like in the South, and they had fought on Lincoln's side of the Civil War. This Waukesha story, which occurred when Mother was in her early twenties, is one she repeated from time to time as I was growing up. That experience had revealed an uncomfortable truth—even in a northern, officially integrated town with a newspaper founded by Abolitionists, her own dear friends held racial prejudices she did not share nor understand.

I loved every black woman that came into our home. They were warm and natural with me and had an ease with their bodies that I admired. Helen cleaned house for us when I was in elementary school. She was young and pretty, and I loved her. Once, when alone with her at the kitchen table, I asked if I could look at her hand. I flipped it one side to the other, running my finger across the lines of her pinkish palm before placing her warm hand against my cheek.

"Helen, how come the insides of your hands aren't the same color as the outsides?" It looked like the color had been washed off black people's palms. Helen laughed and reached for my hands, "Jane, you ask the strangest questions!" Then she cupped my face in her hands and asked, "How come you got straight hair and your skin be the color it is, huh?" She leaned her face closer to mine and looked me in the eyes, "Our outsides different, but all people the same on the inside. We all got red blood, ain't we?"

Helen cleaned house for my family two or three days a week for about two years sometime in the 1950's until she got married and started a family. I remember being terribly excited when Helen was getting married. I had never been to a wedding, and she had invited my whole family to come to hers. We dressed in our Sunday best and piled into the family car at the appointed date and time.

Helen's wedding took place in a small church somewhere down the River Road a few miles past our house. When we arrived, the church was filled with black faces, no white people other than us, which was as novel to me as being at a wedding. After we'd taken our reserved seats, the music began. It was lively. The whole church rippled with excitement. We craned our heads toward the rear of the church to watch the bridesmaids, all dressed in bright colors, begin their dance-stroll down the aisle, hips rolling, shoulders moving with the beat of the music. Then came Helen on her father's arm. She looked stunning in her red dress and she was laughing as she and her father headed down the aisle, moving more like dancers than solemn processionals.

In the many weddings I've attended since that first, I have never seen a bride who appeared to be having as much fun as Helen. Her River Road wedding was not just celebratory, the whole church rocked with joy.

***

The lens through which I have come to view the complexity of America's racial history and my own biases has widened over the course of my life. In 1970 when I was working at MIT's Education Research Center, a black colleague from Bedford-Stuyvesant taught me to see behind other kinds of masks, not just those worn by southerners. Frank Lennon was smart, confident, and charismatic enough to talk his way into a doctoral program at MIT without the required resume. It is not surprising that our paths would cross at Building-20.

I'd grown up in what I thought to be the epicenter of racism. Now I was in the epicenter of enlightenment and progressive thought. Frank Lennon shattered that assumption. Surprisingly, Frank and I felt more alike than we did with others in Cambridge of either race. We had relaxed ways, similar humor, a sense of fun, and an ease in storytelling. We began to seek out each other's company daily. During the time of our acquaintance, Frank broadened the lens through which I had viewed racism all my life. Though he didn't use the term that so inflames conservatives today, "systemic racism," that's exactly what he was talking about.

"This place is as racist as your rural Louisiana," he told me one day. I was shocked and challenged him, "Come on, Frank, have you ever heard the N-word here?!"

He said it was much deeper than the words people used. "Those folks down South who ride around in pickup trucks with

Confederate flags on the back window are not the ones who scare me. That kind of racist is a bull in a china shop," he said, "I know where he stands. The racists who threaten me are the polite people I pass in the halls of MIT and Harvard who would never use the N-word—not to my face, anyway—but wouldn't want me in their clubs or firms. They don't want to see my name next to theirs on an office door, or my house in the same neighborhood as theirs. It would bring down the value."

I wanted to believe that racism was entrenched in the South, that the Civil Rights legislation of the 1960's would move our country closer toward its ideals. I now realize that Frank was right. Racism is as American as apple pie. Louisiana may still incarcerate more black people than most other states, but murders of unarmed black men by police are committed in states I once considered bastions of liberalism, of democracy—New York, Illinois, Minnesota, Wisconsin…. If I were a black person in America, I'd be mad as hell.

Many weddings and many funerals have passed since I began this memoir, and I find myself wondering if the ways of white people are good for humanity. There seem too many premises that remain unquestioned, too many times we're supposed to set aside our best human impulses, bury joy, grief, and conscience, and recede farther and farther from our core humanity, our capacity for love and generosity, gratitude and glee, wonder and humility.

I have lived my life as an observer and a participant in my times, always with a keen awareness that there is more that came before, and will come after my one, fleeting life. Throughout, children have been my touchstone and compass for what is real and true. Children, before the world corrupts their inner sanctum, are *not* racists. They are infinitely curious at birth and come to us with open hearts and minds ready to learn and to love.

Each of us is a son or daughter of "Life's longing for itself" and is born with an "unalienable right to life, liberty, and the pursuit of happiness," or as Helen once said, "We all got red blood, ain't we?"

Jane Goette

Bio

Jane Goette grew up in Donaldsonville, Louisiana. After graduating from the public school system, she briefly attended LSU before transferring to the University of Wisconsin and completing a B.A. in English in 1969. She moved to Boston and worked at MIT where she got involved in the Women's and Free School movements. She helped start a summer learning center for working class children. The "real" teacher got pneumonia after the first week, so Jane assumed responsibility for this mixed age, mostly black, group of children the rest of the summer before returning to her job at MIT. She bided her time, earned state residency, and saved enough money to go to graduate school in the Integrated Day Program at University of Massachusetts. Two years later Jane moved to New Orleans and taught a K-2 Integrated Day class at Country Day for four years before marrying and settling in Blacksburg, Virginia. She continued her career in education and began writing while raising three children. All her endeavors, personal and professional, stem from a lifelong love of children, words, social justice and the natural world.

Made in the USA
Columbia, SC
07 April 2022

58575021R00205